GEORGE WASHINGTON'S EXPENSE ACCOUNT

BY

General George Washington

&

Marvin Kitman, Pfc. (Ret.)

PERENNIAL LIBRARY

Harper & Row, Publishers, New York
Cambridge, Philadelphia, San Francisco
London, Mexico City, São Paulo, Singapore, Sydney

First PERENNIAL LIBRARY edition published 1988.

LIBRARY OF CONGRESS CATALOG CARD NUMBER 88-45125

ISBN 0-06-097185-1 (pbk.)

88 89 90 91 92 HC 10 9 8 7 6 5 4 3 2 1

A TALLY SHEET OF PRAISE FOR
GEORGE WASHINGTON'S EXPENSE ACCOUNT

OTHER BOOKS BY GEORGE WASHINGTON

*George Washington's Rules of Civility and
Decent Behaviour in Company and Conversation*

*Journal of My Journey over the Mountains
While Surveying for Lord Thomas Fairfax*

*Daily Journal of Major George Washington in 1751–1752,
Kept While on a Tour from Virginia
to the Island of Barbadoes, with his Invalid Brother,
Maj. Lawrence Washington*

*Journal of Colonel George Washington, Commanding
a Detachment of Virginia Troops, Sent by Robert Dinwiddie,
Lieutenant-Governor of Virginia, across the Alleghany Mountains,
in 1754, to Build Forts at the Head of the Ohio*

The Diaries of George Washington, 4 volumes

The Writings of George Washington, 39 volumes

———————

OTHER BOOKS BY MARVIN KITMAN

The Number One Best-Seller
You Can't Judge a Book by Its Cover

Acknowledgments

I would like to acknowledge briefly the people and institutions who helped me with this work.

First, I am in debt to my editor, Richard Kluger. Without his expense account, which provided nourishment and warmth at Fraunces Tavern during long years of struggle as a starving writer, the book never would have been possible.

My wife, Carol, did not type the manuscript. She gave up a promising career as a teacher to serve as an unpaid consultant and editor.

Of the Washington scholars, I would especially like to single out for honorable mention James Flexner. He was a constant source of encouragement and solicitude as we worked side by side on Washington books in the right wing of the Frederick Lewis Allen Room of the New York Public Library. The Fred Allen Room was my home away from home, and I am grateful to the library staff for the free office space in the high rent location of Fifth Avenue and 42nd Street.

Professor Richard Morris of the Columbia University department of history was helpful in allowing me to audit his course, G6662y ("The Era of the American Revolution, 1754–1789"). He promised to completely ignore me, and more than fulfilled that promise during the term. Like most newcomers to the world of scholarship, I have tried to make up for any inherent shortcomings by the competence of my research; I have stolen many of the controversial ideas in this book directly from Professor Morris's lectures, which in turn were taken from his last book.

Professor James Shenton of Columbia University, Professor B. C. Jones of the University of Florida and Professor Eric C. Goldman of Princeton were supposed to read the manuscript. Their comments would have been typical of the nit-picking and back-biting so commonplace amongst true scholars.

A number of historians, professional and amateur, gave of their time at cocktail parties where I frequently managed to have George

Washington talked about between 1966 and 1969. I won't bother again Professor Carl Resek of Sarah Lawrence College, Victor Navasky, Roger Jellinek, Dr. Ann Lane of Douglass College, Richard Lingeman, Arthur Kretchmer, Sam Vaughan of Tenafly, Murray Fisher, Dennis Ainsworth of Mississippi State, Donald Sterling, Martin Solow, Peter Nord, Calvin Trillin, Peter Edmiston, Alan Levin, Richard Beebe, Robert Fresco, Timothy Adams, and Howard Hirschhorn, my accountant.

My research assistant, Bonnie Lynn Perloff, did superior work at the Library of Congress in Washington. The highest recommendation I can give is her phone number: 202–338–4016.

The family of George Washington wasn't very helpful. I tried to get them to enjoin publication of this book before, rather than after, it was written. It worried me that I might accidentally damage the family's reputation, something no writer has the right to do unless he's making a fortune out of it. Actually his descendants were hard to find. There were a few Daughters of the American Revolution with vague claims to the Washington line, but nobody worth speaking to. The only people who seem to have anything at stake in protecting the Washington name today seem to be the Port Authority people in New York. If George Washington fell from favor, they'd have to rename their bridge after some other patriotic businessman, say, Alexander Hamilton.

I have been unkind to the marksman Aaron Burr in this book. To his descendants I would like to say that I really believe he did not kill Alexander Hamilton. The former Secretary of the Treasury died from poor medical attention.

Finally, I would like to acknowledge my gratitude to the Guggenheim Foundation, the Fund for the Republic, the Ford Foundation, the Rockefeller Brothers Fund, the Mellon Foundation, the National Institute of Health, and the other foundations and organizations which did not give me a grant to write this book. It was truly a labor of love.

M. K.

This book is for Private Haines of the First New Hampshire Regiment.

At the Battle of Bemis Heights (also known as the Battle of Stillwater and the Battle of Freeman's Farm), north of Albany, on September 19, 1777, Private Haines distinguished himself by climbing astride the muzzle of a British brass 12-pounder. As it has been said, he rammed his bayonet into the thigh of a savage foe, recovering to parry the thrust of a second, and, quick as a tiger, dashed the same bloody bayonet through the redcoat's head; recovered again, only to fall from the cannon, shot through the mouth and tongue, lying two nights on the battlefield until thirst, hunger, and loss of blood finally overcame him; landed in the ranks of the dead being made ready for burial; and from all this recovered for three years more service, and a green old age.

Just think what he could have done with an expense account.

Contents

Preface

T he original hardcover edition of this book was published on February 22, 1970, by those two great Americans, Simon and Schuster. It was, I can say in all modesty, the best selling expense account in history (four printings, 40,000 copies). I used to say, jokingly, that the DAR was buying all the copies—and burning them.

The original volume had great impact. By addressing itself to and perhaps eliminating the guilt feelings associated with expense account writing, it unleashed a flood of spending that may have led to the great bull market of the 1980s. It had, some say, at least as much impact as David Stockman and President Reagan's slideside economics. I could be reading the papers, and suddenly I knew: *that man read the book.* I'm sure, for example, one of the first copies must have gone to Richard M. Nixon, my President in 1970. He may even have had the advance galleys, come to think of it.

One of the lasting achievements of the Nixon years, even greater than the Watergate tapes, was President Nixon donating his presidential papers to the National Archives in 1972 and claiming a $576,000 tax deduction. Because of this gift, as Anthony Marro,* then a member of *Newsday*'s Washington bureau, explained, "This enabled him to pay federal income taxes of only $793 and $878 in two of the years that he was living in the White House, drawing a salary of $200,000 a year and accumulating the assets that have made him a millionaire."

The papers in question—some 1,176 boxes containing about 600,000 documents, as Marro explained—dated back to Nixon's years as a senator and vice president. They included papers dealing with his trips to Latin America and with the Alger Hiss spy case. They also contained, as Marro noted, many routine documents and memoranda such as the 27,000 invitations he accepted or rejected during those years.

When the matter was disputed, Nixon argued that his deduction was conservative. And he offered to take the documents back. "I'll pay the

---

*Newsday, December 30, 1973.

tax," he said, "because I think they're worth more [than the $576,000 tax deduction claimed]."

This had greater impact on society than Watergate. Because of Nixon, loophole pluggers in the tax law ended deductions for donations of papers. Many of us scholars, not so farsighted as President Nixon, got stuck with our papers. My papers are now truly worthless, thanks to Tricky Dicky.

But the man's thinking was so Washingtonesque in spirit.

I keep seeing many new examples of ways of doing business with the country that could only come from a perusal of the general's work. The fruition of all the general was trying to say in the "Expense Account" came to light in the General Dynamics investigation of 1985.

One of the nation's leading defense-manufacturing companies, General Dynamics had been building such things as F-16s, M-1 tanks, and Trident submarines—the latter costing about $1.3 billion each. Among the costs added to the taxpayer's bill for the Trident, it turned out, were kennel fees for a dog named Fursten ($155 a day), an $18,000 country club admission fee, and a $571.25 charge for a king-size Serta Perfect mattress so a company director's feet wouldn't stick out at a motel in St. Louis when he came to the General Dynamics headquarters for discussions about the rising costs of Tridents.*

Even the general would have sat up and taken notice of that achievement.

I'm not saying the president of General Dynamics read the book. But his bookkeeper sure did.

The Defense Department was withholding at one time in 1985 $244 million in payments to General Dynamics, alleging they represented improper billings for entertainment, travel, and personal expenses, such "overhead" costs as a $14,975 party at a suburban Washington country club, and the baby-sitting expenses of one of its officials.†

It was not just General Dynamics. A team of auditors uncovered $109.7 million in dubious claims against the Pentagon by seven giant defense contractors in 1985, the House Armed Services Committee reported. (General Dynamics, Sperry Corporation, Newport News Shipbuilding and Dry Dock Company, Bell Helicopter, McDonnell Douglas Corp., Rockwell International, Boeing Co. . . . all the biggies.)

At the same time, the Defense Department was concluding its investigation of the overcharges by General Dynamics. "The Defense Department's imprecise and ludicrous guidelines were partly to blame," said Assistant Secretary of the Navy Everett Pyatt. "They were simply doing what our procedures would allow them to do."‡

Admiral Rickover's wife, recipient of a $1,125 pair of General Dynamics diamond earrings, couldn't agree more.

Time, April 8, 1985, p. 23.
†*Ibid.*
‡*Time,* August 26, 1985, p. 13.

You also see the influence of the book in government spending in general at the Pentagon. Was it coincidence that in the early 1980s we saw the first $7,662 ten-cup coffee maker, the famous $74,165 ladder, the $600 toilet seat, the $435 claw hammer, the $243 pair of pliers, the $44 refrigerator light bulb, and the $2,043 nut for a screw that had such little value that spares were thrown away rather than returned to the Defense Department inventory? The general was not the last of the big-time spenders, as all of this explains.

Government auditors in 1985 examined a total of $3.6 billion in claims for "overhead expenses" by seven corporations. It concluded, according to Rep. Bill Nichols (D-Ala.), that up to $1 for every $33 submitted to the government for overhead expenses was questionable. I'm surprised it was so low.

These charges included costs of haircuts for senior executives at one company and $62,071 for a public relations campaign to counteract negative publicity caused by the crash of an airplane it had built. Firms now charge the Pentagon for everything. My favorite: Boeing billed the Pentagon for $36,200 in 1982, which included donations to the Salvation Army and tickets to social functions ranging from a Boy Scout golf tournament to a Hanukkah dinner hosted by the Jewish National Fund.*

Rep. Fortney H. "Pete" Stark, Jr. (D-Calif.), whose office released the audit, said, "The contractors either take us for fools, or they're incapable of understanding what constitutes a legitimate bill."

Auditors and Congressmen have not done their homework. The Expense Account explained what this was all about.

Forty-five of the one hundred largest military suppliers were under criminal investigation by 1985, the Pentagon has revealed.† It is a most auspicious time for republication of General Washington's classic work!

And then there was the crowning achievement. What a thrill it was to read the headline in the *New York Times* of January 6, 1987:

REAGAN SENDS $1 TRILLION BUDGET TO CONGRESS, AND BATTLE IS JOINED

The $1 trillion plateau had finally been reached. It was a good thing the Reagan administration was committed to a bare-bones approach and scraps-for-the-poor mandate, a crusade to eliminate big spending in Washington.

It is also not coincidence that the yuppie phenomenon began shortly after the publication of George Washington's latest book. The current generation of overconsumers was coming of age when the book was first being widely circulated and discussed. If ever there was a group of readers who would benefit from the general's wisdom and example,

---

*Bergen Record, April 29, 1985, Washington Post News Service.
†*Time,* May 2, 1985, p. 60.

laying down basic principles and codes of behavior, it was the young consumers—Yuppies—or "Great Americans," as General Washington would have called those patriotic individuals dedicated to buying everything ever made.

The republication of *George Washington's Expense Account* is making accessible to the new post-Yuppies generation the basic rules of spending and morality in matters of entertainment, travel, and personal expenses, as seen through the eyes of the man who wrote the book, so to speak.

The republication could lead to a spurt in the economy the likes of which we haven't seen since the invention of the plastic credit card.

It is the unborn Yuppies of 1970 to whom I respectfully rededicate this new edition.

This book is for my British friends John Cleese and Michael Palin, who encouraged me to have the general's most important work republished to keep alive the dream of every Anglo-American child: to someday grow up to have an expense account.

And, finally, it is for the late Sir Huw Wheldon, the original book's biggest fan, who, while serving as the head of the board of governors of the London School of Economics, told me at an expense account lunch at the Garrick Club in London in 1983, "Without expense accounts and third-class mailing privileges, the whole system would collapse."

Marvin Kitman
Somewhere in New Jersey
July 1988

Note to the Reader

I am leaving the original version of the book intact, with the occasional typographical errors, as well as errors of commission and omission. Expense account analysis was in its infancy in the late 1960s when the work was done. Now it's more sophisticated.

I stand, or sit, by the conversion rate (see page 99). Admittedly, this is an oversimplification, subject to debate. Economists, arbitragers, and bankers will point to the complexities of arriving at the value of the Continental dollar vis-à-vis other currencies. Comparative figures are just as difficult to ascertain today as in 1969. I want to point out one important new fact about the money situation. The conversion rate in the original book was based on the 1969 Consumer Price Index. Based on the latest available figures (1986), the Consumer Price Index has at least tripled since 1969.

Therefore, where "today's dollars" are mentioned, simply multiply by three.

The general's expense account is thus three times more impressive, revisiting it today.

I

Introduction

1.

A MAN'S expense account needs no introduction; it usually speaks for itself. Still a few general words are in order about this revealing form of autobiography.

One of the great American institutions, the expense account, can make even a square-jawed, clean-cut American businessman or civil servant who rises early, works hard and always has his employer's interest at heart feel vaguely un-American. It doesn't matter that he hasn't done anything wrong. The concept of sleeping, eating and forgetting about the cares of a hard day away from the office at no expense to oneself seems immoral. General recognition of this negative attitude can be seen in the widespread usage *within* business and government communities of the phrase "swindle sheet."

The fact is, there is nothing nefarious about the expense account. It is not, as some may have supposed, the product of a Machiavellian or Eastern European mind. Indeed the classic in the field was handed in by that pillar of rectitude George Washington, for his work as father of his country.

Like most American schoolboys, I had heard the story of how George Washington offered to serve his country during the Revolutionary War without salary. In one of the most stirring speeches in the annals of patriotism, he explained, after his election as Commander in Chief of the Continental Army in June 1775, that all he asked of his new country was that it pick up his expenses.

In his own immortal words, which were written by his speechwriter, Edmund Pendleton:

As to pay, Sir, I beg leave to Assure the Congress that as no pecuniary consideration could have tempted me to have accepted this Arduous employment (at the expense of my domesttic [sic] ease and happiness) I do not wish to make any Proffit [sic] from it. I will keep an exact Account of my expences. Those I doubt not they will discharge, and that is all I desire.*

* See original text of speech in Pendleton's hand, with the exception of one single interpolation, in 52 *Papers of Continental Congress,* Pt. I, 1, Library of Congress (LC). Washington undoubtedly specified that Pendleton make it a plain speech. He also asked the Virginia lawyer to draw up his will, which some critics suggest was not a rousing vote of confidence in Congress' decision.

Nothing much is heard in the classrooms about the equally stirring expense account General Washington submitted after the war.

I found this copy of his ledger book in the stacks of the New York Public Library, where for the past few years I have been researching a larger work, titled "The Making of the Prefident 1789" (to be published as part of the bicentennial celebration), about the way the Mount Vernon machine engineered the first national presidential election. It was what scholars call a very exciting discovery.

I am no historian. So I have to be very cautious about getting involved in the issues which Washington scholars have quibbled over for the past century. Was Washington soft on civil rights, as his 212 slaves might suggest? Or do his private letters, in which he said he detested the institution of slavery, qualify him as a prenatal member of the NAACP? Was he guilty of using profanity at the height of the Monmouth Court House battle, when he purportedly cursed Gen. Charles Lee, "Get your fat ass out to the battlefield"? Or was he simply issuing a command regarding the disposition of military vehicles? Did he marry the widow Martha Custis on January 6, 1759,* for her money? Or for her land-holdings? Who really nominated him to be commander-in-chief with his earlier military record, John Adams of Massachusetts or Thomas Johnson of Maryland—and why?

But I *am* a free-lance writer. And if there is anything free-lance writers are authorities on it is expense accounts. Editors have said that some of my most creative writing goes into the composition of expense accounts accompanying my articles. Internal Revenue men have been known to whistle in admiration at some of my interpretations of what is just.

There has been a tendency on the part of modern historians to belittle Washington's accomplishments in war and peace. But expense account writing is the one area in which the man was second to none.

As I leafed through the yellowed, brittle pages of this priceless document, the refrain of a song I remember hearing while working for the government as a draftee† in the same army the Virginia planter founded drifted back:

> You're in the army now.
> You're not behind the plow.
> You'll never get rich,
> You son of a bitch.
> You're in the army now.

* See letter to Sir Isaac Heard, May 2, 1792 in *The Washington Papers,* ed. Saul K. Padover, p. 22.

† Mess hall, Co. M, 47th Infantry Regiment, 9th Division, Fort Dix, N.J., October 23, 1953.

That Washington was able to function as an artist in a place that traditionally offered so few growth opportunities told me that I was in the presence of true greatness.

While it made me sad to discover that much of what I considered original in my work in the field was derivative, I think it is only right that we give credit where it is due. Just about everybody who writes expense accounts today—the so-called "expense account crowd"— is following in George Washington's hallowed footsteps. I might even go so far as to say that General Washington's expense account is the obviously revered model for the nation's current defense budget.

Washington's expense account isn't perfect. There are 43 basic principles governing the art of writing this kind of introspective literature, and Washington has used only 42 of them. Still, he holds the record.

Some modern expense account writers believe the only principle they ever follow is that *each one should be higher than the next.* In today's military language, this is the escalation principle, which Washington followed scrupulously during the 96 months he was on the expense account.

Now nobody likes to give away one's trade secrets, but some of the less important rules, as demonstrated in the Washington model, are:

★ *Omit nothing.* When in doubt, charge anyway. Put it on the train to Westport, and see if it gets off.

★ *Be specific on the smaller expenditures and vague on the larger ones.* Describe in some depth the purchase of a ball of twine, but casually throw in the line, "Dinner for one army."

★ *Whenever possible, intermingle personal and business expenses.*

★ *Pick up the check for one's associates.* Washington was perhaps generous to a fault this way with taxpayers' money.

★ *Above all, be reasonable. Know what the market will bear.* As Washington undoubtedly heard Tom Paine—a leading PR man of the day (his client was the Declaration of Independence)—say often, "You have to use common sense."

Sometimes General Washington manages to illustrate his grasp of the 42 basic principles in the narrow space of three-fourths of a single page (see my accompanying translation). By no means do the items in the ledger book suggest that Washington invented the expense account—I want to make that clear—only that he may have been the founding father of the American way of life known as "expense account living."

My purpose in seeing now to the reprinting of this watershed document in the history of commercial writing is not in the spirit of boasting of one's Revolutionary War antecedents, although I am proud to establish yet another link to the first President. (The first one is that he passed, in great haste, within a block of my house in Leonia, New Jersey, in 1776 on the retreat from Fort Lee to Hackensack, Paramus and eventually, Valley Forge.* My purpose, rather, is to aid in rehabilitating Washington's name.

The average fellow in our expense account crowd today thinks of Washington about as much as Millard Fillmore. After reading this book, I hope every drummer and influence-peddler in Washington will make a pilgrimage to Mount Vernon to pay his respects at the shrine of this great writer—and on somebody's expense account.

With this new appreciation of Washington, the monument and the man, I also hope to revive interest in him amongst the young. My coauthor was the Ché of Fairfax County, Virginia, a dangerous revolutionary who was willing to risk everything—foxhounds, slaves, beloved shrubs and rose gardens—to overthrow the establishment. He was a radical of no political party, without program or ideology, except perhaps a belief in the magical ability of the weed tobacco to solve his problems. His relations with his mother were strained.† The way Washington fought the war on an expense account also should have great appeal to radical students of today who ask for amnesty in their insurrectional activities.

2.

THIS IS ONE of the most inspiring books to come out of the War for Independence, or any other war. Yet for some reason it never caught on with the public.

It was first published by the Chief Clerk in the Register's Office of the Treasury Department in June, 1833, under the title, "Accounts, G. Washington with the United States, Commencing June 1775, and ending June 1783, Comprehending a Space of 8 Years." Despite the sensationalism of the title, it must have struck readers of that era as just another government handout. The account book was not quickly established as a classic American document nor its author as one of the literary heroes of the war.

* William S. Baker, *Itinerary of Gen. Washington from June 15, 1775 to December 23, 1783,* passim (Philadelphia: 1892).

† See every Washington biography and all volumes of Washington's writings. Some historians say Washington was not a favorite son. Others suggest that he hated his mother for non-political reasons dating back to his childhood. Mary Ball Washington refused to let him go to sea as a midshipman. Whatever the reason, there was little love lost between them. Whenever Washington gave his mother a little money, he entered it in his memorandum books as a debit.

Eight years later, the book was reissued in a new package. It had all the juicy parts, the dry-as-martini statistics, but a new title: "A Monument to Washington's Patriotism." Published by the Trustees of the Washington Manual Labor School and Male Orphan Asylum, as a fund-raising project, this facsimile edition was enhanced by a number of advance reviews from authorities on spending federal funds, from President John Tyler and secretaries of the departments, down to members of the House of Representatives. They were all raves.

"This simple memoir is full of instruction," wrote Representative John Sergeant of North Carolina. "It teaches all, and especially the young, that economy, order, and unusual conscientiousness even in the smallest matters . . . not only may be consistent with the greatest capacity and most splendid achievement, but are indispensable to their perfection. . . ."

Levi Woodbury, Secretary of the Treasury under Tyler and later a Chief Justice of the Supreme Court, said of his reasons for enjoying the ledger: "The first one is the example so very laudable which it sets to the rising generation of accuracy, care and punctuality in monied matters, however small. The other [reason] is the model it furnishes of disinterestedness in the public service. . . ."

No wonder it turned off the kids. On closer examination than the reviewers gave it, this book would have explained why economizers in government—from President Tyler, whose administration promised to cut federal spending, to President Nixon*—face such a hopeless task.

Actually the publishing history of this book may be one of the earliest cases of news management. If the government had tried to suppress this long forgotten chapter of the war, it might have had a decent chance to become a best-seller. By making it available to the public—only 43 years after the statute of limitations ran out—the government's strategy may have been that nobody would read it. The book's impact since 1833 more than fulfilled the government's high expectations.

Although I haven't finished reading all the 39 volumes of Washington's collected papers† yet, I did my homework by reading this ledger through. It differs from his other work the way a company's annual report differs from its president's expense account. The difference in this case was so striking, I read the expense account again and again.

The prose Washington is most remembered for always seems to have been written by somebody else. A busy man during the war, Washington employed at least 32 private secretaries in batches of

* Richard M. Nixon, *First Inaugural Address*, January 20, 1969.

† *The Writings of George Washington*, ed. John C. Fitzpatrick. Bicentennial edition (Washington: 1931–44).

four and five.* These were divided into riding and writing aides. This latter group was composed of corresponding secretaries and secretary-treasurers who also kept his books. Alexander Hamilton, the bright, young Columbia (King's College) lawyer, later the Ted Sorenson of the first Washington administration, was one of those who served with distinction as a ghostwriter at Headquarters. Although Colonel Hamilton is credited with being the hand behind much of Washington's writing on economics after the war, there is little doubt about who penned this masterpiece.

The key to the authenticity of the authorship is in the orthography, which has Washington's special touch. At the age of thirteen† Washington wrote a famed guidebook for self-made men, "Rules of Civility and Decent Behaviour in Company and Conversation," in which he advised, "Never tell a lye." He had a fantastic system of spelling, but the code can be broken by keeping in mind that he was never able to get the *i*'s and *e*'s right, in the words like *ceiling.* He wrote *blew* when he meant the color blue, and oil was *oyl.* It shouldn't be supposed that this was typical of eighteenth century scholarship. Alexander Hamilton, Thomas Jefferson,‡ and Benjamin Franklin could spell and use grammar perfectly. George Washington was an elementary school drop-out, and paid the price.

Historians are not clear on how long George Washington went to school; we can safely assume he got some schooling between the ages of seven and eleven, and that he did not go on, like many of the other founding fathers of Virginia, to the College of William and Mary (except for a kind of adult extension course in Surveying I). In that light, his compositions are quite good, although none of the 300 or so written for this book can match the raw talent displayed in his diary of March 15, 1748. On a field trip, the sixteen-year-old surveyor's assistant wrote:

> We got our suppers & was Lighted into a Room & I not being so good a woodsman as ye rest of my company, striped myself very orderly and went into ye Bed, as they calld it, when to my surprize, I found it to be nothing but a little straw matted together without sheets or anything else, but only one thread bear blanket with double its weight of vermin, such as Lice, Fleas &. I was glad to get up . . . I put on my cloths & lay my companions.

He seems to have made a deliberate effort to clean up the spelling when submitting the expense account to a learned body like Congress. Still a basic military word like *reconnoiter* continually evaded him in the expense account compositions. He also misspells the

---

* Roger Butterfield, essay, "The Long Lost Letters of General Washington," *Life* (Washington's Birthday Issue, 1967).

† *The Washington Papers,* ed. Saul K. Padover (New York: 1967), p. 5.

‡ See example of his work in *The Declaration of Independence* (Philadelphia: 1776).

names of friends and other proper nouns regularly. Young Washington once referred sardonically to Williamsburg as "the great Matrapolis." He is always in the same ballpark with a proper noun, unlike some of the New England privates whose diaries, we will see later, immortalized Markis Delefiat (Lafayette), Dullerway (Delaware), and Hushing (Hessians).

General Washington received a degree from Harvard in 1776: an L.L.D. It was probably the most comprehensive degree ever awarded by an American institution of higher learning, making him "Doctor of Laws, the Law of Nature and Nations, and of Civil Law."* Since I expect Harvard Business School, as well as Wharton School of Finance, graduate students to use this book as a required text, I have taken the liberty, as part of my contribution to this joint effort, to improve Dr. Washington's compositions. The periods dropped into run-on sentences are mine.

Dr. Washington's strength was in the science of numbers. He loved arithmetic as other boys of his period loved Marlowe (or Shakespeare). His mind as a boy was crammed with important facts and figures—avoirdupois, pints and gallons, cords of wood, pecks of peas, multiplication tables, and the conversion rates of pound sterling to Spanish dollars. He never learned French, but even as a boy he knew how to draft a bill of sale, a power of attorney, a promissory note. He wasn't what we call today an idea-man, but few scholars would deny his preeminence as a thing-man. George Washington was first among American statesmen in counting things.

One of the more moving passages in his diaries† begins: "Took a list today all my Negroes, which are as follow, at Mt. Vernon.

HOME HOUSE

Will . . . Val de Chambre . . . 1
Frank
*Austin . . . Waiters in the House . . . 2
Hercules
Nathan . . . . Cooks . . . 2
Giles
*Joe
Paris-boy . . . Drivers & Stablers . . . 3
*Doll
Jenny . . . Almost Past service 2
*Betty
*Lame Alice
Charlotte . . . Sempstresses . . . 3

And so forth, down to "the carpenter, Sambo." (The asterisks denoted "Dower Negroes," *i.e.*, Martha Washington's contribution

---

* David A. Lockmiller, *Scholars on Parade* (New York: 1969), p. 220.
† *The Diaries of George Washington*, ed. John C. Fitzpatrick, entry for February 18, 1786 (Boston and New York: 1925).

to the household.) Slaves were sold then like used cars today, and it was very important for the Virginia planter-industrialist to keep a careful record of the condition of his property.

Every penny he owned and every foot of land was set down over and over again, in the most orderly, meticulous way, in memorandum books he carried inside his tunic. Washington's spirit of inquiry knew no limits. He counted and listed "the no. of Paynes" in each window at Mount Vernon. At one time when he was managing five plantations and seven hundred slaves he calculated laboriously the number of seed in a pound Troy weight of red clover (71,000). He was the Robert McNamara of the Continental military establishment.

So there is no reason to think Robert Morris, the Superintendent of Finance (equivalent to our Secretary of the Treasury), could have had General Washington in mind when he complained to the President of Congress in 1782 that military officers thought keeping books was "rather beneath their dignity."* The expense account clearly shows the influence of one of the most widely-read books in Washington's private library: "Book-Keeping moderniz'd: Or, Merchant-Accounts by Double Entry, according to the Italian Form. Wherein the Theory of the Art is Clearly explained, and reduced to a Practice, in Copious Sets of Books, exhibiting all the Varieties that usually occur in Real Business."† This was his bible, perhaps second only to the book he ordered from London, soon after he married Martha: "a small piece in octavo, called 'A New System of Agriculture, or a Speedy Way to Grow Rich.'"‡ His 900-volume library was filled with all the get-rich-quick handbooks of the day.

I have gone on at such length about General Washington's qualifications as a bookkeeper to disarm those critics who might lack faith in the reliability and accuracy of his figures. Personally, I believe he actually spent every farthing he listed. With his reputation for candor, there is no reason to doubt it.

The modern expense account writer, who sits down to straighten out his financial affairs at the end of a busy week, may wonder if order was imposed on confusion. This expense account is neatly written in Washington's fine Italian hand, as if at one very long sitting. That the General was able to keep all his notes and receipts on where he ate, slept, etc., through the eight years of battles and retreats is yet another reason why everybody in the field must look up to this paragon.

He wrote the book, as we say.

* Robert Morris to President of Congress, April 20, 1782; in *Official Letter Book C,* Morris Correspondence, LC, pp. 198–201. Anything Morris wrote or said must be taken with a grain of salt.

† *A Catalogue of The Washington Collection in the Boston Athenaeum,* ed. Appleton P. C. Griffin (Boston: 1897), p. 134.

‡ *The Writings of George Washington,* ed. Worthington C. Ford, II (New York: 1889–1893), p. 129.

3.

THIS EXPENSE ACCOUNT is filled with tales of violence, sex, and camaraderie; of betrayal and espionage; of night patrols and hot pursuits; of men living on the edge of death or capture by the hated tyrant. There is a cast of thousands, whose exploits are documented. Like most good novels, expense accounts don't spell everything out for the reader, but trigger the thought processes.

Washington's tour de force has the power to evoke more than the rattle of sabres, the roars of muskets, the smells of damp defective gunpowder that our profiteers were foisting off on the army. It evokes the aromas of dinners cooking in the special dining hut the General ordered built for his wife's visit to Valley Forge, the rustle of clean sheets in the numerous inns he slept at while forced to live the dull bachelor life for eight years, the romance and mystery of far-off places such as Perth Amboy, the Paris of New Jersey, during the Revolutionary period.

In many ways, the expense account is also a morality play. More than the TV western or professional baseball and football—the current favorites of critics seeking hidden meanings—this document explores the roots of American society. Once we read of Washington's "true blue values," the moralistic simplicity of his work, it is hard to feel a sense of alienation with the state of the nation as it is today.

Some of the passages are pure poetry. They can bring tears to the eyes of patriots. It can be argued that a line like this one (from Valley Forge, the winter of 1777 to 1778)—"To Capt. Gibbs . . . Household Expenses . . . $2,000"—may not be literature, but it is living journalism, crammed with vital statistics. This novel-morality play-poetry-journalism is written in translucent, terse, idiomatic business English, which modern expense account writers will immediately identify with and interpret on the basis of their own experience in the field.

It is not easy to summarize the contents of this book any further, other than to say that it tells the complete story of the war from the first day the General went on the expense account to the last time he picked up the tab for a lunch catered by Fraunces Tavern in the field at Orangetown, New York, some thirty miles from Lower Broadway.*

* Henry R. Drowne, pamphlet, *The Story of Fraunces Tavern* (New York: 1966), p. 20. These were unusual expenses. "Fraunces, shortly after the

Some of the financial items do not readily work as history. For example, when Washington notes that he spent a few dollars of an afternoon at "J. Sparhawk's," the reader may not know that (1) John Sparhawk's was the Georg Jensen's of Philadelphia and (2) that Washington bought a book on the art of war, a legitimate purchase for a top general. Perhaps this was the book that helped influence the General's troop information and education policies: "Field Marshal Count Saxe's Plan for new-modelling the French Army, reviving its Discipline and improving its Exercise, In which are shewn the Advantages of the Roman Legion."*

From other sources, one has to learn that General Washington was an earnest advocate of flogging for almost every offense from disobedience and dishonesty to playing cards. Corporal punishment of 39 lashes was considered stern discipline in a volunteer army composed of Minutemen and farm boys; Washington therefore introduced sergeant punishment. Looking through his *Orderly Books,* one finds 100 lashes, or even 300. On some occasions he added, "to be well washed with salt and water after he has received his last 50."†

When Washington describes the march of the army from Valley Forge, it is not clear that the orderly formations were due to the sweat and tears of Friedrich Wilhelm Ludolf Gerhard Augustin, Freiherr von Steuben. The arrival of the creator of the American *wehrmacht* is not noted directly in these pages. The stout, balding, big-nosed baron, resplendent in a new blue uniform upon whose breast flashed, as large as a saucer, the dazzling jeweled Star of the Order of Fidelity of Baden, arrived in camp without knowing a

---

news of the cessation of hostilities and preliminary treaty of peace, April 19, 1783, came up from the city, on some two or three occasions, to provide for the American officers and their British guests, who met to arrange matters relative to the withdrawl of British troops in the vicinity of New York," Drowne writes. "In May, 1783, when General Washington and Sir Guy Tarleton met near Tappan, a Philadelphia newspaper comments on the expense of the entertainment as amounting to the modest sum of five hundred pounds.

"On the 4th of May, 1783 General Washington, Governor Clinton, General Scott, Lieutenant Colonels Trumbull, Cobb, Humphreys and Varick, after having visited General Knox, then in command at West Point, were furnished on their arrival at Tappan, with a repast provided by Fraunces. On the 6th of May also, the meeting quoted as taking place at Orangetown about 4 P.M.— General Washington, Governor Clinton, Egbert Benson, John M. Scott and Jona [sic] Trumbull, Jr. being present 'when a most sumptuous dinner was served to about thirty who ate and drank in the Peace and good fellowship, without drinking any toasts.' "

* In the Boston Athenaeum collection of Mount Vernon books. The Comte de (Herman Maurice) Saxe was Marshal of France when he wrote this manual, published in 1753. As far as I have been able to determine, Washington modeled himself after not Saxe but Frederick the Great, with less than Prussian thoroughness.

† John Whiting, *Revolutionary Orders of Gen. Washington.* Selected from the MS., pp. 39, 64.

word of English. He did have a 17-year-old French secretary, Pierre Duponceau, two aides, a German servant and an Italian greyhound.* Baron von Steuben taught drill on the muddy fields of Valley Forge from three in the morning until six in the evening. Those who didn't shape up, according to the *Orderly Books,*† were "relegated to the awkward squad to learn manners."

The need for stern discipline and drill pained George Washington, though probably not nearly as much as the men, and a good case could be made for forgetting about this unpleasant aspect of our history. Since General Washington's views on law and order in the army were well known when the expense account was written, as reflected by the sharp decline in enlistments, there is no point in not mentioning what happened to those guilty of petty crime. By going into this aspect of army life, I also hope to disabuse you of the notion that our patriotic ancestors were all sadists; many of them must have been masochists.

Perhaps the most serious shortcoming of the book is that it fails to explain how George Washington got the expense account in the first place. Some of what happened in that election in Philadelphia is now clear.

In May 1775, when the 43-year-old George Washington arrived at the second session of the Continental Congress, his rank was that of delegate, or congressman, representing the Fairfax district. He was one of sixty-three assembled in Carpenter's Hall, "a respectable looking building . . . originally constructed for the hall of meeting for the Society of House Carpenters."‡ Later the building housed the first national bank, founded by some of Washington's influential army and congressional friends.

Washington had seniority as a congressman, having also served in the first Continental Congress in 1774. The Virginia delegation was a powerful one, including such well-known orators as Patrick Henry, Peyton Randolph, Richard Henry Lee, Edmund Pendleton, Richard Bland and Benjamin Harrison. But it was Washington's words that were being discussed in the smoke-filled tavern rooms of Philadelphia that spring.

A South Carolina congressman, Thomas Lynch, reportedly observed the election campaign for delegates in the House of Burgesses at Williamsburg on his way up to Philadelphia. "He told us that Colonel Washington made the most eloquent speech at the Virginia Convention that ever was made," recalled John Adams, the congressman for Braintree, Massachusetts. "Says he, 'I will raise

---

* George F. Scheer and Hugh F. Rankin, *Rebels and Redcoats* (Cleveland: 1957), p. 352.

† A. Lewis, *Orderly Books,* p. 6; in Charles K. Bolton's *The Private Soldier Under Washington* (New York: 1902), p. 231.

‡ John F. Watson, *Annals of Philadelphia,* I (Philadelphia: 1830), p. 419.

one thousand men, submit them at my own expense, and march myself at their head for the relief of Boston.' "*

These were more stirring and practical words than "Give me liberty or give me death." A better and more timely speech could not have been made. The evidence suggests that it wasn't. Adams is the only contemporary who recorded Lynch's report of the speech. Others must have discounted it as campaign oratory on the part of the South Carolinian, a known friend of Washington's. The sentiments undoubtedly were Washington's, but the financial details, in the light of his acceptance speech, were probably garbled.

His colleagues in Philadelphia called him Colonel Washington. While Washington was a veteran of the French and Indian War, the title then had as much prestige as esquire has today. All Virginia politicians were called "colonel."

Colonel Washington hadn't drilled a soldier in a decade. The last time he was on active duty with the Virginia militia he was credited with the capture of Fort Duquesne (Pittsburgh, such as it was in the autumn of 1758). Some historians tend to deprecate this accomplishment since the fort was empty at the time. The French and Indians had pulled out secretly the night before Washington marched his troops in. Whether the young colonel knew that, history does not tell us.

Two years earlier, Washington had been responsible for the planning and erection of Fort Necessity, near the present Uniontown, Pennsylvania. The site he selected was the bottom of a valley, by the side of a creek, with higher ground all around it. The French and Indians, hiding in the surrounding woods at higher elevations, could see the interior of the fort at all times. Even in a moderate rain, with water draining from the surrounding slopes, the fort became a muddy pond. After nine hours of siege by the French and Indians during a heavy rain storm, Washington was forced to surrender Fort Necessity. Military experts today say that the raw colonel made every conceivable military error, save one: capitulating, thus saving his men from drowning. But that is hindsight.

Colonel Washington was allowed to walk back to Virginia with his 350 men. As one of the conditions in the surrender agreement, the French demanded that Washington swear not to build another fort on the Ohio for the period of a year. It was easy to see why the French lost that war.

There was some resentment about the way Washington ran the Virginia militia during the French and Indian War. The troops drank and caroused too much, immorality was rife in the ranks—the usual complaints from the Church of England crowd in Virginia, which eventually made the newspapers. Some one named "Centinel X" wrote an article in the *Virginia Gazette,* in which Washington's

* *The Works of John Adams, Second President of the United States,* II (Boston: 1850–1856), p. 360.

management of military affairs was denounced as inefficient. But the young colonel wasn't mentioned by name.

Despite this relatively undistinguished war record, Washington's name was one of those being considered by Congress for the great honor of Commander in Chief. Few would have known enough of the details of those frontier battles to have called George Washington a George Plimpton of war. The poverty of his experience, besides, was more than compensated for by his wealth.

In those days being rich was not the suspicion-breeding handicap it is today. The Congress, which later passed a declaration of independence with high-minded words about equality, felt no general could command the respect of either his own soldiers or his enemy unless he had an independent income and social prestige. Like most plantation owners, Washington had met payrolls. They were the only Americans at the time with the managerial ability and experience in giving orders and caring for hundreds.*

Still, the army besieging Boston, some members of Congress felt, should be led by a Northerner. Troops from the New England colonies were manning the trenches. As their first major contribution to the war effort, Southern congressmen wanted to send a Southerner to the front at Boston as supreme commander. The orators in the Virginia delegation persuasively explained it to John Adams, the leader of the New England bloc in Congress. Seeing the logic of the Virginia position, Adams began a talent hunt on the floor of Congress for a Virginia general.

There was Colonel Washington, who by making the offer to finance his own private army had shown that he was ready to risk everything he had striven so hard to build. That was a declaration of open rebellion, even if the squire of Mount Vernon hadn't said it in quite those words. Adams became Washington's unofficial campaign manager.

Most of the opposition to Colonel Washington seemed to come from the Virginia delegation. The favorite son of the Virginians was Colonel William Byrd of Westover. He had succeeded Colonel Washington as commander of the Virginia militia after the French and Indian War, and had been an active soldier while Washington was growing rich as a tobacco planter and speculator in western lands. Washington's coldest critics during the war years always seemed to be his neighbors. While it may have been that the old Virginia colonels thought they knew more about the art of war than Washington, it also may have been the human inability to see grandeur in one's neighbors.

Colonel Washington did not campaign for the job. To the end, he denied that he was a candidate. His letters home to his constituents, especially to his wife, Martha, made that clear. Still the New Eng-

---

* Jackson T. Main, *The Social Structure of Revolutionary America* (Princeton: 1965), p. 155.

land delegates couldn't forget about him. "Col. Washington appears at Congress in his uniform," Adams wrote to his wife, "and by his great experience in military matters is of much service to us."*

At the time Washington was not serving in a military capacity, but as informal chairman of the equivalent of our House Armed Services Committee, drafting rules and regulations for the new national army. Every visitor to Carpenter's Hall who looked through the doors asked: "Who is the tall gent in the uniform?"†

Washington scholars argue about the exact color of the uniform.‡ It was probably the buff and red (or blue) of the Virginia militia, which stood out smartly against the delegates' buff and brown. Such attendance by a member of a deliberative body dressed in an old service uniform, however, would be regarded as startling today. Think of Representative Richard Nixon sitting at the House Un-American Activities Committee sessions in the late 1940s in his Lieutenant-Commander's naval uniform.

Through the hot weeks Washington was silent in speech and loud in military garments. The 6′3″ statuesque figure undoubtedly cast a spell over Congress. He certainly was no office-seeker in the common sense, since he was on the record as being against giving the job to himself. What Colonel Washington was doing showing up in his uniform every day was expressing his hawkish attitude towards the war. "It was the highest aspiration of patriotism," explained Charles Francis Adams, the grandson of John Adams and a military historian who served as a Brevet-General in the Civil War, "offering to meet danger in any situation which such services as he could render might avail to defend his country. Viewed in this light, then, it would seem as if, when answering the much agitated question 'Who nominated Washington to the chief of command?' it might be affirmed that he most unconsciously nominated himself."§

The question is still open, as far as I am concerned. Colonel Washington's name was officially placed in nomination on Friday, June 16, some historians say, by John Adams. Others say he was nominated by Thomas Johnson, a Maryland congressman who was Washington's partner in the Potomac [Canal] Company and later a Supreme Court Justice in the first administration.‖ Whoever did it,

---

* John Adams, *Familiar Letters of John Adams and His Wife Abigail During the Revolution*, ed. Charles Francis Adams (New York: 1876), p. 59.

† W. E. Woodward, *George Washington: The Image and the Man* (New York: 1926), p. 259.

‡ Douglas S. Freeman, *George Washington*, III (New York: 1951), p. 426, n.

§ Charles F. Adams, in Proceedings of *Massachusetts Historical Society*, IV, p. 10.

‖ Herbert B. Adams, paper, "Washington's Interest in the Potomac Company," Johns Hopkins University, *Studies in Historical and Political Science*, 3rd Series (January, 1885), p. 82, Baltimore. See Washington's investments in the Ohio Company, the Mississippi Company, Great Dismal Swamp Company, and most other speculative real estate ventures of the period. Washington

the fact remains that the hero of Fort Necessity seemed genuinely surprised by the maneuver. He rushed out of the room during the nominating speech and hid in the library until after the results were in. (One wonders how Representative L. Mendel Rivers, the present chairman of the House Armed Services Committee, would have reacted if, after donning his old World War I uniform, he had been elected to head the Joint Chiefs of Staff in the Vietnam War.)

George Washington, then, was probably the first man in the history of the American army to be drafted.

4.

SINCE "no pecuniary consideration" could have tempted General Washington to accept the arduous employment, as he said in the Expense Account Address, it is obvious that he didn't take the job for the money. A study of the pay table that Congress voted the same day that General Washington became 1-A in the draft indicates this was not as great a financial sacrifice as it may seem.

"That the pay of officers and privates be as follows," the act of Congress read:

> "Privates . . . . $6⅔ per month
> Drummers . . . . Same
> Corporals $7⅓
> Sergeants $8
> Lieutenants $13⅓
> Captains . . . . $20"

Of the general officers, brigadiers were rated at $125 and major generals at $166 a month. All were "to find their own Arms and Clothes."* The pay scale for soldiers in the colonial period was

---

bought land claims given his soldiers in lieu of salary during the French and Indian War, and continued this sound policy even at Valley Forge. As he wrote to his brother John Augustine in 1780, when the bottom had dropped out of the real estate market (some critics say because of his military leadership): "It ever was my opinion, though candor obliges me to confess it is not consistent with national policy, to have my property as much as possible in lands. I have seen no cause to change this opinion; but abundant reason to confirm me in it; being persuaded that a few years peace will inundate these States with emigrants and of course enhance the price of land far above the common interest of money." Those who say Washington would have done anything for money are in error; I can't vouch for the man on land.

* Peter Force, *American Archives,* IV Series, pp. 1847, 1849.

generally below the income of lawyers, but more than the income of other professional men.*

Congress had voted $500 a month for the Commander in Chief. Alarmed that the people would think the salaries extravagant, John Adams was very relieved as he wrote home to his wife the good news that the General had "accepted the mighty trust" and would not accept "a shilling for pay."† Obviously Adams saw the General's service as a petty cash item. Congress miscalculated, in much the same way it projects military expenditures today.

As a gentleman volunteer under Braddock, Washington had given the British Army his services without pay. But that was because the British War Office refused to hire him as an officer. Now he was repeating the gesture on a grander scale.

Being disinterested in "the proffit" motive, Washington's only other possible motive in giving Congress this deal was psychological. Declining the salary set him apart at once from all the other officers who had to take their pay, since they needed the money to live. It was a patriotic action, of course, but it was also a snobbish action.

General Washington wasn't born with a silver spoon in his mouth.‡ He had to make his own way, to fight, even as you and I, against social and economic forces which tended to drag him down. As a thirteen-year-old, while his friends the children of Colonel Fairfax rode to the hounds, he was forced to learn a trade as a surveyor. They didn't have child-labor laws in those days, perhaps the reason so many of Washington's admirers today disapprove of such legislation. The youth had to struggle to accumulate his slaves one by one, until he made a fortunate match with the wealthiest widow in Virginia. In dress, equipage, etiquette, dances, he always wanted to be in fashion. In the years since he had inherited Mount Vernon, he had managed to convert a simple Virginia cottage into a pretentious mansion. As much as we admire Washington, we must admit that he was a status-seeker, an authentic big spender, and the prototype of the great American consumer. His lust for the best in shelter, food, and high-minded recreation, on credit, is admired because his taste excelled. But it kept him on the brink of bankruptcy in the prewar and postwar years.

"I wish, my dear Steward," he wrote to a London shopkeeper shortly after the French and Indian War, "that the circumstances of my affairs would have permitted me to have given you an order . . . for £400 . . . or even twice that sum . . . But, alas! to show my inability in this respect, I enclose you a copy of Mr. Cary's [another London merchant] last account current against me, which

---

* Main, *op. cit.* p. 104.

† John Adams, *Works*, IX, pp. 357–59.

‡ Gerald W. Johnson, *Mount Vernon: The Story of a Shrine* (New York: 1953), p. 53.

upon my honor and the faith of a Christian, is a true one. . . . This upon my soul is a genuine account of my affairs in England. Here they are a little better, because I am not much in debt. I doubt not but you will be surprized at the badness of their condition unless you will consider under what terrible management and disadvantages I found my estate when I retired from the publick service of this Colony; and that besides some purchases of Lands and Negroes I was necessitated to make adjoining me (in order to support the expences of a large family), I had Provisions to buy for the first two or three years; and my Plantation to stock in short with every thing;—buildings to make and other matters which swallod up before I well knew where I was, all the money I got by marriage, nay more, brought me in debt." The same wolf scratches at the door in the suburbs today.

After the Fort Necessity campaign, the House of Burgesses gave Washington a vote of thanks, and a sum equivalent to $3.60 apiece to his men. War was a lot cheaper in pre-Revolutionary War America. Going off to war again, the rebel leader was now faced with the choice of returning to the salad days, or fighting valiantly to maintain his normal standard of living, which was roughly that of a king. He didn't lose face.

5.

FOR THE EIGHT YEARS of the war against British tyranny, General Washington turned in an expense account of $449,261.51.*

All of Washington's bill for his services, I want to point out right away, wasn't for actual expenses. It included the interest (at 6 percent per annum) he charged the government for the money he laid out from his private purse to cover his expenses the first two years of the war. He also threw in a surcharge for depreciation, which was caused to some degree by a loss of confidence in his military leadership.

This sum of $449,261.51 may seem staggering when compared to the $48,000 General Washington would have received had he gone on the payroll for eight years like the other patriot generals. But not when you compare it to what the expense account is worth in terms of today's buying power.

---

* This may actually be only $447,220.92, depending upon which system of accounting you use. Since this is a work designed to enhance Washington's reputation as an expense account writer, I am using the larger of the two. For further comment, see "Financial Note," beginning on page 97.

Those were Continental dollars Washington was writing about, much harder money than we have today. Historians have always had trouble deciding just how much sounder the dollar was in the nation's darkest days than now. Let us assume, however, that General Washington had a meal today at Fraunces Tavern, which is still frequented by army officers who work at 39 Whitehall Street, a cannon ball's distance away from the tavern in downtown New York. For argument's sake, let us assume further, the General took a girl to lunch. His secretary, or some USO girl. And picked up the tab, like the gentleman this book will prove that he was. Washington, we also will soon see, was a hearty eater. Even if he stuffed himself like a pig, a study of Fraunces Tavern menu today shows that the bill wouldn't run to more than $70 or $80. In 1775, Washington bought a whole pig for three and a half Continental dollars. Of course, this might have been a prize pig.*

Continental money has a nice ring to it today. Whether we use the conservative scale of appreciation—say 10 times the 1969 dollar—or the Galbraithean scale, more appropriate in an affluent society, of 50 times, we can see that what we're talking about here is *millions*.

If the crafty Alexander Hamilton, who was to be Washington's principal adviser on economic affairs, had invested the General's expense account money in IBM stock, or even U.S. savings bonds, we would be talking about billions.

But this is mere speculation.

General Washington wasn't one of those soldiers of fortune we're always reading about in history. It is important to remember that he was taking a risk by not being paid as he went. If the war had been lost, he would have been out quite a lot of expense money. In that case, however, he would have been hanged as a traitor anyway. So I guess that isn't too strong a point in his favor.

By deferring payment until the end of the war, rather than accepting the Continental paper dollars that the other soldiers were getting (on the rare occasions when there was money in Congress' war chest), General Washington at least had a fighting chance of getting paid in specie. It was shrewd thinking like this which makes George Washington's portrait on the dollar bill such a fitting monument.†

---

* Despite the man's inherent honesty, he submitted bills to substantiate all purchases under $25. They are mixed in with the *Washington Papers* in the Library of Congress. Unfortunately, the receipt for this purchase doesn't say whether it was a little pig or a big pig.

† See Federal Reserve Note, B35398918H, Series 1963 B, Kathryn O'Hay Granahan, Treasurer of the United States.

6.

BEFORE WE BEGIN reading this story of life, liberty, and the pursuit of happiness on an expense account, there is one further matter that requires explanation, especially for veterans and others who think they understand what war is all about.

From time to time, we will come across items like:

"To a Reconnoitre of the East River, & Along the Sound as far as Mamaraneck . . . $411."

and

"To the Expence of Reconn'g the Country as far as Perth Amboy . . . $754."

This will confuse ex-GIs because it has always been assumed that looking for the enemy was part of a soldier's rotten job, not a deductible expense. And as impressive as are these interpretations of trying to find the whites of British eyes, they don't hold a candle to General Washington charging the country for fleeing the enemy:

"To sundry Exp.'s paid by myself at different times & places in passing from the White plains, by way of King's ferry to Fort Lee—and afterwards on the Retreat of the Army thro' the Jerseys into Pennsylvania & while there . . . $3,776."

The genius of Washington in making these charges, for seeking the enemy and then running away from him, has never been fully appreciated by the military. If Washington's leadership in bookkeeping tactics had been followed, with the added democratic touch of allowing enlisted men as well as generals to hand in chits to the paymaster after every patrol, we wouldn't be in Vietnam today. The cost of running an army would be so prohibitive that not even a country with our resources could wage war without bankrupting itself. He was truly FIRST IN PEACE. His critics say that Washington's thinking seemed hazy—when you look for an Adam Smith, a Ricardo, a Rousseau, a Locke. But the quality of his mind can't be discounted. It compares favorably to the average big city banker of today.

Some of the things Washington was trying to say in this work may have escaped even me. I'm no financial wizard. No free-lance writer is. It could even be argued that a literary man shouldn't undertake a study of this kind; it is more properly the work for an FBI man.

That is what Washington scholars would call "a little hatchet job." I wouldn't want to be involved in anything that would tend to undermine the expense account way of life, the backbone of American society. If I occasionally have erred by bending over backwards to explain away some minor inconsistency in the pages that follow, I can only say in my defense that George Washington would have done the same thing for himself.

Speaking for my silent partner and myself, I trust that you will give the expense account more attention than the traditional July Fourth oratory. It is perhaps the most definitive statement ever written about American integrity.

—MARVIN KITMAN
(For George Washington)

Leonia, New Jersey
October 1969

II

ORIGINAL VERSION

*Accounts, G. Washington with the
United States, Commencing June 1775,
and Ending June 1783, Comprehending
a Space of 8 Years*

* *

TREASURY DEPARTMENT,
REGISTER'S OFFICE, *1st June,* 1833.

√

General WASHINGTON's Account of Expenses during
the Revolutionary War, in his own hand writing, is on
file in this office.   *The annexed is a fac simile copy of it.*

[signature]

Chief Clerk in the Register's Office.

* *

Accounts,

G. Washington - with the

United States,

Commencing June 1775,

and ending June

1783,

Comprehending a Space

of 8 Years.

1) Dr. The United States...... in		Penn^a	Law^
			2,6, Dollar
1775 June. No 1	To the purchase of five Horses (two of which were had on credit from Mr James Mease) to equip me for my journey to the Army at Cambridge — & for the service I was then going upon — having sent my Chariot and Horses back to Virginia.	£239 —	
22 No 2	To a light Phaeton bot of Doctr Renaudet	55 —	
3	To double Harness ford bought from Mr Todd	7.15 —	
4	To Cash paid for Sadlery, a Letter Case, Maps, Glasses, do do do for the use of my Command	29.13.6	
5	To Mrs Beny a Hammens for keeping the above Horses	5.6.2	
July No 6	To the acct of Thomas Mifflin Esqr for money expended by him in the journey from Philadelphia to Cambridge in which the Expences of General Lee, Colo Reed &c were included	129.8.2	
	Amt carrd forwd Dr	£466.2.10	

with ..... G Washington .... Cr 2

1775		Lawful
		cp dollars 6/
ly	By Cash for a Gun and	
	accoutrements - - - - - - - - - - -	£ 3 0 0

Am car for £ 3 0 0

3) Dr. The United States ... in

		Penna	Law
1775			
July	To amount brot forward $466..2.4		
No 7	To Sundry Sums paid by my self in the aforesaid Journey - amountg. to		34 8
No 8 5	To R. Parbauks acct		2 8
„ 9	To Saml Griffin Esqr	1..15.4	
„ 10	To the Expences of myself & party reconnoitrg the Sea Coast East of Boston Harbor		18 13
„ 15	To 333⅓ Dollars given to _____ * to induce him to go into the Town of Boston ; to establish a secret Correspondence for the purpose of con- veying intelligence of the Enemys move ments & designs		100 -
12	To Cash paid for cleaning the House which was provided for my Quarters & wch had been occupied by the Marblehead Regmt		2 10
13 19	To Ditto to Mr. Ebenr Austen the Steward for House hold Expences †		10 ~
14 24	To Ditto - paid a French Cook		2 5
„ 15	To Ditto - paid Mr Austen for Household Expence		2
	An carrd forwd - £ 467. 18. 2 $172 - 5		

* The names of Persons who are employed within the Enemys Lines, or who may fall within their power cannot be inserted

Æ------ G. Washington --- Cr (4

		Lawful		
4	By amount bro.ᵗ forward ___	£ 3	0	0
19	By. Cash of Ies.ᵈ Trambull Esq.ʳ			
	Commissary General ____	200	~	

By amᵗ carrᵈ forward. £ 203 | 0 | 0

+ This, and every other sum which will
be found charged in Rescacᵗⁿ to Mᵒʳ
Custis, are credited in his Book of
Household Expenditures, herewith
given in as a Voucher. ___

5) Dr. The United States

1775			Pers.ª	Lᵘ	
July	To amount broᵗ forward		£467-18-2	172	5
Novʳ 26	To Mʳ Austen for House Expences			10	
	2.	To Mʳ Honer. accᵗ		5	9
Aug 1		To Mʳ Austen — Houseʰᵈ Exp		2	
18 — 5		Ditto .... Ditto		8	
19		To washing at sundry times		4	12
20		To Servants at Ditto		4	16
21		To Mʳ Willᵐ Vans accᵗ		81	11
22 — 8		To Danⁱ Isley pᵈ accᵗ		6	
23 17		To Giles Alexander Dᵒ		1	
24 18		To Reuben Colburn		10	
25 20		To Mʳ Austin ... Hᵈ Expᵗ		10	
26		Ditto ..... Ditto		2	8
27 — 21		Ditto ..... Ditto		18	
28 23		To James Campbell — necessaries for the House		1	10
29 25		To Jehoiakim Jenkin Dᵒ Dᵒ		1	10
30 29		Td Mʳ Austen — Hᵈ Expᵗ		12	
31		To Paper, Sealing Wax &ᶜ of Severals		6	10
Sepʳ 1		To Cash for recovering my Pistols which had been stolen, & for repairing them afterwards		1	10
33		To Mʳ Sparhawks accᵗ		22	1
34 7		To Mʳ Purce assᵗ to Genᵉˡ Gates — Wages		4	
35		To Reuben Colburn		16	8
36		To S. B. Webb Esq. for Majʳ French (a Prisoner) his Expᵗ to Hartford		12	
37		To Mʳ Austen — Hᵈ Expᵗ		6	
38 — 18		To The Expᵗ of myself and Party in reconnoitring the South & west shore of Boston Harbor		16	8
39		Amᵗ carᵈ forwᵈ	£467.18.2	435	17

Pr with ..... G. Washington ... Cr ⑥

		Lawful		
1775				
July.	By amt. bro.t Forw.d 3	£203	—	
28	By Cash to Thos. Mifflin Esq.			
	aid de Camp — advd. by Jos.h	5		
	Trumbull Esq. Com.t Genl ...	32	—	
2	By Ditto from the Paymaster			
♀21	Genl. Warren .... 1000 Dollars ~	300	—	
	By Ditto from Mr. Oswald — Balt			
	of money put into his hand			
	to bear his Exps. to Recorde			
	20ga .... — — — —	1	17	3
	By Ditto from James Barry for			
	a Musket	3	—	
	Amt. carrd. forward £	539	17	3

7) **Dr. The United States** ....

1775			Benja.			Lawfu		
Sep.		To amount bro.t forn.d ____ £	467	18	2	435	17	—
40	28	To Mr. Austin ___ H.d Exp.s ___				12		
41	—	———— Ditto ____ Ditto ___				6		
42	—	To Ebenr. Frey				6		
43	—	To Mr. Willm. Van ___				35	6	11
44	—	To Capt.n Osnald — p.a Con-						
		stant Harts — rec.t				3	7	3
45	Oct 1	To Blacksmiths acc.t al						
		sundry times to the date				3	6	4
46	—	To Servants ___ Do ___ Do				1	16	—
47	—	To Washing ___ Do ___ Do				6	11	4
48	—	To Servants Wages in						
		part — 74. dollars				18	4	—
49	2	To Expens at My stick ___				2	16	4
		Ditto for servants ___				1	8	9
50	—	To a Field Bedstead & Cur-						
		tains, Mattrass, Blan-						
		kets &c.a &c.a had of						
		different Persons ___				22	—	—
51	3	To Walter White Esq.r for						
		a Riding Mare ___				18	—	—
52	5	To Mr. Austen ___ H.d Exp.s				6		
53	—	To Halters — &c.a				2	4	
54	6	To Mr. Ritchie ___				28	—	
55	—	To Expens of My self & Party						
		visils. the shores about						
		Chelsea ___				8	5	6
56	10	To Mr. Austin ___ H.d Exp.s				6		
57	—	To Wm. Ryan's acc.t				2	16	—
58	16	To Mr. Austin H.d Exp.s				16	10	
59	23	Ditto ___ Ditto ___				6		
60	27	Ditto ___ Ditto ___				2	2	
61	30	Ditto ___ Ditto ___				12		
62	—	To Cash gave servants at						
		different times ___				2	8	—
63	—	To Josiah Fessendon ___				6		
64	—	To Moses Fessendon ___				5	4	
		Am.t carr.d forn.d — £	467	18	2	704	13	7
						705	13	7

acc. with ... G Washington ... C.^r (8)

			Lawful		
1775					
Aug.	By amount bro.^t forw.^d ... £	539	17	3
Oct. 6	By Cash from the Pay master			
	Genl ... 500 Dollars = ...	150	—	—
	Am.^t carr.^d forward — £	689	17	3

9) Dr The United States .... ½ acc

1775			Pers.	Law
Oct.	To Am.t bro.t forward --- £	467. 18.2	704	13
Nov 5	To Geo: Bayler Esq.r			
x. 65 ---	p.r acc.t		3	9
66 7.	To Mr. Austin --- H.d Exp.s		9	
67 10.	Ditto Do		9	
68 20	Ditto --- Do		12	
69 —	To Exp.s at Roxburg ---		6	2
70 —	To Mr. Austin --- H.d Exp.s		12	18
71 22	Ditto Do		12	
72 30	To Elijah Bennet ---		18	
73 Dec.1	To Oway Byrd Esq.r ---			
	p.r Rec.t - & by order ---		31	
74	To Servants wages ---		9	
75 5	To Mr. Austin --- H.d Exp.s		26	8
76 —	To Mr. John Dunlap ---	11.11.6		
77 —	To Washing ---		4	13
78 —	To Barber at Sundry times		6	10
79 .12	To Mr. Austin --- H.d Exp.s		36	
80 19	To Mr. Van ---	37	18	
81 28	To Sam.l B Webb Esq.r for			
1776	Sundries - House use		10	6
Jan.9	To Mr. Austin --- H.d Exp.s		32	8
83 —	To the Farrier - attending			
	My sick Horses ---		7	10
84 ---	To the Relief of the distress			
	sad wives & children of			
	the soldiers from Mar-			
	blehead ---		15	
85 ---	To Ditto of Ditto Cape Ann		10	
86 17	To Mr. Austin --- H.d Exp.s		32	8
87 20	To Paschal Smith Esq.r ---		75	
88 25	To Mr. Matth.w Irwin ---		14	2
89 29	To Barber ---		3	15
90 —	To Geo: Bayler Esq.r - Exp.s to			
	& from Norwalk on busin.s		21	5
91 Feb 1	To Oway Byrd Esq.r - p.r ord.r		30	10
92 ---	To Washing ---		3	16
	Carr.d forward. £	479-9 8	1177	12

with ---- G. Washington --- Cr ⑩

1775			Lawful		
Oct.	By amⁿᵗ broᵗ forward ----	£689	17	3
Dec 19	By Cash of the Paymaster			
	General ---- 1600 Dollars -	300	—	
26.	By Ditto returned from Colᵒ			
	Fry's Regiment overp᷎ ----	22		

10.

Amᵗ carr᷎ forwᵈ ---- £1011 17 3

JJ) Dr. The United States ____ in ac

1776			Pensa		Lawful		
Feb.		To amount brot forwd ___	£479-9-8		1177	12	
93	5.	To George Bayler Esqr per Sundry articles purchased by him for the use of the Family ___			6	17	
94	7	To Mr. Austin ___ Hd Expo ___			32	8	
95		To Saylering for my ten ___			8	12	
96		To Postage of Letters ___			3	12	
97	22.	To Mr Austin ___ Hd Exp			40	10	
98	Mar 2	To Thos Patton ___			6	1	
99	4	To Expo of my self and Party recce 9. Dorchester Heights previous to our possessing them ___			10	10	
100		To Sadlery ___			2	0	
101	12	To Mr Austin ___ Hd Expo			32	8	
102	19	To Mrs Wm Bartlett ___			38	12	
103	23	To Cash advanced the Baron De Woodhte ___			3	12	
104	25.	To Mr Wm Hollingshead ___			37	1	5
105		To Mr Austin ___ Hd Expo			18		
106	28	To Mr Josh Hanbury ___				16	
107	30	To Cash advanced Lieuts. Birmingham, Wm Burr & Timothy Seely Rifle= men from Quebec ___			6		
108	31.	To Washing ___			3	12	
109	2	To Barber ___			1	10	
111	Apl 1	To amount of Sundry ho pd Messrs for secret Services to the date ___			232		
112	2	To Captn Oakley to bear his Exp. to Providence			1	4	
113		To Steacy Reed ___ Sundries			3	5	
114		To Mr Hastings Postage			3	5	
115		To Mr Austin ___ Hd Expo			35	9	
		Carrd forward £479-9-8			1704	19	

with ---- G. Washington ---- Cr. (12

1775			Lawful		
Dec. 2	By am.t bro.t forward ------	£	1011	17	3
1776 Feb.17	By Cash of the Pay master General -- 1000 Dollars --		300	—	
Mar.14	By Ditto from D.o -- 1000 D.o --		300	—	
29	By Ditto rec.d from Dum.n Newet -Ball.o of money put into his hands by warrant to purchase arms -------		116	6	6
30	By Ditto rec.d from Col.o Mitchell on a similar acc.t --		85	10	—
e.r 3	By Ditto rec.d from M.r James Barrett. & others -- D.o --		182	14	—

£ 1996 7 9

13) Dr. The United States ... in Acc

1776			Pers.ª	Lawfu	
Aprl	To amount broᵗ forwᵈ --- £479-9-8			1704	19
Nº 116	To Expⁿ in visiting the several Islands in Boston Harbor - after the Evacuation of the Town by the Enemy ---			8	15
117 4	To Mr. Austin - for Balᵉ of his accᵗ as Steward to the date - and my leaving Cambridge for New York ---			9 2 4	
18 ---	To Barber - in full ---			5 18 4	
	To Washing --- Dᵒ ---			7 4 8	
119 6	To Cash paid Govⁿ Cooke at Providence p. acᵗ ---			15 —	
120	To Mr. Fessenden. Express Rider - twice ---			5 14	
121 13	To Expⁿ on the Road from Cambridge to New Gᵏ by the way of Provid. & alsᵗ the Sound p. Mr. Palfrey ---			53 15 2	
122 —	To Ditto paid by myself in Providence dᵒ exclu- sive of the above ---			12 10 9	
123 —	To the Expⁿ of Maj. Wary & Harrison - My Aids de Camp on the upper, or Commⁿ Post Road with Mrs. Washington ---			45 6	
124 15	To Mr. Philips for Riding Express to Commodore Hopkins at New London ---			3 —	
125 --	To Expⁿ of a Party of Oneida Indⁿ on a visit to me - & for presᵗ for them ---			15 1	
	Carrᵈ forward £479-9-8			1886	1

with ----- G. Washington ⫶ Cr (14

		Lawful	
776	By amount brot forward — £ 1996-7-9		
2ᵈ.	By Cash of the Pay master		
	General -- 1000 Dollᵐ --	300 --	

Carrd fornᵈ -- £ 2296-7-9

15) Dr. The United States ..... in acc

			Pensª		Lawfu
1776					
Apᵒ	To amⁿ broᵗ forward — £	479-9-8		1886 10	0
	Deduct 25 p Cᵗ to redu				
	Penᵃ to Lawful — —	95.17.11		383 11	9
		Yorkℓurᵈ			
nᵒ 25	To the Expˢ of myself				
26	& party reccᵈ 9 the				
	Seᵛˡ Landing places				
	&ᶜᵃ on Staten Island —	16—10—			
May 11	To Robᵗ Porter — — £7 5				
nᵒ 128	To Benj. Harbeson 13.11.6			16 13 2
	20 16.6 by &c — — — —				
129	To Expˢ of a tour on, and				
	reccⁿ ɟ of Long Island —	26-8-6			
130	To Washing — dᵒ ᶜᵉ	8 3 4			
131	To Mʳ Plunket Fleesonˢ				
	accᵗ £64.2.6 Penᵃ eqᵗ			52 6	—
132. 28	To Mʳ Jnᵒ G Frazer for				
	a Trunk to pack my				
	Papers in			2 16	—
June 4	To Mʳ Sparhawk for a				
133	Collection of Maps &c				
	ver to the Book £14.18 eqᵗ			11 18 6
134	To the Expˢ of myself painit				
	to, at, & from Philᵃ				
pᵈ Mʳ Harrison — —	87-18-8			
135	To Washing & other Accⁿ				
	paid by myself amɟ				
	pᵈ Bills to — — —			10 5
136. 14	To Georᵍᵃ Baylen Esqʳ —	=		35 3
137. 26	To Abᵗ Durgee — — —	7.10.6		
138	To Expenˢ in Reccɟ the				
	Channel & landings on				
	both sides the Nᵒ River				
	as high as Tarry Town				
	to fix the defenses thereⁿ	10.18—		
	Carrᵈ forwᵈ — — £	157-9-0		2398

with ..... G. Washington 6.ᴺ (16)

1776		York Cy.	Lawful	
May	By amᵗ broᵗ forwᵈ ----		£2296	7	9
	By Sundry Sums advancᵈ			
	by Thoˢ Mifflin Esq.			
	Qᵉ Mʳ Genˡ to Mʳˢ Smith			
	the House keeper at			
	New York, for House			
	held Expences --- viz			
	Apˡ 12 ...100 Dollˢ at 8/ 40-0-0			
	18 -- 100 -------- 40 ~			
	23 --200 --------- 80 ~			
	May. 1 --100 ------- 40 ~			
	———			
	50.0			
Juneˡ	By my draft in favor of			
	Messʳˢ Mease & Caldwell			
	Penˢᵃ Curʸ. £100 ~			
	diffᶜᵉ of Excha.. 20. -------- ✓ 80 ~			

| Corᵈ Forwᵈ .. £200 ~ | 2376 | 7 | 9 |

57) Dr. The United States __ in acc

1776		York.	Law[?]
June Nº 139	To amo't bro't forward	£157-9-0	2398
	To a Recconoitre of the East River _ & along the Sound as far as Mameraneck _ _ _ _ _ _	-16.9.4	
140 26.	To Capt'n Gibbs for House hold Exp' _ _ _ _ _ 91 Doll'		-27 6
July 8.	To -Ditto _ _ _ D° -120 D°		-36
42 15.	Ditto _ _ D° -200 D°		-60
143 _ _	To Timothy Wood _ _ _ _ _	-4 15-	
144 _ _	To Mrs Smith the H° Kee per -5:0 Dollars at differ't times fr'm Thos Mifflin Esqr & Mr Ger. as p° Contra _ and 909 Dollars by myself thro' Capt'n Gibbs _ In all 1409 Dollars a 8/-	563.12	
145 _ _	To Guns bought _ _ _ _ _		13 10
146 _ _	To Lieut. Lewis _per lan dries for y' use of the H°	-2.8-	
147 _	To my own _ & Parties ex pences lay ing out Fort Lee _ on the Jersey side of the N° River _	-8.15~	
48 23.	To Capt'n Gibbs for House hold Expences 200 D'		60~
149 _	To the Expence of Reconn the Country as far as Perth Amboy _ _ _ _ _	-19.10-	
150 Aug 9	To Cap: Gibbs. H° Exp 500 D'		150
Sep 1 151	To Servants at Sundry times _ 42 Dollars _		12 12
	Carr'd forward. £	772.18.4	2757.12

with ---- G. Washington ------ Cr (18

1776		York.	Lawful		
June	By amount broᵗ forwᵈ £200 —	✓2376	7	9
Aug 9	By Cash from the Pay			
	master 1000 Dollars ___ ___	300 —		
	Carᵈ forwᵈ .. £ 200 —	✓2676	7	9

59)	Dr The United States ... in acc		York		Lawful	
1776.						
Sep.	To amot brot forward ---- £	772-18-4	2757	12	4
Oct 2.	To Richd Peacock --------	2.11 -			
153 ..6	To Capt Gibbs H Exp 500		150	-	-
154 ..2	To Exp at Valentines				
	Mile Square --20 Dol		6		
..5	To Mr Fleeson £4..6-c Rx				
	deduct 25 pCt--17.2		3	8	10
156 ---	To Barber at sundry times -	5-10			
157 - -	To Cash advanced Monr				
	Imbart French Engin		6		
Dec.	To Household Expences				
	paid by May Cary an				
	Baxler in 6 & 8 part				
	of Novr while Capt				
	Gibbs was absent with				
	the Bagage -- p acc				
	settled - viz 725½ Dol----		217	13	-
	York Cury red to Lawful	£780-19-4	3140	13,14	2
		195-4-10	585	14	6
	Expenditures of the }		£3726	7	8
	Years 1775 & 6 -- }				

No 104 £37..1..5
.. 106 - 0..16..0
         37..17..5 Penna Cury Estimated at Lawful £7..11..5
                   different ---------- }
Page 7 Short added - - - - - £1..0..0
" 19 ----- Ditto - - - - - 0..1..0   1..1..0
              Deduct -----   6 10 5
                                  £ 3719 17 3

with ---- G. Washington ---- 6.ᵛ ⟨20⟩

1776		York	Lawful
Aug.ᵗ	By am.ᵗ bro.ᵗ forward £200 —	2676	7 . 9
Oct 9.	By Cash from the Pay: master Gen.ˡ 1000 D.ˡˡ		300 —
	York Cur 7 ⅓ d.ᵗ to Lawf.ˡ	£200 — 50 —	2976 7 . 9 150 —
	Amount of the Money rec. from the Public in the Years 1775 & 6		3126 7 9
	By Ball.ᵉ due G. Washington & carr.ᵈ to acc.ᵗ for 1777	*	599 19 . 11
		£ 3726	7 . 8

* This Ball.ᵈ arises from the Expenditures of my private purse. — From which (as doth appear from the dates of the public debits against me) my outfit to take the Command of the Army at Cambridge — The Expences of the journey thither — and disbursements for some time afterwards were borne. — It being Money which I brought to, and rec.ᵈ at Philadelphia while there as a Delegate to Congress, in May & June 1775

G.º Washington

27)

(22

23) Dr. The United States—in acc.

		Dollars	Lawful		
1777 Jan 1	To Balc of the last acct accs for the years 1775 &6	---	£599	19	11.
N.1	To Colo Jos h Reed pr accs rendered the Paymastr Genc	---	37.	10	~
"2	To Sundry Exps paid by myself at different times & places in passing from the White plains by the way of Kings ferry to Fort Lee—and afterwards on the Retreat of the Army thro' the Jerseys into Pensylvania—& while there	---	126	4	3
"3	To Secret Services since the army left Cambridge in April—while it lay at New York—and durg its Retreat as above	1050 & 284	---		
4–12.	To Sundry Exps paid on the March from Trenton to Morris Town & during two days halt at Pluckemin—Vr Memm Book	98 & 35	10	-	
Feb. No.5	To Colo Weeden—leathr for the use of his Regt	500			
Mar 8	To Captn Gibbs—Hhd Exps*	-130			
7	Ditto——Ditto	260			
8	To Mr Thompson the Hhd keeper for like purposes	-10			
"2d 11	To Captn Gibbs—Hhd Exps	1000			
"	To Servants—at sev. times	-46			
1	To Benja Hennings's acco Pena Curry 7. £5 "12~11 dedg diff of Exe 1. 2. 7.	---	4	10	4
3 19	To Specie to Majr Genl Greene for secret Services—5	---	3		
May 22	To Captn Gibbs—Hhd Exps	1000			
	Am. carrd forwd	4094	£1090	14	6

* This & every other sum which is charged in these Accs Household Expenditures, which

with ---- G. Washington ---- Cr (24

1777		Dollars	Lawful
Jan.	By Cash of Robt. Morris Esqr. in Specie p̄ Acct.	----	£124-7-8
Feb. 14	By Paper Dollars of Maj. Genl. Sullivan — being the Balle. of Money put into his hands to pay the Bounty of some of the Eastern Regiments at Trenton — in Sartt. Cast	2610	
Decr. 11	By Cash of the Paymaster General ----------	1000	
	By Ditto ---- from Ditto-	1000	
	Amt. carrd. fowd. ----	4610	£124-7-8

nts to Maj. Gibbs, will be found credited in his Book of
er in as a Voucher.

25) Dr. The United States ___ in ac

			Dollr	Lawf	
1777					
May	To amount brot. forward ___		4094	1090	14
June 1	To Secret Services to this date ___		846 &	135	__
16 ___	To Mr. Parke Custis Esqr. for a riding Horse ___		333⅓		
17 Aug 4	To Colo. Moylan for Ditto having lost two of mine with the distemper that raged ___		200		
18 8	To Captn. Gibbs ___ H.d Exp.s ___		1000		
19 28	Ditto ___ Ditto ___		1000		
20	To Secret Services while the two armies were Manauvering in the Jerseys—& till the British Sailed for the H.d of Elk ___		580 &	52	10
21 ___	To Expenditures pr. my Mem Book on the march from Middle brooks in the Jerseys to Smiths Clove,—and from Smiths Clove in the State of New York to the Cross Roads in Pensyca ___		167 &	44	5
22 ___	To Expended in a tour to examine Mud Isld. Red bank and Billingsport ___		60⅔		
23 ___	To Ditto—going to Marcushook ___		86		
24 ___	To Ditto on the march from the Cross Roads to Wilmington in the State of Delaware exclusive of other acc ts ___		234		
25 ___	To the Expence of a Reconnoitre to the head of Elk, with a large party of Horse when the Enemy's were abt. landing there ___		185 &	22	1
	Carr.d forward ___		8786 &	1345	4

...ith ‒‒‒‒‒ G Washington ‒‒‒‒ C.ʳ 26

		Dollʳˢ	Lawful
77			46 10	£ 124 ‒ 7 ‒ 8
ʸ May	By amount bro.ᵈ forⁿᵈ ‒‒‒‒	46 10	£ 124 ‒ 7 ‒ 8
ly 30	By Warr.ᵗ on the Paymas ter General ‒‒‒‒‒	1000	
º 7	By Ditto ‒‒ on Ditto ‒‒‒‒‒	100c	
	By Cash rec.ᵈ from Col.º Reeder ‒ am.ᵗ of what he had borrow.ᵈ ‒‒‒‒‒	500	
28	By Ditto ‒ of the Paymaster General ‒‒‒‒‒‒‒‒	1000	

Carr.ᵈ forⁿ 8110 £ 124 ‒ 7 ‒ 8

27) Dr. The United States.....cr

1777		Dolls	Lawf
Aug. 3	To am.t bro.t forward	8786	1345 4
Sep 14 No 26	To Expenditures after the Battle of Brandy Wine untill we arrived at German Town — p.r mem.m Book	1128	15 6
27 —	To Cash advanced to Serv.ts at sundry times	52	—
Oct 11	To Capt.n Gibbs for H.d Exp.s	1000	
Dec 25 No 29 —	To Expenditures in the different & continual movements of the Army from the time of its march from German town Sep.r 15th till we Hutted at Valley forge the 25th of Dec.r p.r mem.ms	10374 78 10	
1778. 30 Jan. No 35	To Secret Services since the Enemy's Landing at the Head of Elk to the present date	1415	20 10
31 29	To Capt.n Gibbs — H.d Exp.s	2000	
Ap 10	Ditto — Ditto	1000	
June 5	To Capt.n Barry p.r acc.t	356	
34 16	To Maj.r Gibbs H.d Exp.s	2000	
35 18	To Secret Services during the Enemys hold P. Phila.	450	220
3 Aug. No 36	To Sundry Expenditures on the march of the Army from Valley forge June 18th (by the way of Monmouth) till its arrival at the white plains the latter end of July	3244 46	
Sep No 37	To Cash paid in Recon. g the Custm. ab.t the Plains, betw.n the N.o & East Rivers	133	— —
	Carr.d forward	18,665	1725 15

th ----- G Washington ------ 6. Nᵒ 28

		Dollᵈˢ	Lawful		
77	By amᵗ brot forward ----	8110	124	7	8 0
..10	By Cash from the Paymas- ter General ---------	1000			
23	By Ditto --- from Ditto --	1000			
c 21	By --Ditto -- from Ditto Warrᵗ in favor of Geo Baylor Esqʳ Novʳ 12. 1776 -	1000			
78					
.29	By Ditto --- from Ditto ---	2000			
30	By Ditto ----- Dᵒ	1000			
el 10	By -- Ditto ---- Dᵒ---	1000			
ay 7	By -- Ditto ---- Dᵒ --	2000			
ne 16	By -- Ditto ---- Dᵒ--	2000			
y 3	By -- Ditto ---- Dᵒ--	2000			
	By Ditto from Danᵈ Sulli- van return of Money which had been advan- ced him by Warrᵗ on the Paymaster Genᵈ 11ᵗʰ of Feby. last-------	100			
h	By Cash in Specie --- } 500 Guineas ----- }		900		
	Carr forward -	21,210	824	7	0

29) Dr. The United States...

					Dolr.	Lau
1778. Sep.			To amount bro.t forward		18,665	725.
N.o 38			To Expenditures in visiting the Post at West Point		130	..5
39	2		To Maj.r Gibbs — H.d Exp.s		1000	
40	6		To 25 Guineas sent Brigad.r Gen.l Scott — Commanding the light Troops on the Lines — to enable him to escape some of the Inhabitants betw.n him and the Enemy to watch their moovem.ts & apprize him of them — to prev.t Surprizes			35
41.	25		To 25 Guineas sent him for the like purposes			35
Oct.4. N.o 42.			To Exp.s of my self & Party of Horse from Fredericksb.h to Fishkiln, where I was detained Two days on Bus.		434	..5
43.			To Ditto to Danbury		240	
44.	22		To 25. Guin.s sent Brig. Gen. Scott for the purposes above mentioned - Sett			35
45 Nov.	2		To a Second trip to Fishkiln		320	
46	20		To Maj.r Gibbs — H.d Exp.s		2000	
47			To the Expences which were paid by my self on the March (sometimes with, & sometimes apart from the Army) from Fredericksburgh to Middle brook, to our Winter Canton.mts; & on my return back to the N. River upon the movem.t of General Clinton up it		420	35
			Carr.d forward		23,209	1877

For Port.t see letter this acc.t

James 2

with ---- G. Washington ---- C^r -- (30)

1778		Dollars	Lawful		
Sep -	By amount bro.^t form.^d ---	21,210	824 - 7 - 0		
	By Cash of the Pay master				
	General - - - - - - - - - - -	1000			
Nov.	By Ditto --- from Ditto ---	2000			
Dec.^r	By Ditto --- from Ditto ---	2000			
	Carr.^d form.^d ---	26,210	824	7	0

31) Dr. The United States ..... in acc.

		Doll.	Lawful	
1778				
Dec. 3	To am.t brot forward -------	23,209	1877	4 4
No. 48	To Maj.r Gibbs ---- H.d Exp.s	2000		
1779				
Feb 6	To my Exp.es in Phil.dto wch			
No. 49	place I was called by Con-			
	gress, & remained from the			
	22.d of Dec.r to this date --	990	35 10 ~
50 -- 15	To 50 Guineas sent Gen.l			
	McDougall at West Point			
	by Mr. Lawrence Esq.r for			
	secret Services ---------		70 --
Mar. 3	To 150 Ditto — sent D.o at			
No. 51	D.o by Col.o Malcom ----		210	
52. 15	To Maj.r Gibbs. Money rec.d by			
	him of Mr. Mitchell Esq.r			
	D, 2.d M.r Gen.l in Phil.a to			
	purchase necessarys			
	for the use of the Family	500		
53 27	To -- Ditto ----- H.d Exp.s ---	2000		
Apr. 29	Ditto ----- Ditto ---	2000		
June	To Expences in going from the			
No. 55	Contour.n at Middle brook in			
	the Jerseys to New Windsor			
	& to West point — preceeding			
	the army upon Gen.l Clintons			
	moving up the N. River			
	to Verplank's point ----	1400		
56 3	To Major Gibbs ---- H.d Exp.o	2000		
July.	To Expences in Recon.g the Ene-			
No. 57	mys Post at Stony Point pre-			
	vious to the Assault of it,			
	& on a visit to it after it was			
	taken ---------		10	
Sep. 12	To Major Gibbs ---- H.d Exp.o	2000		
Oct. 14	To 120 Guin.s p.d Maj.r Talmadge			
No. 59	at diff. times to y.e date for the			
	purpose of Establish.g a line of			
	Com.n by the way of long Isld			
	& for defraying the Exp. thereof			
	with my spies in New York --		168 --
	Carr.d forward --	36,099	237. 7

(32)

with ----- G. Washington ---- Cr.

		Doll.rs	Lawful.		
1778 Dec.	By am.t bro.t forward -----	26,210	824	7	0
1779 Mar. }	By Money of the Paymaster Gen.l upon Warr.t ----	2000			
Feb.y 28th	By Specie ---- 1000 Dollars -----		300		
March 5	By Paper Dollars - received by Maj.r Gibbs in Phil.a from Jn.o Mitchell Esq.r D.Q.r M.r Gen.l - & credited in his acc.t of Expenditures -----	500			
ap.l	By the Paymaster Gen.l upon my warrant --	2000			
June.	By Ditto ---- Ditto -----	3000			
	By Specie - rec.d by the hands of Maj.r D'Epanier 500 Guineas -----		700		
Sep.12	By the Paymaster Gen.l Cont.tl Dollars upon a warrant -----	2000			
	Carr.d forward	35,710	1824	7	0

33) Dr The United States....... ex acc

		Doll.s	Lawful		
1779					
Oct.	To amount bro.t forward.	36,099	2371	4	4
Nov 6	To Major Gibbs --- H.d Exp. 60	3000			
Dec 23	Ditto ----- Ditto 61	3000			
1780					
Jan 29	To Major Gibbs -- H.d Expa.	3000			
Mar 14	Ditto ----- Ditto 63	3000			
28	Ditto ----- Ditto 64	3000			
Ap 14	Ditto ----- Ditto 65	3000			
N.o 66	To Expences of a Visit to				
	Eliz.a Town & Posts on line	100	7	12	6
May 2	To Major Gibbs --- H.d Exp.	4000			
13	--- Ditto ----- D.o	4800			
June 1	Ditto ----- D.o	4300			
Ju 15	To Expenditures while the				
	Army was moving ab.t				
	Springfield - & the Enemy				
	about Elizabeth Town -		36	15	
Aug 20	To Major Gibbs --- H.d Exp.	5000			
29	To Col.o Graham of the York				
	State Troops p.r acc.t		12	1	1
Sep 2	To Col.o Meade's disbursem.t				
N.o 73	p.d Acc.t rendered (inclu-				
	ding 1505 Dollars retur-				
	ned to, & credited by				
	Maj.r Gibbs in his Acc -	10,000			
74 11	To Rich.d Humphrey's				
	acc.t p.d Col.o Biddle's				
	rec.t Perg.a £53.10.0				
	ded.d diff.o of Exch 10.14 -		42	16	
75	To The Expence of a Recon-				
	noitre as low as the Town				
	of Bergen - into the Neck		12		
76.27	To Major Gibbs --- H.d Exp	5000			
77	To Col.o Meade's Acc.t of Ex-				
	penditures to Hartford				
	When I went to meet the				
	Except.s Ct. de Rochambeau				
	& Adm.l de Terney Includ.g				
	416 D.rs ret.d to Maj.r Gibbs &				
	credited in his acc -	8000			
	Carr.d forward -	95,299	2483	3	

with ——— G. Washington ——— Cr. (34)

1779				Dollrs.	Lawful		
Sep.	By amount brot. forward			35,710	£1824	7	0
Nov.	By the Pay master General upon a Warrant ———			3000			
Dec. 2	By Ditto ——— Ditto ———			3000			
1780 Jan. 29	By — Ditto ——— Ditto ———			3000			
Feb. 4	By — Ditto ——— Ditto ———			5000			
Mar. 14	By — Ditto ——— Ditto ———			3000			
28	By — Ditto ——— Ditto ———			3000			
Apr. 13	By — Ditto ——— Ditto ———			3000			
May 2	By — Ditto ——— Ditto ———			4000			
13	By — Ditto ——— Ditto ———			4800			
*	By Cash ———				133	16	
June 1	By the Pay master General upon Warr. 2 ———			4300			
15	By — Ditto ——— Ditto ———			10000			
Aug 20	By — Ditto ——— Ditto ———			5000			
Sep. 14	By — Ditto ——— Ditto ———			8000			
27	By — Ditto ——— Ditto ———			5000			

* This sum stands in my
acct. as a credit to the Public — but I can find no
charge of it against me
in any of the Public
offices — where the mis-
take lyes I know not
but wish it could be
ascertained, as I have
no desire to injure
or be injured

| | | Carr.d forward | | 99,810 | £1958 | 9 | |

35) Dr. The United States _____ in Acc

		Dollr	Lawful		
1780 Sep. No. 79	To amount brot. forward	95,299	2483	3	11
	To Specie paid on my Journey to Hartford & back and during 4 days stay at that place _____		34	6	8
Oct 16 No. 80	To Cash paid Mr. Jno. Mercereau of Woodbridge in New Jersey (including 5 Guineas to Baker Hendricks) pd. Rects. for Exps & rewards of himself & others (whom he was obliged to employ) to open & carry on a Correspondence with persons within the Enemys Lines by the way of Staten Island _____	327.62	179	10	—
81	To Ditto paid Majr. Tolmadge towards the Expences of the Communication with New York by the way of Long Island _____		56		
82 — 16 83	To Colo. Lewis the Caughnawaga Indian — a presd _____		2	8	
Nov.	To the Expenditures on a Journey (after the Army left the Field for Winter Quarters) to Morris Town — Fleming Town — Halkets Town — New Germ Town — Sussex Ct. House &c. to the Cantonment at New Windsor — pd. Men	476	102	14	
84 15	To Major Gibbs ___ Hs. Exp. recd. from Colo. Pickering —	1000			
85	To Taylors acct. for my Servants _____	745			
	Carrd. forward	100,796	2857		

with _ _ _ _ _ G Washington _ _ _ Cr. (36

1780		Doll.s	Lawful		
Sep.	By amount bro.t forward	99,810	£1958	3	—
Nov 15	By Cash advanced Maj.r Gibbs by Col.o Pickering 2 m. 9 d	1000			
Dec 14	By Specie by the hands of Col.o Tilghman		79	4	—
	Carr.d forward	100,810	2037	7	—

37) Dr. The United States .... in acc

1780		Doll.	Lawful		
Dec. 2	To amot. bro't. form'd	100,796	2858	2	7
1781 Feb. 3 No. 86	To Lieut. Colfax – Ball'e of 9260 Doll. rec. on a warr't. & retained in his hands. *	3260			
Mar. No. 87	To the Expenditures on a Journey to Rhode Island on a Visit to the French army – p. Col. Tilghman	19,848½			
88	To Specie expenditures in this Journey – p. my mem. Bk. – where Paper w'd not pass		68	12	—
May No. 89	To the Expence of a Journey to Weathersfield for the purpose of an Interview with the French Gen'd d'arm'e – see Colon. Tilghmans acc'a as above	8376½			
" 90	To Specie expended in this Trip		35	18	—
Aug. 2	To Secret Services		146	—	
92	To Cash advan. Cap. Dobbs & other Pilots, to carry them to Monmouth Cty. to await the Arrival of the French Fleet – then ly expected		18	13	4
93 25	To Cash paid Mrs. Thompson the Housekeeper, in part of her Wages – viz – 25 Guineas		35	—	
94 28	To Expenditures on my march from y White Plains, or Dobbs Ferry by y way of Kings ferry to Brunswick inclusive		38	15	
95	To Washing & other sm'l accounts at Philadelphia		6		
	Carr'd form'd	132,281	320		

* This and all the sums which will be found accounts, which a

with ———— G. Washington ———— Cr (38

1780		Dollars	Lawful
Dec.	By amount brot forwd———	100,810	2037-7-
1781 Feb—	By the Paymaster Genl upon a Warrant———	9,264	
Mar.	By Paper Dollars recd by Colo Tilghman at Hartford of Mr Burwell———————	20,000	
apl	By Cash in Specie 500 Dollars—————		150
May	By the Paymaster Genl upon a Warrant—	20,000	
Sep 7.	By Specie—500 Guineas—————		700 —
	Carr'd forwd———	160,074	2887-7-

ged to Lieut. Colfax in these accts are credited in his
will rendered as Vouchers.

39) **Dr. The United States ---- in acc** 2

1782.		Doll.n		Lawful.		
Sep. 6.	To am.t bro.t forw.d ---	132,281	3207	10	11
	To Household Expences from the close of Major Gibbs's acc.t Nov.r 21. 1780 till the commenc.t of them by L.t Colfax the 6 of Sept.r 1781 – amounts from the best acc.ts & Estimates that can be had & from recollection (exclusive of what was obtained by bartering a little Salt w.ch was put into the hands of the Housekeeper for that purpose) to at least ✱ ---------		800		
	Carr.d forward	132,281	4007	10	11

✱ This business during the above Interval was in such a variety of hands for want of a proper Steward (w.ch Six vain by myself & others endeavoured to obtain) – And the accounts were not only irregularly kept but many of them were lost or mislaid, & some of them so defaced as not to be legible, that it is impossible for me to make out a statement of them; But as it comprehended that space of time in which the French & American armies formed one Camp at Philipsburgh & our Expences were at the highest; and as this sum corrispond as nearly as can be expected with the average Expenditures p. month as will appear by Lieut.t Colfaxs acc.ts since – the above Sum is charged under these Circumstances, upon the principle which seems most equitable to do justice to the public, and no injustice to myself

nth ----- G: Washington ---- Cr. -- (40

		Doll?s	Lawful		
1781. Sep. Oct.	By a mou$t bro? ferd— By Cash rec? of Mr. Dav? Rofs at York Town it Virginia for a sett of Bills by Tho? Pleasants Jur? in favor of Rob? Mor= ris Esq ---------	160,074	£2887 - 7 -		
			320 —	
	Carr? ferw.d ---	160,074	£3207 - 7 —	

45)   Dr. The United States ----- in acc

1781.		Doll.	Lawful		
Sep.	To amt. bro.t forward ----	132,281	4007	10	11
Nov. 8	To Danl. Grant (Baltr.) his acct. £13-3-3. eql to ----		10	10	7
"2 ---	To my own Expences - toge ther with one Aid Camp & three Serv.ts on the R. from Baltim.e to my H.d ---		6	8	4
"3	To my Secretary & two Aids their Exp.s friend to D°.		8	8	5.
"4 17	To Exp.s on the Road p.d Col. Smith £55-4-3 Penn.a red.d is £44-3-5 & £49.6.8 Lawful . together - is ----		93	10	1
"5'	To Sundries exclusive of the above, paid by myself for the Road to Wmsburgh in wch. M.r de Rochambeaus Exp.s who travelled in Comp.a with me) were generally included ---		59	10	-
6 ---	To the Expences of a Trip to the French Fleet of Cape Henry — to fix upon a Plan of operation with Count de Grass ----		25		
"7 27	To Washing & other small Exp.s in Williamsburgh		5	2	
8 Oct.r 3	To Secret Services ---		86		
9 - 31	To Taylors acc.t for serv.s		2	9	-
10 ---	To an Express . 3 Guis ---		4	4	
11 ---	To Expended on a second Visit to the French Fleet after the Siege of York ---		22	10	-
Nov. 1	To John Likley's acc.t				
12 ---	for 20 lbs of Tea - it be ing for Public use ---		18	-	
	Car.d forw.d --	132,281	4349	3	4

with ------ G: Washington --- Cr. (42

1781.		Dolrs.	Lawful		
Oct.	By amt. brot. forward --	160,074	3207	7	-
Nov.	By Sundries from the British Stores in York Town Virginia for my private use, but charged in the Public account ----------		28	—	
	Carrd. forwd. ---	160,074	3235	7	0

43) D.ᵣˢ The United States ..... in acc

1781		Doll.ˢ	Lawful		
Nov	To amount bro.ᵗ forward	132,281	4349	3	4
Dec 1 N°13	To Col.º Trumbulls acc.ᵗ of Travelling Expences from York Town in Virg.ᵃ to Mount Vernon & from Mount Vernon to Phil.ᵃ £29.0.8 Lawf.ˡ & £73.9.5 Penn.ᵃ eq to £58.15.8 and together		87	16	4
N°14	To Col.º Smith for his Expenditures on the said Journ.ᵉ		15	6	9
15	To Cash paid by my self on Ditto		18	5	-
16	To Ditto paid M.ʳˢ Thompson Housekeeper 25 Guin.ˢ		35	-	
17. 16	To Ditto advanced Lieut.ᵗ Colfax for Household Expences from Septem.ʳ Inclusive to the date		182	12	-
18	To Ditto advanced Ditto upon a warrant sec.ᵈⁿ		300	-	
1782					
Jan. 7	To Saddlers acc.ᵗ £3.5.0 eq to		2	12	-
Feb. N°.19	To Lieut.ᵗ Colfax — Warr.ᵗ on the Treasury - 1000 Doll.ˢ		300		
Mar 20 N°.20	To Gen.ˡ Lincoln — Col.º John Laurens draft for 35. Guineas - amount of Tin Plates - a Telescope &c.ᵃ brought from France for my use		49		
21	To Lieut.ᵗ Colfax — received from the Treasury for Household Expences		300	-	
22	To Sundry small acc.ᵗˢ and Expenditures during my residence in Philodel.ᵃ since the month of Nov.ᵃ To the date		46	12	-
	Carr.ᵈ forward	132,281	5686	7	5

with _ _ _ _ _ _ _ G͟.͟W͟a͟s͟h͟i͟n͟g͟t͟o͟n͟ _ _ C.ʳ 44

		Doll.ʳ	Lawful		
1781					
Nov.ᵃ	By am.ᵗ bro.ᵗ forward _ _ _	ˇ160,074	ˇ3235	7	ˑ
Dec 10	By Cash from the Treasury or a Warr.ᵗ in favor.ᵗ of Col.ᵒ Tilghman 1000 ᵈᵒˡˡ	_ _ _ _	ˑˑ300	~	
1782					
Feb.	By Ditto _ from Ditto paid to Lieut.ᵗ Colfax _ _ _ _	_ _ _ _	300	~	
Mar 16	By Ditto _ from Ditto _ to the same _ _ 1000 Doll.ⁿ	_ _ _ _	300	~	
21	By Ditto _ from Ditto _ in Notes _ _ _ _ 4000 Doll.ⁿ	_ _ _ _	ˇ1200	—	
	Carr.ᵈ forward _	ˇ160,074	ˇ5335	7	ˑ

45)

		Dr. The United States --- in acc		Doll.n	Lawful		
1782							
Mar	To amount bro.t form.d --			132,281	568 6	7	5
No 23	To Wm Eagles &c.t				1	8	
May.	To Servants -- viz Philt.						
No 24	Ramsley & others						
	their Wages --				16		
Iune.	To my Expenditures in a						
No 25	Tour to Albany - Sarato						
	ga & Schenectady on a						
	visit to our North.n Posts				32	8	
July.	To my Expences in going to						
No 26	to the Interview with Count						
	de Rochambeau at Phila						
	-- viz - going -- £. 20.7.1,						
	Evans's acc.t - 69 - 7 - 6						
	Wash. for others - 6 - 15 --						
	mah aco.ns						
	Capt. to Potsgrove -- 1 - 13. 4.						
	Bethlehem &c.a -- 3. 17. 6						
	Col. Trumbulls ⟨ 7. 14 - 9						
	acc.t of Exps ⟩						
	Maj.r Walkers Do 29 - 6. 9v						
	Rxfyl a £139 - 1. 11						
	diff.o of Excha -- 27 - 8 - 6.				111. 13	5	
Aug.t 17	To Capt.n Pray - p.r Rec.t	potts		v	14	--	--
Sep..	To Maj.r Talmadge - Do	potts		v	9	--	--
No 29	To the Expences of a Recon						
	noitre as far as Philips						
	burg & thence across						
	from Dobbs ferry by four						
	with a large Party of Horse				32	8	
Oct 10	To the Expences of a visit						
No 30	to the Post at Dobbs's fer						
	ry &c.a --				7	10.	
Nov.r 1	To Secret Services to the						
No 31	date - p.r Mem.m Book --				175		
	To Col.o Tilghman for old Con						
In C E Acc.t No 8 & 9	tin. Money returned & now						
	handed in --			27,775			
	Carr. forward --			160,056	608 5	14	10

with _____ G. Washington _____ Cr. 46

		Dollars	Lawful		
1782.					
Mar.	By amount bro.t form.d	160,074	5335	7	—
1783 Feb 25	By Cash in Specie of the Dep.t Pay m. Gen.l 250 Guineas _____		350		
Mar	By Ditto _ from Ditto 200 Dollars _____		60		
	Carr.d forward	160,074	5745	7	

47) Dr. The United States __ in acc

1782		Doll.ʳˢ	Lawfu...
Nov. 12 Nº 32	To the am.ᵗ from the other side	130.056	6085	14	10
	To the Expences of a tour to Poughkeepsy — thence to Esopus & along the Western Frontier of the				
1783	State of New York -----	-----	43	10	4
Jan 1 Nº 33	To Sundry Sums advanced Lieut. Colfax for House hold Expen. betw.ⁿ the M.º of June & the pres.ᵗ date p.ʳ his acc.ᵗ — Y. Cur.ʸ £610.6.0 ded.ᵍ diff.ᵉ of Excha. 152.11.6	-----	457	14	6
Mar.10 Nº 34	To ____ Sheldon's acc.ᵗ p.ᵈ Col.º Trumbulls Rec.ᵈ ____		6	7	6
Apl. Nº 35.	To the Expences of a Trip to meet the Secretary at War at Ringwood for the purpose of making arrangements for libe- rating the Prisoners -- &ᶜ	-----	8	10	8
.36	To Expenditures upon an Interview with Sir Guy Carleton at Orange Town exclusive of what was paid by the Contract.ⁿ — viz				
	at Birdsalls --- £5.2.6				
	May Blankets for the use of his N.º Furniture &c.ʷ 10 Guin. a 37/4 --- 18.13.4				
	Gave the Dragoons to carry them to their Quarters - 5.12 -				
	Gave the Serv.ᵗˢ to travel up by Land to H.ᵈ Quarters --- 3.4.0				
	Y. Cur.ʸ £32:11:10 eq.ᵘ to ---		24	9	
	Carr.ᵈ forw.ᵈ ---	160,056	6626	6	

with _____ G Washington _____ Cr (48

1783		Doll.ⁿ	Lawful		
Mar	By amount bro.ᵗ forward	160,074	5745	7	0
29	By Cash from the D. Pay master Genᵈ 500 Doll.ⁿ		150		
May 3	By Ditto __ from Dᵒ __ 500 Dᵒ		150		
June 9	By Ditto ____ Dᵒ __ 1000 Dᵒ		300		
	By Ditto ___ Dᵒ __ 350 Dᵒ		105		
	Carrᵈ forward	160,074	6450	7	

49) Dr. The United States..... in acc.²

		Doll.ˢ	Lawful.		
1783. May	To amo.ᵗ bro.ᵗ forward ----	160,056	6626	8	10
July 1. N.º 37	To Cash advanced Lieut.ᵗ Colfax for Household Expences between the 5.ᵗ of Jan.ʸ and this date p.ᵈ his accounts. --				
	G.ᵗ Currency £592-11-8 ded.ᵈ diff of Exch 148-3-2	------	444	8	6
	To Balance ----- as ac counted for the Both	160,056 18	7070	15	4
1783 July 1	Amount of the Expendi tures for the Years 1777, 8 & 9 and 1780, 1 & 2 and to the pres.ᵗ date	160,074	7070	15	4

E Excepted

G Washington

July 1.ˢᵗ 1783

Cr ------- G. Washington --- C^n (50)

1783		Doll^s	Lawful		
June	By amount bro^t form^d ----	160,074	6450	7	-
July 1 1783	By Bal^ce due G Washing ton - & carr^d to acc^t folio 65	--------	620	8	4
		160,074	7070	15	4

Note,

Before these acc^ts are finally closed, justice and propriety call upon me to signify that there are Persons within the British Lines - if they are not dead or removed, who have a claim upon the Public under the strongest assurances of compensation from me for their services in conveying me private Intelligence; and which when exhibited, I shall think myself in honor bound to pay. —

Why these claims have not made their appearance 'ere this unless from the of the causes above mentioned - or from a dis inclination in them to come forth till the B. force is entirely removed from the United States, I know not - But I have thought it an incumbent duty on me to bring the matter to view that it may be held in remembrance in case such claims should hereafter appear

G^o W^n.

51) *Recapitulation . . . . . or*
of the accounts for the

	Dollar	Lawful		
To Household Expences (Exclusive of the Provisions had from the Commissaries & Contractors _ and Liquors &c.ᵃ from them & others).				
viz				
Mr Austins Acc.ᵗ Nº 1 £496–19-4				
Mrs Smiths Dº ___ 2				
£563–12–9 ³/Cr.egᵗto ----422–14–				
Major Gibbs's ----- 3 — 489–6-4 _ 65,990				
Captn Colfax ---- 4 - 198–4 15-+ _ 3260	3387	14	4
Total H.ᵈ Expenditures _ 69,250+ 3387	14	4
Expended for Secret Intelligence __*___ 7617+ 1982	10	—
Ditto in Reconnoitring _ & in travelling — sometimes with, & sometimes without the Army _ but generally with a Party of Horse ---------- 42,755½ 1874	8	8
Miscellaneous charges amounts p.ᵣ accˢ to __ 40,451½ 2952	10	1
Total ---- 160,074 10,197	3	1
To 160,074 Dollars extended in Lawful money according to the Scale of depreciation _ p.ᵣ Contra		6114	14	—
Expenditures of 8 Years __ _ £16311	17	1

* 200 Guineas advanced Gen.ˡ Mc Dougall
for the like purpose is not included in this
sum as I have had no controul of it & know
nothing of the Application. _

Gener. Statement (52

Years 1775, 6, 7, 8 & 9 — and for 1780, 1, 2, & 3

		Doll.ᵗˢ	Lawful
1775 a 1777	By amount of several Sums received p. acct. to the date here of		£3126-7-9
1783 July 15	By Ditto received since to the present date	160,074	£6450-7-
	By 160,074 Dollars turned into Lawful money by the Scale of depreciation Adopted by Congress as follows — viz		

When Rec.		Dollars		Value in Law. Money	When Rec.		Dollars		Value Law. Money
Year	Month	Nomia	By depr. scale	Law.d Mon	Year	Month	Nom.	By depr scale	Law. Money
1777	Feb d	2610	2610	£782.10-0	Bro.t up	28710	16441	£4989-18-0
	Apr	1000	1000	300		Apr	2000	180	54
	May	1000	1000	300		June	3000	220	66-12
	July	1000	1000	300		Sep	2000	110	33
		1000	1000	300		Nov	3000	129	38-14
	Aug	500	500	150		Dec	3000	114	34-4
		1000	1000	300	1780	Jan	3000	102	30-12
	Oct	1000	911	273.6		Feb	5000	130	39
		1000	911	273.6		Mar	3000	78	23-8
	Dec	1000	754	226.4			3000	75	22.10
1778	Jan	2000	1370	411		Apr	3000	75	22.10
		1000	685	205.10		May	4000	100	30
	Apr	1000	497	146.2			4800	120	36
	May	2000	868	260-8		June	4300	108	32-8
	June	2000	756	226.16			10,000	250	75
	Aug	2000	574	172-4		Aug	5000	125	37-10
		100	29	8-14		Sep	8000	200	60
	Sep	1000	250	75			5000	125	37-10
	Nov	2000	366	109.16		Nov	1000	25	7.10
	Dec	2000	314	94.4	1781	Feb	9264	231	69.6
1779	Mar	2000	200	60		Mar	30,000	750	225
		500	50	15		May	20,000	500	150
		28710	16,441	4989-18-0			160,074	20,393	Am.t J. £o 6114-14-0

| 1783 July 1 | By Bal.e due G. Washington & carr.d to New Acc.t Folio 65 | | 620-8-4 |
| | | £ 16311 17. 1. |

Note, 104,364. of the above Dollars were received after March 1780 — and also credited also for 1 many of them did not fetch 1 for a hund.d — While 27,775 of them are return'd with.t deduct.g any thing from the above acc.t G. Washington

65)

Dr.... The United States .... in a

1783.				Lawful		
July	1.	To Ball'd brot from folio 50 ------		£620	8	4
		To Interest of £599 .19 .11 being the Ball. due me Dec. 31st 1776 — The amount having been applied to Public uses in the preceding year — from thence to art July 1st 1783 I charge Int. at 6 P. Ct. P. Ann ------		288		
		To Mrs Washington's travel.g Exps. in coming to & return.g from my Winter Quarters Pr. Accts rendered — The Money to defray which being taken from my private Purse, & a brought with her from Virga .. ✱		1064	1	0
			£	1972	9	4

✱ Altho' I kept Memms. of these Expenditures I did not introduce them into my Public accounts as they occurred — the reason was, it appeared at first view, in the commencement of them, to have the complexion of a private charge — I had my doubts therefore of the propriety of makg. it — But the peculiar circumstances attend.g my Command, and the embarrassed situation of our Public affairs which obliged me (to the no small detriment of my private Interest) to post-pone the visit I every year contemplated to make my Family between the close of one Campaign and opening of another — and as this expence was in-cidental thereto, & consequent of my self denial I have, as of right I think I ought, upon due con-sideration adjudged the charge as just with respect to the Public as it is convenient with respect to my self. and I make it with less reluctance as I find upon the final adjustmt of these accts (which have, as will appear, been long unsettled) that I am a considerable looser

— Mrs

Dr with ____ G. Washington ____ Cr. No 66

—My disbursements falling a good deal
short of my receipts, & the money I had upon
hand of my own —, For besides the Sum I
carried with me to Cambridge in 1775 (and
which exceeded the aforementioned Ball. of
£599~19-11.) I received Monies afterwards on
private Acct in 1777, ^and since^ which, except small Sums
that I had occasion now & then to apply to private uses, were all expended in the Public
Service — And thro' hurry, I suppose, &
the perplexity of business (for I know not
how else to acct for the deficiency) I have
omitted to charge — whilst every debit
against me is here credited

July 1st. 1783.   G Washington

III

FINANCIAL NOTE

WASHINGTON struggled with a wide variety of currencies circulating in the United States during the war. These accounts had to be reduced to a common basis, so he translated them into "Lawful," or coin currency value, generally called "hard money."

The rate of exchange, unfortunately, varied throughout the war, from place to place and from week to week. The difficulty was further compounded by each colony's having its own currency.

While in New England Washington kept his accounts as he had started them, in Pennsylvania currency. (He later switched to New York dollars.) The New England rate of exchange at the beginning of the Revolution was six shillings to the Spanish milled dollar, or piece-of-eight of seventeen pennyweight; but specie value itself fluctuated during the war and computation of the exchange was ever an exasperating task.

' I am grateful for the help of John C. Fitzpatrick, the late curator of the Washington Papers in the Library of Congress, in compiling the above information. Frankly, I don't understand it either. If a man like Fitzpatrick, who spent his lifetime as a scholar trafficking in Continental currencies, couldn't write a clearer description of what a 1780s dollar was worth in terms of today, it is obviously a subject requiring the highest authority.

For a more useful statement, I went to the people who should know, the office of the U.S. Comptroller of the Currency. They referred me to the Federal Reserve Bank of New York. The Board of Governors passed the buck by referring me to their research staff, who wouldn't say. It's not that they didn't care to remember what a dollar used to be worth; reliable comparisons dated back only to the 1820s. Even the U.S. Army's Criminal Investigation Division (CID), which I approached on the off-chance they might have a file on "Washington, George, Gen. (Deceased), serial number RA 001," would not hazard a guess.

Jackson Turner Main, in "The Social Structure of Revolutionary America," writes that "the following table is accurate for 'lawful money' from the end of the 'French and Indian' war through the 1780's":

	Value of the Spanish Dollar	For Sterling, Subtract
The English pound sterling	4s 6d	
New England and Virginia	6s	1/4
New York and North Carolina . . .	8s	9/16
New Jersey, Pennsylvania, Delaware, and Maryland	7s 6d	3/5

This will be useful for anybody who has access to a computer.

"New England jailers were authorized to spend between 4/6 and 5/- lawful money weekly for the support of debtors in prison," Main writes of the cost of living during the Revolutionary period. This, of course, is the lowest rung on the economic ladder, and a minimum starvation diet. A shilling a day (£18 lawful per year), Main adds, probably was the more usual outlay.

The single man who lived alone needed not over £10 to £13 annually for food. Clothing and lodging cost about £10. Thus a bachelor could survive on £25, though the well-to-do merchant or lawyer might pay £40 or more a year for room and board alone, according to the *Samuel Holten Papers, Bills, Accounts, and Receipts, 1780–1789,* in the Library of Congress, and the Virginia *Herald* of June 19, 1788. "Anyone who wished to live in some comfort required at least £100," Main writes. "This was the sum regarded as 'sufficient support' by the Society for the Propagation of the Gospel in Foreign Parts, and as the expected housekeeping cost of a planter's family by the author of 'American Husbandry.' "

Albert S. Bolles, in *Pennsylvania: Province and State* (Philadelphia: 1899), reports a statement of William Penn in 1775 that the ordinary expenditures for running the whole state of Pennsylvania in peacetime was £3,000. As late as 1774, £5,000 was the cost of government in New York, according to *Documents Relative to the Colonial History of the State of New York,* edited by O'Callaghan (Albany: 1853–1887).

The most graphic statistic dealing with pounds that I came across during my research was "209." That is how much George Washington weighed when he broke camp at Newburgh, New York, in 1783—a net weight gain of 28 pounds from his prewar vital statistics. Of the staff officers who joined Washington for dinner on the old expense account on a fairly regular basis, General Henry Knox grew most in stature, winding up the war at 280 pounds. Gen. Benjamin Lincoln weighed 224. Col. David Humphreys 221 pounds. "All of which figures were a scandal of the high command and staff," Freeman notes (*George Washington,* V, p. 453) when compared with Eben Huntington's 132 pounds. (Brig. Gen. Ebenezer H. Huntington was one of the thousands not on the expense account.) Like businessmen on the tab today, General Washington and his friends had to fight the battle of the bulge, with the usual results.

Most of us would still prefer an expense account translated into simple dollars. Fortunately, one authority was able to supply a conversion rate. Washington himself uses one, as cited on pages 51–52: £1 = $26 (approximately). Twenty-six Revolutionary dollars could take care of the average modern expense account writers' monthly American Express bills a lot better than that "new green money" the credit card company is always writing about.

Some economists may argue with the conversion rate. A gloomy man by nature, they will say, Washington always took a dimmer view than most about how bad off money was in his day. Still it is hard to believe that Washington ever sold the dollar short.

Whether the dollar value for each expenditure has been under- or over-estimated a few bob one way or another by using Washington's arithmetic seems immaterial. It is *what* he charged for as well as how much that made the eight years of the Revolutionary War the golden age of expense account writing.

IV

A TRANSLATION FROM THE OLD ENGLISH TO THE NEW ENGLISH

*Accounts, G. Washington with the
United States, Commencing June 1775,
and Ending June 1783, Comprehending
a Space of 8 Years*

For it is fixed principle with me,
that whatever is done should be well done.

—GEORGE WASHINGTON
Yorktown, Virginia, 1783

1775 — June
No 1

> To the purchase of five Horses (two of which
> were had on credit from Mr. James Mease) to
> equip me for my journey to the Army at
> Cambridge—& for the Service I was Then
> going upon—having sent my Chariot and
> Horses back to Virginia $6,214

The records show that James Mease was a Philadelphia merchant, who later served as Commissary to the Pennsylvania troops and eventually rose through the commercial ranks to Clothier-General of the Continental Army.

However, there is no record of Paul Revere charging the government for the purchase, or rental, of horses on his famed ride to Lexington and Concord. He borrowed Deacon Larkin's horse. (See Longfellow, *Paul Revere's Ride.*) Men of Revere's ilk are the bad guys in this Revolutionary tale.

Not surprisingly, Paul Revere was later accused of cowardice and disobedience [at the battle of Penobscot, Massachusetts in 1779] and lost his commission as a lieutenant colonel of artillery in the Massachusetts militia. For three years, the pots-and-pans man fought for a court-martial, which finally cleared his name. But where there's fire there's smoke.

What Washington was doing in this item about horses is executing one of the basic principles of sound expense account writing: *If you get stuck in a shoestring operation, charge for the shoestring.*

1775 — June 22
No 2

> To a light Phaeton bot [bought] of Doct.
> Renaudet at $1,430

Washington considered a phaeton a suitable chariot for riding to war. It saved him the fatigue of riding in the saddle to the front.

Dr. Peter Renaudet was a Philadelphia physician. In terms of today's dollars, the Renaudet phaeton is the equivalent of roughly twelve Cadillac broughams.

In mythology, Phaëton was the son of the Greek god Helios and the nymph Clymene. He once tried to drive his father's chariot but could not control the horses. Falling, the rig dried the earth of the Libyan Desert.

In military science, there was a risk involved in riding a phaeton, too. As it moved up to the front, through the Toryist Jerseys, the phaeton was a sign of great rank. It was as dangerous as a lieutenant wearing his bars on his helmet in Vietnam today, an inviting military target. But Washington was fearless.

As generals of industry today must have their costly limousines, so Washington always looked to it that his carriages should be of the finest quality, with the latest accessories, all imported. He described these high standards to Robert Cary & Company, his purchasing agent in London, on June 6, 1768:

Gentn: My old Chariot havg. run its race, and gone through as many stages as I could conveniently make it travel, is now rendered incapable of any further Service; The intent of this Letter therefore is to desire you will bespeak me a New one . . .

As these are kind of Articles, that last with care agst. number of years, I would willingly have the Chariot you may now send me made in the newest taste, handsome, genteel and light; yet not slight and consequently unserviceable. To be made of the best Seasond Wood, and by a celebrated Workman. The last Importation which I have seen, besides the customary steel springs have others that play in a Brass barrel, and contribute at one and the same time to the ease and Ornament of the Carriage; One of this kind therefore would be my choice; and Green being a colour little apt, as I apprehend to fade, and grateful to the Eye, I would give it the preference, unless any other colour more in vogue and equally lasting is entitled to precedency, in that case I would be governd by fashion. A light gilding on the mouldings (that is, round the Pannels) and any other Ornaments that may not have a heavy and tawdry look (together with my Arms agreeable to the Impression here sent) might be added, by way of decoration. A lining of a handsome, lively cold. leather of good quality, I sh'd also prefer; such as green, blew . . .*

The new chariot was shipped to Washington in September 1768. Two years later, he complained to Mr. Cary that he had been cheated. "The wood so exceedingly grien [green] that the panels slipped of the mouldings before it was two months in use—split from one end to the other."†

* *The Washington Papers,* ed. Saul K. Padover, pp. 70–71.
† *The Writings of Washington,* ed. Worthington C. Ford, II, p. 285, n.

This charge for a chariot illustrates a basic principle of expense account writing: *Let your employer know you are a good liver, so it won't come as a shock when your expense account is turned in.* When you eat with the boss, before leaving on your first business trip, it is important not to order hamburger steak to show that you are an economy-minded businessman, but duck à l'orange and champagne.

The congressional watchdogs saw Washington riding around Philadelphia in the government's new phaeton, and there was never any friction in the employer-employee relationship. The phaeton was a best buy.

1775 — June 22

No 3

To double Harness for D bought from Mr. Todd . $201.50

This harness from William Todd was neatly ornamented with brass. We don't know from the records whether Washington was stock-piling harnesses because we don't know from the records whether Renaudet's phaeton was new or used, in which case it might have already come with a less ornamental harness. The sum also included undescribed alterations and "a chair saddle." The businessman on an expense account today follows this basic principle when he rents a car without specifying that it was a Shelby Ford GTO with air conditioning.

1775 — June 22

No 4

To Cash paid for Sadlery, a Letter Case, Maps,
Glasses, &c &c &c. for the use of my Command . . $831.45

The saddlery item was for leather work and canteen repairing, saddle, bridle, stirrup leathers, coat straps, and other items purchased from Elias Botner, William A. Forbes, and Christopher Binks. The letter-case, or portmanteau, was of genuine Russian leather and was bought from Robert Aitken, a Philadelphia bookseller and publisher, at a cost of £3, or $78.

What is of more importance in this passage is that it marks the introduction of the basic expense account word "etc.," or as Washington phrased it, "&c, &c, &c." This is one of the most powerful words in the expense account vocabulary. The closest thing we have today in the expense account language used in business and government, to my knowledge, is "miscellaneous." Like commerce and politics themselves, this category often seems to combine elements of nonfiction and fiction. As we run into this phrase often in Washington's work, we will have ample opportunity to expand on "etc." as a major theme in the genre.

1775 — June 22

No 5

To Mr. Benj Hemmings for keeping the
above Horses $137.95

Benjamin Hemmings was a Philadelphia stableman. He performed the service of minding government property so well, Washington appears to have taken him to the front at Cambridge on the expense account as a kind of parking lot attendant.

This marks the end of what appears to have been a long day in the military history of the United States Army. The next time you suddenly are asked to give an impressive speech on the heritage of the Land of the Free, or date a Daughter of the American Revolution, you might want to go over this hallowed ground of Washington's facing the sharp-eyed Philadelphia merchants in a series of skirmishes which military analysts might call "a shopping expedition." He refused to give an inch on procuring the basic necessities for leading a rebel army.

In other wars, a bomber gap or a missile gap developed. But Washington had done his best to prevent a horse gap, a phaeton gap, a harness gap, or a portmanteau gap—at least temporarily. (As we will see, he ran out of these items.) By the end of that first day on the expense account, he spent more than the average rebel general's annual income in Philadelphia's Abercrombie & Fitches'.

Buying wasn't the only action Washington saw that first day on active duty. He was also selling. The list of credits on the page opposite the debits (see page 2 of facsimile of original version) indicates that he sold his gun. This was a puzzling thing for a man going to war to do. Fitzpatrick solves the mystery by reporting Washington sold the gun "to a chairman of one of the committees appointed by several of the counties of Massachusetts to purchase arms for the militia." Perhaps the weapon was defective in some way.

All of this was taxpayers' money well spent. At the time Philadelphia was a hotbed of Toryism. The sporting goods store owners undoubtedly spread the word of General Washington's purchases. With the usual optimism of soldiers going off to war, Washington's confidential dispatches to Martha at Mount Vernon reported he expected to be home in the fall, or at the latest during the winter. But the Philadelphia shopkeepers could see that he was expecting a longer war by the way he laid in supplies, which, as will be seen, escalated once he reached the shops up front at Cambridge.

The intelligence that the revolutionary's gear included "To a Field Bedstead & Curtains, mattrass, Blankets &C, &C. &C." (see my comments on item No. 50) must have thrown terror into the British War Office. In these expenditures for interior decorating may be the origin of modern psychological warfare.

Washington's reliance on craftsmen in the better shops of wherever he traveled on the expense account also led to the lucrative alliance between the military and industrial we can still see in evidence today. A lot of people mistakenly attribute the term "military-industrial complex" to General Eisenhower because, with his gift for the right phrase, he so labeled it in his famed Farewell Address of 1960. The comparison is limited only to the way both generals spent taxpayers' money.

1775 — July

No 6

> *To the acc[ount] of Thomas Mifflin Esq. for*
> *Money expended by him in the journey from*
> *Philadelphia to Cambridge in which the*
> *Expences of General Lee, Col. Reed &c. were*
> *included* *$3,364.42*

At first you might think some of these travel items are for the whole army. But this couldn't be true, as the above itemized entry demonstrates conclusively.

George Washington was the first to put his secretary on the expense account. Like most secretaries today, Joseph Reed did more than take dictation. He was Washington's confidant, a master manipulator of people and protocol, a trouble-shooter who solved many minor problems during the early days of the war, allowing the boss to free his mind for the larger problems. A Philadelphia lawyer who kept his office open while he was at the front, Reed did not seem to suffer politically from military service. By 1781, he was President of the State of Pennsylvania.

The general also picked up the checks for Thomas Mifflin, an Aide-de-Camp who was to become Quartermaster General of the army. Before casting his lot with the rebels, Mifflin had been a junior executive in the counting house of William Coleman, a prominent mercantile establishment of Philadelphia. He had just returned from a tour of the Continent, according to Beard in *An*

Economic Interpretation of the Constitution of the U.S., where he had studied commercial affairs.

Mifflin was one of those bright, sharp young men still seen hanging around Washington today, who see government service not as an end in itself, but as a stepping stone. He served Washington well as a liaison man with Congress. Whenever the General's military policies needed explaining, which was quite often in the first few years of the war, he sent Mifflin to Philadelphia. A smooth-tongued politician who could talk congressmen's language, Mifflin was a master salesman. As the Quartermaster General in Boston, he won additional fame for being one of the first to introduce the practice of buying *and* selling provisions—in other words dealing with himself.* "I have taken occasion to hint to a certain gentleman in this camp, without introducing names, my apprehensions of his being concerned in trade," Washington confided in a letter to Reed, who had left camp to conduct some law business in Philadelphia. "He protests most solemnly that he is not, directly or indirectly, and derives no other profit than Congress allows him for defraying expenses, to wit 5 per cent on the goods purchased." Mifflin seems to have been the government figure who served as a model for the former Secretary to Congress, Bobby Baker.

Despite the slander, smears and innuendo heaped on Mifflin during his army career, he prospered in business after the war, becoming a founding father of the Philadelphia Society for the Encouragement of Manufactures and Useful Arts, which played the same constructive role in the 1780s as the National Association of Manufacturers (NAM) does today. It lobbied vigorously for high tariffs at the Constitutional Convention of 1787.

The "&C" refers to an unspecified number of others (probably one) sharing Washington's treat. According to Fitzpatrick, one of these was Maj. Gen. Philip Schuyler, whose landholdings at the start of the war included a large part of the State of New York. As a group, these men constitute the first official recognition of what we call today "the expense account crowd."

Two-thirds of the army was ill-fed, ill-clothed and ill-housed in 1775. By making it a practice to include only the affluent men of good breeding, like himself, in his inner circle, Washington was exercising a non-inflationary brake on the economy. Under the influence of money, the poor traditionally will do or write anything, and don't take their financial obligations seriously. A study of the major credit card company policies on eligibility requirements—anybody who is regularly employed and earns $12,500 a year is considered a good credit risk, even though he may lie, cheat and drink excessively on the job—shows how sound General Washington's thinking was on deadbeats.

---

* Freeman, *George Washington,* IV, p. 73.

The entry is also significant because it introduces the concept of telling as little as possible about major expenses. Washington improved on this basic principle of expense account writing by telling nothing at all. From Fitzpatrick, we learn that among the expenses Washington didn't specify was a loan to General Lee of £6 13s. 6d., or $164.45, from public funds, the repayment of which does not appear elsewhere in these pages. Such largess was to earn Washington the reputation in the expense account crowd of being the first of the big-time spenders, one of a long list of firsts in the man's career.

1775 — July
_____

No 7

To Sundry sums paid by myself in the aforesaid Journey—amounting to *$734.20*

This modest item is for out-of-pocket expenses incurred while moving up to the trenches at Boston. It complements the previous one, like the shoe one waits to hear drop.

"Sundry" is a military word meaning the acquisition and replacement of war materiels, such as powder for wigs. It is a word in Washington's vocabulary second only to "&C."

In this instance, further investigation shows, the sundry sums covered expenditures for wine: £7 10s. 6d., or $195.65, seemingly purchased from Abraham Durfee, a member of the New York Chamber of Commerce. An "upholder," Joseph Cox, seems to have done upholstery work on the General's carriage.* A portmanteau trunk, writing papers, sealing wax, and other stationery supplies were also bought. As Washington's massive correspondence during the war indicates, he was one of those military men who believed that the pen was as mighty as the sword.

I don't think too much should be made of the actual figures in this item. Young Mifflin did the shopping for Washington. He may have dealt with himself, and given the General the wholesale price. Still it can be safely said that wherever Washington traveled on the expense account he seemed to become a major force in the economy. These figures are impressive when you consider that Washington spent only one night in New York City on business.

On June 24, the expense account crowd had halted at New Brunswick, New Jersey, enroute to where the war was going on, for the Commander to ponder on which of three roads to take into New York City. This was one of the most dramatic decisions covered by the expense account. If the General chose wrongly, the ledger would have been not a book, but a slim pamphlet.

* See Volume 16, *Papers of George Washington,* 65, LC.

Washington's anxiety about being captured was real. His Majesty's ships were in New York Bay. The rebel New York Congress was still formally loyal. The city was the residence of the royal governor. King George's civil servants had been especially vigorous in protecting the working class people against their oppressors, the Wall Street lawyers who were solidly behind the Revolution. New York City was not a citadel of Americanism the way it is today. But that was politics.

New York was a bastion of another kind of freedom then, as it is today. It stood for the sanctity of personal freedom. Anybody who has been around Manhattan at night recently has seen these freedom-fighters in action. The Copacabana! The Four Seasons! Toots Shor's! The Hilton! The Americana! Those are the great battle-grounds the very names of which send a shiver up the spine of today's expense account troops. Like Washington and his guerrilla band, they travel around in squads of four and five, the password for the night being "Give me Liberty or Give Me Death." Wife and kids at home. Free at last. Some of these marauders from out of town, reveling in their New York freedom, have been known to fall apart. They drink too much, have no respect for authority, and abuse the privilege of being able to charge, the highest honor a corporation can tender. These men represent the lunatic fringe of expense account writing.

I can't speak for a man like General Charles (Good-Time Charlie) Lee—the military adventurer who fought for Stanislas Poniatowski, the King of Poland and former lover of Catherine the Great. Lee made a name for himself in Warsaw, Moldavia, the Hungarian spas and Italian beaches before volunteering for service in the Revolutionary cause. He may have been looking forward to living it up in New York on the General's expense account. Young Mifflin wasn't one of your average stay-at-home executive types either. But Washington's mind was strictly on business, as the record of his expenditures will prove. There isn't a single bill for nightclubbing.

Rather than circle around the city on their bellies under the cover of darkness, the party of rebels on the way to the rebellion dispatched an express rider to notify the New York Congress that the high command was planning to pay a call. The morning of June 25, Douglas Southall Freeman reports in *George Washington* (III, p. 462), the expense account crowd rode to Newark *without* stopping for breakfast. Though it was a Sunday, the New York Congress hurriedly met and sent an escort to conduct the guerrilla band by "the most prudent crossing" into downtown Manhattan for the equivalent of a ticker-tape parade.

The high command didn't take the Staten Island Ferry.* To

* *New Jersey Historical Society Proceedings,* new ser., v. 7, p. 109.

avoid, if he could, the chance of being seized on the ferry by a boat's crew from one of the royal ships in the harbor, General Washington followed the advice of the New York congressional committee and came across the Hudson at Hobocken (also known as Hobocok, Hocken, and today as Hoboken). It was a tense moment. General Washington prepared for it by putting on a new purple sash with his blue uniform, and laid aside his travel hat for one that bore a fine plume.*

What complicated the landing was that everybody knew the royal governor William Tryon was also due in town that day, having sent word from a ship in the harbor of his intentions to resume his residence at the Governor's mansion. "A clash between the supporters of the two causes," Freeman writes, "on a summer Sunday afternoon, when the streets were full of strollers, might transfer the battle of Charlestown to New York. It was not a pleasing prospect, but certainly not one over which Washington would hesitate."†

There is no record of who paid the Hoboken ferry tolls. We do know the rebels hit the beaches of New York at a remote part of the city (14th Street). The secrecy aspect of the mission was a failure, as the beaches were crowded with radical supporters. The famished men didn't go to Washington's favorite New York restaurant, Fraunces Tavern, to break their fast. They were escorted instead to the home of Colonel Leonard Lispenard, located on a hill overlooking the Hudson where Canal Street today crosses Desbrosses and Hudson streets.‡

All historians agree the rebels ate heartily at Lispenard's table. From this mansion, after the mid-afternoon meal was finished, Washington's carriage was escorted by hundreds of radicals down the present Greenwich Street to the Fields (now City Hall), where he probably spent the night at another great expense account place, the house of William Smith, General Schuyler's cousin.

This must have been the site where, as Fitzpatrick observes in *George Washington Himself* (p. 170), "A dinner at the public expense, engineered by George Clinton, was tendered to Washington." There is much confusion about where Washington actually slept that night. *The New York Gazette and Weekly Mercury* (July 3, 1775) reported he stayed at a tavern further uptown. Local historians have him at Cox's Tavern (Broadway and 230th Street). In *Washington's Journey of 1775* (p. 39) he reportedly slept at Hyatt's Tavern (also known as Kingsbridge Inn), at the intersection of Broadway and 223rd Street. The possibility should not be discounted that he stayed at all these places that one night. This at

* Mrs. Richard Montgomery, *Biographical Notes Concerning Gen. Richard Montgomery*, pp. 5–6.
† *George Washington*, III, p. 462.
‡ *The Celebration of the 139th Anniversary of the Journey of Washington from Philadelphia to Cambridge*, p. 73.

least would explain the great number of houses the General reportedly slept at during the war.

Less easily explained is what the British navy was doing while all of these things were going on. None of the historians say why a force of marines wasn't put ashore to end the insurrection right there on the streets of New York. A purple sash and a plumed hat wouldn't have lasted too long against the might of the Royal Navy. The Tories in town, judging by their writings at this time, fumed at the crime in the streets. My guess is that the British, like New Yorkers today, didn't want to get involved.

That same evening, at nine o'clock, Governor Tryon landed at the Exchange and was welcomed by Judge Thomas Jones, a justice of the Supreme Court of New York, clergymen of the Church of England, and the rest of the court crowd. Judge Jones wrote later, "But strange to relate, yet strange as it is, it is nevertheless a fact that those very people who attended the rebel generals in the morning and conducted them from place to place with repeated shouts of approbation, congratulated them on their respective appointments to such principal commands in so virtuous an army, upon so important an occasion, wished them joy on their safe arrival in New York, prayed God to bless their great and glorious undertaking, and to grant them success in all their measures in the management of so great and necessary a war. These very men—now one and all joined in the Governor's train and with the loudest acclamation attended him to his lodgings, and with the utmost seeming sincerity, they shook him by the hand, welcomed him back to the colony."* Judge Jones said this was "cursed hypocrisy! a farce!" Yet it suggests why New Yorkers later in their history could love both the Giants and the Dodgers in the same baseball league.

From all reports, General Washington's carriage was more impressive than Governor Tryon's in the battle for New York. It scarcely matters, as Freeman correctly observed, "but there is doubt whether it was a four-wheeled phaeton, for which he procured harness in Philadelphia, or a two-wheeled sulky, in which he was said by Mrs. Montgomery to have entered New York."† The wife of General Richard Montgomery, soon to die in the rebel invasion of Canada, was a great admirer of the Commander in Chief and his equipage. She also said Governor Tryon nearly fainted when he saw General Washington pass by his house later in the night.

The important thing for students of great expense account writing in all of this is that there is little doubt in the confusion of events in New York that Washington somehow managed to defray his expenses. Here we have another basic principle of the art: *Live off the land*. The money you don't spend for dinner by eating hors

---

* *History of New York During the Revolutionary War*, I, p. 53.
† See her *Biographical Notes*, pp. 6–7.

d'oeuvres at some manufacturer's cocktail party, you can spend tomorrow.

Washington slipped out of New York with his neck the next morning, in either a phaeton or a sulky. He cut expenses further by being the soldier-in-residence at Yale College on June 28. The local volunteer Yale militia unit, a forerunner of the SDS chapter at New Haven, paraded on the green for the rebel leader. One of the crazies was Noah Webster, who played either the fife or drum, depending on which historian you read (Webster later applied for a job as a secretary at Mount Vernon, but was turned down, possibly because of his radical notions about spelling). On June 29, General Washington spent the night in New London, Connecticut, at the home of Silas Deane, the Connecticut congressman. Deane was to be one of the leaders of the free enterprise system in Congress, a man whose private business dealings while part of the government were to set the standards by which congressmen judge themselves today. On June 30, the General was the guest of honor of the Massachusetts Bay Congress in Springfield. His hosts included Dr. Benjamin Church, a Raynham, Massachusetts, physician who had the distinction—in England, at least—of being the new nation's first traitor. Dr. Church's mistress betrayed him. The General finally arrived at his field headquarters in Cambridge the night of July 2, only sixteen days after his election.

There were no ceremonies on his arrival. A welcoming committee composed of the cream of the patriot army had been on hand in Harvard Yard the two previous days for the General's arrival, which had been expected hourly. The ceremony, trumpet flourishes, and roll of drums were dispensed with, in view of the unexpected delays in travel during war time.

One thing the expense account doesn't tell us is what was going on in the country during that first business trip: the battle of Bunker Hill, which actually took place on Breed's Hill.

1775 — July 5

No 8

To N. Sparhawk's Acc[ount] *$62.20*

This wasn't the first July Fourth weekend in American history. General Washington celebrated it anyway in the traditional manner. He went to the seashore at Salem, Massachusetts. While there, he forged another link in the military-industrial complex by shopping at the mercantile establishment of Vans & Sparhawk. One of the shopkeepers, Nicholas Sparhawk, is on record as having sold him 9 yards of Damascus cloth. The material was not used for flags. Betsy

Ross, the flagmaker, is another bad guy in this history, for not charging for cloth, stars or stripes in her contribution to the war effort. She certainly can't be faulted for not handing in a bill for her services as a design consultant on the flag project, since a man named Francis Hopkinson seems to have come up with the winning design. Mr. Hopkinson could have used a publicity agent.

Fitzpatrick says the Damascus cloth was for table linen for Washington's field headquarters. George Washington was first in piece goods in the Continental Army.

For what he spent for the Damascus cloth, in terms of today's dollars, Washington could have written off a trip to Syria and picked up twice as many yards in the bazaar. A transcript of the negotiations between Sparhawk and Washington is not available. Nevertheless, I tend to think that Washington held his own at the bargaining table. His sense of dignity rarely prevented him from exercising common business sense.

Washington's stature as a trader dated back to one of his feats during the French and Indian War. Part of the price demanded by the French at the surrender of Fort Necessity was his interpreter, Captain Van Braam, a Dutchman who knew French. Washington resisted, but the French were unyielding. Before delivering his part of the bargain, he sold Van Braam a dress uniform, which the British historian Marcus Cunliffe has noted, "he might otherwise have found a nuisance to carry away with him. It was not a shameful transaction, but it was a brisk one." (*George Washington: Man and Monument,* p. 6.)

Washington's neighbor, Richard Henry Lee, once refused to sell the squire of Mount Vernon a horse, for fear that he would receive less than the prevailing market value. Where money was involved, at least in the days before he married Martha, Washington had a reputation for being tight, even stingy.

Of Washington's tendency to work on holidays—another of the basic principles of inventive expense account writing—we will see many other finer examples.

1775 — July 5

No 9

To Sam. Griffin, Esq. *$45.93*

Samuel Griffin's account closes the pages on the memorable trip to the front. It is not known what other contribution Griffin made to the Revolution.

We can now see that the actual costs of Washington going into combat—from the day he moved out of Philadelphia to when he dug in at Cambridge—totaled £165 11s. 6d. (or $4,146.55), excluding the costs of equipping himself to lead what was then known as the Eight Months Army (enlistments were up in December).

This may seem a trifle high in comparison to what the Minutemen charged when answering the cry that the British were coming. Some of these hotheads didn't charge a farthing, simply grabbing their flintlocks and powder horns, leaving the ploughs in the furrow, buckets at the well step, fodder at the door of the cattleshed and rushing off to the front. The Minutemen as a group are therefore also villains in this Revolutionary story. Their intemperate actions cast a pall on the great events described in General Washington's account of the war, and we will ignore them, except when the results of their rashness—the plundering and looting for food and clothing beginning the first winter—make it impossible.

Not all of the troops were fiscally irresponsible Minutemen. "An Act for Embodying, Supplying and Paying the Army of Observation Ordered to Be Raised for the Defense of the Colony," passed by the Rhode Island General Assembly the first Wednesday in May 1775, recognized that even a volunteer army needed financial help. The act read:

> That each able-bodied effective man who shall enlist in the service, and find himself a Small-Arm, Bayonet & other Accoutrements, shall be allowed & paid 40 shillings [$52] as a bounty; and each able-bodied effective man, not finding himself a Small-Arm Bayonet & Other Accoutrements shall receive 24 shillings [$31.20] as a bounty.*

The "Accoutrements," in the eyes of the Rhode Island legislators, were thus worth 16 shillings ($20.80). It was assumed that the Rhode Island troops would walk to the front outside Boston.

In Massachusetts a gun and bayonet were estimated to be worth £2, or $52.† In Virginia, a gun was reckoned at £3 to £5 ($78 to $130). At this time, £5 would buy about 15 cords of wood, pay a laborer for two weeks work, or purchase some 50 bushels of coal.‡ When a militia soldier provided his own firelock his contribution to the cause was considerable for those days. Next to gunpowder, guns were what the rebels needed. Armaments were a constant drain on the new country's financial resources.

On the face of it, then, General Washington's spending on travel may have shown poor military judgment. Washington, of course, was doing more than demonstrating the luxury of mobilization for future generations. His circuitous trip to the Boston war zone can be viewed in terms of a recruiting tour. He was showing himself to the people, much the way the administration today shows Nelson Rocke-

---

* Force, American Archives, 4th Series, II, pp. 1847, 1849.

† *Journals of the Continental Congress,* October 25, 1774.

‡ *Virginia Historical Magazine* (January 1899), pp. 280–83.

feller to the people of Latin America or the U.S. Navy shows an aircraft carrier in the Middle East. His answering the call to arms in this way, in terms of its propaganda value, can be measured by this patriotic song, which Moore, in *Songs and Ballads of the Revolution* (pp. 99–102), says the people sang in his wake:

> When Congress sent great Washington
> All clothed in power and breeches,
> To meet old Britain's warlike sons
> And make some rebel speeches.
>
> 'Twas then he took his gloomy way
> Astride his dapple donkeys,
> And travelled well, both night and day
> Until he reached the Yankees.
>
> Away from camp, 'bout three miles off
> From Lily he dismounted.
> His sergeant brushed his sun-burnt wig
> While he the specie counted.
>
> All prinked up in *full* bag-wig,
> The shaking notwithstanding,
> In leathers tight, oh glorious sight!
> He reached the Yankee landing.
>
> The women ran, the darkeys, too;
> And all the bells they tolled;
> For Britain's son, by Doodle doo,
> We're sure to be consoled. . . .
>
> Full many a child went into camp,
> All dressed in homespun kersey,
> To see the greatest rebel scamp
> That ever crossed o'er Jersey. . . .
>
> Upon a stump, he placed himself,
> Great Washington did he,
> And through the nose of lawyer Close
> Proclaimed great liberty.
>
> The patriot brave, the patriot fair,
> From fervor had grown thinner
> So off they marched, with patriot zeal,
> And took a patriot dinner.

Which sounds to me as if it came out of the Minutemen's PIO office.

When we look at the trip in the light of recruiting, Washington's skill in writing this part of the expense account can be appreciated. "It cost £ 12 10s. just to send a recruiting officer to England," Prof. John Shy of Princeton found in researching the War Office Papers in the British Public Records Office for his book, *Toward Lexington*. A trip to Europe, then, must have been thirteen times cheaper than

Washington's Expense Account odyssey. This is still a good mark to shoot at for new expense account writers who are at sea on what to charge for their first business trip. The basic principle is: *Don't travel on a troop ship.*

1775 — July 5

No 10

To the Expences of Myself & Party reconnoit[er]
the Sea Coast East of Boston Harbor $484.85

This is a fine example of another important principle of expense account writing: *Avoid fancy writing.* Never call attention to your exploits with flowery words.

Washington could have boasted of his adventures here. After all, it is the first time he is on record as having visited the front. With characteristic modesty, he resisted the temptation to describe graphically the perils that might have befallen him and his party on the scouting patrol. Instead he stuck to a dry account that almost makes it seem like a joy ride to the seashore. He is not guilty of blowing his own horn here.

The "East of Boston Harbor," an army investigation team empowered to award battlefield medals would have discovered, is through Winnisimet, or what is now Chelsea and East Boston, across the river from Bunker Hill. The stated purpose of this mission over the hot July Fourth weekend was to take a look at the position of the British army, many of whose troops were aboard ships in Back Bay. He finally had seen the whites of the British eyes!

1775 — July 15

No 11

To 333⅓ Dollars given to ——— to*
induce him to go into the Town of Boston, to
establish a secret correspondence for the
purpose of conveying intelligence of the
Enemys movements & designs . . . . $2,600†

---

* *The names of Person who are employed within the Enemy's Lines or who may fall within their power cannot be inserted.*
—[G. W.'s note]

† *Washington does not mention what kind of dollars these were: Spanish or American. This is only one of the mysteries connected with this item. Since he also supplies the amount in lawful money (£100), I have translated it by the common rate of exchange for consistency's sake.*

"———," as Washington refers to this unsung hero, was the country's first successful spy. Unlike Nathan Hale, one of the most prominent failures in the history of spying, "———" has been treated shabbily in the annals of patriotism.

———'s last immortal words, possibly "If I don't get a raise, George, I quit," have never been publicized like Hale's. "If I had ten thousand lives, I would lay them all down, if called to it, in defence of my injured, bleeding country," he said at the gallows, according to a reporter in the Essex *Journal* of Newburyport, Massachusetts (February 13, 1777). This was because of Washington's attitude towards this distinguished profession.

As the expense account shows, he refused to name names even after the war was over, as if there was something shameful about the practice of informing. To err is human, and Washington has made a number of mistakes in this expense account. This is one of his worst.

Selling out one's associates and neighbors is a rich American tradition, widely encouraged by the FBI and numerous congressional committees. Much of the guilt we still feel over accepting a few pieces of silver, or more tangible psychic rewards, may stem from Washington's taciturnity in this area of achievement. By deleting the names of the few, Washington by inference is giving credit to all our forbears. The expense account could have cleared up the mystery of which sons of the Revolution were the truly great informers in American history. Did the Cabots speak only to the Lowells? As it stands now, all we have is the hearsay of historians which vaguely implicates fine men like a Mr. Hitchborne and James Lovell, later a delegate from Massachusetts to the Continental Congress. They were active in securing intelligence *through* spies, according to Fitzpatrick, making them at least accessories to the crime, if that is what it is.

This item of Washington's also casts a cloud on the loyalty to the free enterprise system of our confessed spies. Was Nathan Hale a paid employee on Washington's expense account, and not a volunteer as we had always been taught? In that case, he would have been giving up not only his life but his salary, too, for his country.

The so-called ———s in this book deserve a better fate than Washington has given them.

None of this is important for modern expense account writers, unless they are industrial spies on the side. The genius in this entry is the way Washington demonstrates the basic principle of intermingling private and office expenses: *When mixing funds make the cover story difficult to verify.*

1775 — July 15

No 12

> *To Cash paid for cleaning the House which was*
> *provided for my Quarters & [which] had been*
> *occupied by the Marblehead Regm [*]* $65

---

* The Marblehead Regiment was the 21st Massachusetts,
commanded by John Glover.

General Washington arrived at the front in Cambridge the night of July 2 and bivouacked in what was known then as "President's house," built by Harvard College in 1726 for its chief administrators. A precedent for future collaboration between the university and military was thus established.

The next morning, at nine o'clock, Washington officially took command of the army on Cambridge Common, although local residents believe it was under the so-called "Washington Elm." Coincidentally it was the 21st anniversary of the surrender of Fort Necessity. He rolled up his ruffled sleeves and got down to work. Historians say Washington's first official act was an inspection tour of the posts occupied by the ragged Revolutionary band at Cambridge, Winter and Prospect hills, and at Roxbury. But there is no record in the expense account for this piece of military business.

At some point soon he must have seen the troops, for on July 27 he wrote to his brother, "I found a mixed multitude of People here under very little discipline, order or Government." He discovered that "some men lived in tents, made from now useless sails from seaport towns." The Reverend William Emerson reported others lived under boards and sail, stone and turf, and birch bush.*

The camp that summer, judging by the diaries I have read, resembled a country fair or gigantic rural picnic. The crowd was interracial (it wasn't until later in the war that Washington tried to discourage blacks from enlisting in the army). There was a lot of drinking, gambling, tall-story telling, singing and smoking going on. A few were taking baths and haircuts. They were an easygoing bunch, but many of the bearded radicals also studied by campfire light and kept up their journals; judging by these, Cambridge in 1775 sounded something like the Woodstock festival at Bethel, New York, in 1969.

The kids who walked to Cambridge for the freak-out against the Establishment included some of the nation's finest idealists. Many were escapists who only wanted to get away from responsibilities at home and at school. Others were shrewd Yankee opportunists out to make a fast Continental dollar off the crowd of 20,000 who

---

* French, *First Year of the American Revolution*, pp. 300–301.

showed up for the rebellion against authority. It was a cross-section of radical America.

The patriot army also must have looked like today's hippies dressed in odds and ends of old uniforms (including British army surplus). It was a war against tyranny, and the troops chose to express their freedom in the individuality of their dress. The Connecticut Light Horse, one of the fancier rebel factions, showed up in gaudy cloaks that made them look like the British cavalry.* At the other extreme were the backwoodsmen who wore their civilian clothes. Others came to the front "dressed as savages." The only uniformity at Cambridge was raggedness; the colors brown and green seemed to predominate.† Washington, dressed in blue, was appalled by the sight. Somebody had to teach those unwashed, long-haired hippies respect for law and order.

Sometimes I think Washington didn't understand his men. The army was a free-floating experience to them. They hadn't read Marshal Saxe on the rules of war. They couldn't understand the importance of marching in straight lines on parade grounds. All they came to Cambridge for was to stand behind trees and stone fences and kill British soldiers. The strategy had worked brilliantly at Lexington and Concord. At Breed's Hill, they had patiently and silently waited until the British were 40 yards away—they had sharp eyes—and did their thing. "Where companies of Grenadiers had stood," the British historian Trevelyan wrote, "three out of four, and even nine out of ten in some places, lay dead or wounded in the long grass."‡ A Scotchman living in Virginia two months later blamed the slaughter of June 17 on the fact that the Americans "took sight" when they fired. The rebel fighting man of 1775 was somebody a Fidel Castro or a Mao Tse-tung would have been proud of.

General Washington's plan was to turn the men into a highly-polished Anglo-Saxon army. He was determined to hammer the farm boys, students and weekend warriors from the militia companies into goose-stepping automatons who would fire by platoons. "Hyde Park tactics," as they were called. Friction was bound to occur.

One of the first issues on which the Commander and his men disagreed was saluting. The bolsheviks who dropped everything to fight for freedom in 1775 refused to salute officers, almost as if it was a confession of their inferiority as a class. The enlisted man's officers, Bolton in *The Private Under Washington* (p. 127) explained, "were not infrequently his intimate friends, or even his inferiors, men who devoted their time to local militia organizations

---

* Dr. Albigence Waldo, "Diary," *Historical Magazine,* June, 1861, p. 169.

† *Historical Magazine,* December, 1860, p. 353.

‡ *The American Revolution,* Pt. I, p. 328.

and had become familiar with drill and tactics while he perhaps was busy with other matters." Privates could not understand why they should salute such neighbors in camp, or why they should ask permission to go beyond the lines.

Some of the politician-officers did not precisely distinguish themselves at Breed's Hill. Discipline depends upon those in command. What could be expected of a company whose captain ordered his men to march into battle at the hill, "promising to overtake them directly" and never appearing until the next day?*

As the chief operating officer of a slack organization, Washington introduced regular board of directors meetings, or court-martials, which dealt with shoddy work performance. His two major enemies at this stage of the war were the army's officers and enlisted men.

On taking command, he had ordered his officers to send in the returns, a list of the men and their availability for duty. The old hippie army never quite knew how many men it had at any given time. The returns, an hour's work, the General complained in his letters, took eight days. Court-martials dismissed officers for carelessness, ignorance, unmilitary behavior, and cowardice at Breeds' Hill. The General also said he was sickened by the way his officers were fraternizing with the employees. Reading through the court-martial records one sees that a Lieutenant Whitney was tried and convicted of "infamous conduct in degrading himself by voluntarily doing the duty of an orderly sergeant." Joseph Reed, of the expense account crowd, reported that a cavalry officer was found guilty "for unconcernedly shaving one of his men." It didn't matter that he may have been a barber back home who was afraid of losing his touch. Washington was determined to give his junior executives a sense of dignity.

He dealt just as firmly with the enlisted men. The first court-martial of a man in the ranks was for stealing 11 geese. There was no excuse for petty crime, even a patriot's hunger, and the fellow was convicted. The hippies were also found guilty for drinking, swearing, whoring, and the equivalent of not obeying *keep off the grass* signs. Flogging, as mentioned in the introduction, was the keystone of the General's law and order program. But it was humane. A surgeon always stood by, it was said, to make sure the disciplinarian (usually a regiment's drum-major) did not go over the prescribed number of strokes; he was also on duty to revive the patriot in case he fainted. For the more serious crimes, an offender sometimes had to "ride the wooden horse." As this was described to me by a military historian, "The patriot was tied a-straddle of the sharp edge of a board or some similar peaked device, raised about six feet off the ground, and weights were put on his feet. The physical effect was something in the nature of a split, though, of

* *Boston in 1775,* ed. Ford, p. 14.

course, the weights were never heavy enough actually to split the patriot in two. Usually he would faint after a few minutes, though some of the hardened veterans could stick it out for an hour."

Whole regiments participated in passing the gauntlet, another innovation in the American Army's penal code which didn't last. Washington may have inspired the inclusion of guarantees against cruel and inhuman punishment in the proceedings at the Constitutional Convention in 1787.

From all reports, the General seemed to prefer ordinary flogging. As he pointed out, with the other disciplinary methods, the men were sometimes permanently injured and of no use to their companies. It took courage for Washington to stick by these reforms. If he ever decided to run for public office after the war, he wouldn't be able to count on the veterans' vote.

The men, understandably, turned surly. The scene was now heavy. They would have to learn who was boss.

During these first few days of de-radicalization, Washington's expense account shows that he was also preoccupied with fixing up his new headquarters. Why he moved from the President's house is not known. Perhaps the decision was dictated by the start of the summer session at Harvard. But it more likely had something to do with Samuel Langdon, the president of Harvard, who had requested permission to continue living in one of the back rooms. (Freeman says he is not sure whether Langdon's wife and five kids also were quartered in the room.) Washington was always uncomfortable in the presence of scholars.

His new field headquarters—formerly the house of John Vassal, a fugitive royalist, renamed the Craigie Mansion and later given as a wedding present to the poet, Henry Wadsworth Longfellow—was large enough to quarter the entire Marblehead Regiment, though probably not very comfortably.

In the room to the right of the front door, where Washington may have jotted down in his memorandum books this item for cleaning, Longfellow wrote some of his most memorable lines, such as "Into each life some rain must fall."

It took eight days, Fitzpatrick says, to render the Longfellow House inhabitable. This may have been an expression of what a Virginia gentleman really felt about "the dirty New Englanders," as they were sometimes called. (See Mrs. Portnoy's method of re-washing dishes after her maid finished eating lunch, in Philip Roth's *Portnoy's Complaint.*)

When he was bringing his young bride, Martha, home to Mount Vernon with her portmanteaus filled with Bank of England stock, he sent ahead a note to the caretaker-steward, John Alton, which read:

"You must have the house very well clean'd. You must get two of the best Bedsteads put up, one in the Hall Room, and the Other in the little dining room that used to be, and have Beds made on them against we come. You must also get out the Chairs and Tables, and have them very well rub'd and Clean'd; the Stair Case ought also to be polished in order to make it look well."

We have no record of how many men (or cleaning women) slaved for eight days to shape up this headquarters for a mere £2 10s. (a sum less than the Damascus tablecloth linen in item No. 8). Nor do we even know whether the work was done by professional cleaners, or a detail of volunteers recruited by a first sergeant in the company day rooms (Brattle Street taverns). These goldbrickers could have easily stretched out a day's work to eight. If that was the case, the £2 10s. may have been the cost of *cleaning supplies,* not labor—a more credible explanation.

I don't recommend that modern expense account writers take this item seriously. To believe Washington actually paid so little for a task force which played such an important role in the history of the Revolution is a slur on his memory.

1775 — July 19

No 13

> To Ditto to Mr. Eben. Austin the steward
> for Household Expences* $260
>
> ---
>
> * *This, and every other sum which will be found charged in these accounts to Mr. Austin, are credited in his Book of Household Expenditures, herewith given in as a Voucher.*—[G. W.'s note]

No other phrase in this book gives such a good quick impression of the range and versatility of Washington's genius as "Household Expences." In two prosaic words, he managed to cover a multitude of sins, such as eating.

The name of Ebenezer Austin looms rather larger here than in most other chronicles of the war. More than Maj. Gen. Nathanael Greene, strategist of the Revolution; Maj. Gen. Charles Lee, the soldier as radical; Maj. Gen. Horatio Gates, the professional soldier; Brig. Gen. John Sullivan, the luckless Irishman, or Brig. Gen. Benedict Arnold, the swine—it was Austin, the civilian, who gave Washington the logistical support without which our Revolution might have failed. From July 18, 1775 until April 4, 1776, Austin served as steward at headquarters. His salary for running Washington's household as smoothly as a restaurant like the Forum of the Twelve Caesars was £7 10s. ($235) a month. But that also included the services of his wife and daughter.

The unsung hero of Cambridge, Austin wrote up his Revolutionary War experiences in the *Book of Household Expences,* which as far as I know is not used at any army war college or general staff school. Washington briefly mentions it as a source material for further study of his accounts. It actually is two small (about 7″ × 8″) paper-covered octavo volumes with hand-ruled pages. Washington's summary of the contents, which he mentions that he is handing in as a voucher, doesn't do it justice.

Opposite is a true copy of the summary, a sample of great accompanying-voucher writing.

I wouldn't change a word of that. It is the closest thing to perfection in narrative, the most difficult area of expense account writing.

<u>*1775 — July 24*</u>

<u>*No 14*</u>

To Ditto—paid a French cook *$58.50*

The French cook, Fitzpatrick says, was Adam Foutz, who later became a member of the Commander in Chief's Guard.

Of the military action going on in July, the only one I have found where a man of Foutz's talents could have been effectively utilized was described by Amory in *Old Cambridge and New* (p. 23) and S. A. Drake, in *Historic Fields and Mansions of Middlesex* (p. 262), as cited by Martyn in *Artemas Ward:*

There was much hilarity and Adjutant Gibbs was hoisted, chair and all, upon a table and gave the company a rollicking bachelor's song, calculated to make the immobile features of the Chief relax . . . Glasses clinked, stories were told, and the wine circulated.

But all the evidence suggests that General Ward paid for this business conference.

The practice in the non-expense account crowd, according to the diary of a Connecticut enlisted man (Simeon Lyman, *Journal,* Connecticut Historical Society Collection, VII, pp. 128–131): "It was my turn to cook."

Dᴿ Mͬ Ebenezer Austin .. Steward .. Nͬ

1775.				Lawful.		
July	19	To Cash to Mͬᵒ Ebenezʳ Austin (who was employed as a Steward) - for Household Expences		10		
	24	To Ditto .... to Ditto		2		
	26	To Ditto ... Ditto		10		
Augᵗ	5	To Ditto ... Ditto		2		
		Ditto ... Ditto		8		
	20	To Ditto ... Ditto		10		
	21	To Ditto .... Ditto		2	8	
	23	To Ditto ... Ditto		18		
	29	To Ditto ... Ditto		12		
Sep	18	To Ditto ... Ditto		6		
	28	To ... Ditto ... Ditto		12		
		Ditto ... Dᵒ		6		
Ocᵗ	5	To Ditto ... Dᵒ		6		
	10	To Ditto ... Dᵒ		6		
	16	To Ditto ... Dᵒ		16	10	
	23	To Ditto ... Dᵒ		6		
	27	To Ditto ... Dᵒ		2	2	
	30	To Ditto ... Dᵒ		12		
Nov	7	To Ditto ... Dᵒ		9		
	10	To Ditto ... Dᵒ		9		
	20	To Ditto ... Dᵒ		12		

1775 — July 24

No 15

> To Ditto—paid Mr. Austin for
> Household Expence $52

The General lacks his usual candor in explaining the substance of these "Household Expences." They are worth going into anyway. At this late date, the risk of giving away any military secrets to the British War Office is slight.

There is nothing unusual in Mr. Austin's book, which is in the stacks of the Library of Congress. The payments he made were for everyday household expenses, primarily food, and a great deal of it. It sometimes looks as if enough was bought to feed an army.

On July 21 to 22, for example, Mr. Austin bought a pig, an illegible number of ducks, "1 dozen pidgeons, veal, 1 dozen squash, 2 dozen eggs, hurtleberries, bisket [sic] and a cork cask." All this seems to prove is that an army officer doesn't live on bread alone.

The basic principle in these recurring "Household Expences" for modern expense account writers is: *God helps those who help themselves.*

1775 — July 26

No 16

> To Mr. Austin for House. Expences $260

Somebody in "the family," as Washington referred to the expense account crowd, must have liked limes. Mr. Austin ordered them by the hundreds. One time he bought 400. As a class, Washington's family probably had fewer cases of scurvy than the army as a whole.

1775 — August 1

No 17

> To Mr. Hower acc[ount] $141.70

William Howe, as he was better known in 1775, was a Cambridge shopkeeper. Washington spent more than the Paymaster-General's monthly salary—$100 a month, according to the act of Congress previously cited—for cloth and thread.*

* Force, American Archives, IV Series, p. 18.

1775— August 5
No 18

　　To Mr. Austin . . . Househ. Exp. $52

The family's menu this month included chickens, oysters, hurtleberries, pears, cucumbers, mending a bolt for the pump, veal,
mutton, eggs, a blanket, bread, milk, and a pepper box & dipper.
(Despite Mr. Austin's skill as a home economist, non-food items
occasionally appear on his market list. Possibly he bought things
like a blanket impulsively.)

　　Family retainers had a better balanced menu than the men on the
payroll. At this time of the war, when food was relatively plentiful,
the troops' menu was "pork and beans" one day and "beans and
pork" the next. How they expected to fight a war on that is beyond me.

　　These early household expense items appear so slight, they are
embarrassing. But collectively they will add up to an impressive
body of work.

1775 — August 5
No 19

　　Ditto . . . Ditto $208

This loses something in the translation.

1775 — August 5
No 20

　　To Washing—at Sundry times $119.60

No 21

　　To Servants—at Ditto $124.80

Besides food stuffs, the *Book of Household Expences* also listed
items of miscellaneous nature, often under the nomenclature "miscellaneous." We know for a fact that "Household Expences" did not
usually include charges for servants. Following the old military
principle that those also serve who only stand and wait, Washington
hired a number of civilians to make his bed, police the area, carry

his duffle bag (or foot locker), and shine the silver buckles on his shoes. He usually listed these items separately.

Washington was an equal opportunity employer, judging by the number of whites who worked like slaves on his staff. He was on a first-name basis with all of his employees. Sometimes he probably called co-workers in the fight for freedom "boy," but even a 60-year-old handyman on the staff knew he meant no harm. The General was a product of his environment.

It is difficult to give with any certainty a complete list of those who distinguished themselves during the Revolution by waiting on the General hand and foot at headquarters in 1775. Those we know, from Fitzpatrick's work in the field, and whom I single out now to assist anyone still trying to trace his ancestry, include by name and rank, without regard to race or creed:

> Edward Hunt, a cook;
> Mrs. Morrison, kitchen-woman;
> Mary Kettel, washerwoman;
> Eliza Chapman;
> Timothy Austin, possibly the son of Ebenezer Austin;
> James Munro;
> Dinah, a woman;
> Peter, a man.

William Lee, Washington's body servant from Mount Vernon, also known as "Billy," was brought to the front at the public's expense. Apparently it wasn't until after the American Revolution that war was supposed to be hell.

1775 — August 8

No 22

To Mr. Will[ia]m. Vans acc[ount]. $1,120.30

This has the rhythm and cadence of Washington's expense account writing at its best. Five words for $1,120, or roughly $224 a word, a rate which puts him in the class of such contemporary free-lance writers as Harold Robbins (for copies of his expense accounts, see the Director of the Internal Revenue). As the war wore on, however, Washington leaves Robbins in the dust.

William Vans, Washington doesn't explain, is the other partner in the military supply depot, Vans & Sparhawk. The requisition was for tea, tablespoons, and (possibly for the hospital unit at headquarters) a cask of Madeira, bottles, corks, and "other sundries."

It is not widely known that during the war Washington continued to drink tea. Some radicals wouldn't have touched that beverage for all the tea in China. By not swearing off tea, as others had done after the Boston Tea Party of 1773, Washington may have been giving his opinion of the issues behind that dispute, which to this day are not clear. Did John Hancock, the noted tea smuggler and insurance man, have a profit, rather than a patriotic motive, in underwriting the expenses (for costumes and entertainment) of that party? A shortage of tea caused by the dumping of 200 chests into Boston Harbor the night of December 16, 1773, by so-called Indians must have increased the value of the inventory in Hancock's warehouse.

No tea company advertised that such and such a brand was the favorite of General Washington. A popular brand at the time, however, was Bawstonaba, a blend of Indian and Ceylon teas, packaged then as now by Davison Newman & Co. Ltd. of London. It still comes in one pound and half-pound canisters, now bearing a copy of the original petition Davison and Newman sent to King George III demanding compensation for the chests thrown into the water by Hancock's paid volunteers, a truly Washingtonesque gesture. Boston Harbour Tea, as it is called today, sells for only $4 a pound in Bloomingdale's delicacies department and at Charles & Co.

At those prices, taking into account the scale of appreciation of money, Washington must have drunk a lot of tea. A better way to explain the tea bill is that the Vans item is a metaphor for a GI party, which could have been better expressed this way:

"To cash for Tea for Two Thousand . . ."

Observers at headquarters usually mention Washington drinking only imported wines. Madeira was his favorite, especially the '59 and '63. Things got so bad during the later war years, he would drink Madeira of any year.

It is not known whether Mary Ludwig Hays or Heis, alias Molly Pitcher, charged the government for the water she served at the battle of Monmouth in 1778. That camp follower is also *persona non grata* in the expense account hall of fame.

1775 — August 17

No 23

To Danl. Isley—per acc[ount] *$156*

Daniel Isley was a Watertown, Massachusetts, carter. Washington paid for transporting the baggage of the then Colonel Benedict Arnold from Casco Bay (Maine) to Cambridge. Some of these fellows on the expense account, like Arnold, seem a little shady to me.

1775 — August 18

No 24

  To Giles Alexander—D[itto] *$26*

Giles Alexander was a tailor employed at headquarters from July 1775 apparently to the end of the war. Keep in mind that business expenses are legitimate deductions no matter how frivolous they may seem to you.

George Washington, even at Valley Forge, was one of the ten best-dressed men in the army. His fatigues were more resplendent than the average enlisted man's or officer's uniform. This was one of Washington's strengths as a general.

As a teen-ager Washington was an awkward, gangly fellow, all hands ("The largest I've ever seen on a human being," Lafayette once wrote) and feet (size 13 shoe), and with no small talk to speak of. He was especially silent amongst women. When he first began wearing uniforms in the French and Indian War, he was a new man. His handshake became like hard steel and his cold gray-blue eyes looked straight at people, in silent appraisal. Whenever he entered a room where he was not well known, everyone wondered who this tall veteran was and sensed that Somebody Special had arrived. He was in uniform on some non-military business in Williamsburg in 1758 when the freshly widowed Martha Custis first caught sight of him.

In light of his later election as Commander in Chief, perhaps there was some significance in the fact that when he posed for his portrait by Charles Willson Peale in 1772, he dressed himself up as a veteran. It could be said this was the equivalent of our campaign photos today. But Washington denied that he was a candidate. It seems more likely that he simply thought that he looked particularly impressive in military garb.

A clothes-conscious generation today would thrill to read the Revolutionary Washington's wardrobe requirements, as described in his purchase orders to his London agent. "Half a dozen pair of Men's neatest shoes, and Pumps, to be made by one Didsbury, on Colo. Baylor's last—but a little larger than his—and to have high heels—" he wrote on May 1, 1759. "Never more make any of Dog leather except one pair of Pumps in a Cargoe unless you send better leather than they were made of before—for the two pairs of Shoes scarcely lasted me twice as many days & had very fair wearing," he complained in a follow-up letter of November 30, 1759.

His fondness for fine clothing went beyond his own wardrobe. Not long after his marriage, he asked for:

 1 salmon colored tabby (a soft plain velvet or silk) velvet of the en- closed pattern, with satin flowers to be made in a sack and coat.

1 cap, handkerchief tucker, and ruffles, to be made of Brussels lace on Point, proper to be worn with the above negligee, to cost twenty pounds.

The above items were for his wife, I hope. Also in this order were "1 doz. most fashionable cambric pocket handkerchiefs," "1000 minikins" (which I'm told were small pins), "8 lbs. perfumed powder," and "2 handsome breastflowers."

When Washington sat on the expensive horses we have already read about, wearing gorgeous military raiment we will be reading more about, remember this was part of his job as a leader. He felt that clothes made the general.

The only flaw in this long-winded justification for this expense item, his critics will say, is that Giles Alexander was paid not for work on the General's wardrobe but on his servants'.

1775 — August 20

No 25

To Reuben Colburn *$260*

This item doesn't sound like the George Washington we all admire. It is for money paid to Reuben Colburn of Gardinerstone, on the Kennebec River, for sawing planks preparatory to building bateaux for Colonel Arnold's expedition to Canada. With item No. 36, which paid the costs of sending a team of bateaux-builders into the Maine woods to nail the planks together, it is an expense which should have properly been included in the nation's war budget for 1775.

The Canadian expedition was an attempt to open a second front. The planks Washington paid for turned out to have been of green timber. The bateaux weighed 400 pounds apiece and had to be carried around numerous waterfalls. "Arnold retained his cheerfulness," Willard M. Wallace writes in an essay in *George Washington's Generals,* "despite the shocking discovery that the bateaux were falling apart and many of the provisions were already ruined. At the Great Carrying Place, with the men's shoulders raw and blistered, downpours turned the portage into a sea of yellow mud. Some men drank the water and came down almost at once with nausea and diarhea."

Arnold and his bateaux-carriers survived anyway. His exhausted, half-frozen, famished men subsisted on meals of boiled moccasin and a gruel of shaving soap. If General Arnold put these sundries on an expense account, I have seen no record of it. Time and time again, we will see that the non-expense account crowd during the war fared badly.

How these national defense items wound up in George Washington's expense account is one of those unresolved mysteries which still haunt the Revolutionary War. My guess is that items like No. 25 and No. 36 are common bookkeeping errors, for which I apologize post-facto in behalf of my coauthor.

1775
August 20
_____

No 26

  To Mr. Austin . . . *H. Exp.* *$260*

August 21
_____

No 27

   Ditto . . . *Ditto* *$62.40*

August 23
_____

No 28

   Ditto . . . *Ditto* *$468*

While these items are written in Washington's inimitable style, there is no record of what they cover. They may have been for a family reunion.

Human nature abhors a vacuum. My speculation here runs along military lines. Arnold, who, most military historians concede, was a great general, though something of a security risk, was off to conquer Canada, which could turn the tide in Boston Harbor. Anticipating the eventual success of Arnold's bateaux panzer to the north, Washington may have broken the monotony of the Boston siege by commissioning a new portrait, a favorite form of relaxation. The pacing of these three items is reminiscent of this passage in his diaries of 1772:

> May 20. I sat to have my picture drawn.
> May 21. I sat again to take the drapery.
> May 22. Set for Mr. Peale to finish my face.

The price also seems about right, checking with his Ledger for 1772:

> May 30. By Mr. Peale Painter. Drawg. my
>   Picte.   .... £ 18. 4s.
>   Minature Do. for Mrs. W ...... £ 13
>   Ditto ..... Do. for Miss Custis ...... £ 13
>   Ditto ..... Do. for Mr. Custis ...... £ 13.

1775 — August 25

No 29

> *To James Campbell—Necessaries for the*
> *House* *$39*

August 29

No 30

> *To Jehoiakim Youkin* . . . *D[itto]* . . . . .
> . . . . *D[itto]* *$39*

No 31

> *To Mr. Austin—Hd. Exp.* *$312*

September 1

No 32

> *To Paper, Sealing Wax, & C., of Severals* *$169*

Campbell's voucher does not specify the necessaries. It may be for paint and canvas.

This is a pure fabrication which has no basis in fact, and is frankly meant to be ridiculous. I include this speculation only to demonstrate the value of a non-specific charge, buttressed by an even vaguer voucher—an unbeatable combination in expense account writing. The charge becomes flexible enough to cover any contingency.

A portrait may not seem essential to Washington's business, in the light of today. But we can be sure that sitting for a picture was very important work to Washington, judging by the number of his portraits currently hanging in museums. I don't have to point this out to modern businessmen who put Fabian Bachrach portraits on their expense accounts, against the day when these must be sent to newspapers.

The basic principle of loose bookkeeping is still practiced today by maitre d's who give their regular customers a blank receipt. They also give them a knowing look. The theory is that the customer is supposed to save the restaurant management time by recording the official record of the meal. It works.

Nevertheless, some critics say this is an institutionalized invitation to exaggerating one's feats at the dinner table, or cheating.

Those who may see a parallel will be dismayed to learn that entries like Mr. Austin's household accounts (item No. 31) were balanced every week or ten days and cleared by warrant of the Paymaster General. An honored guest at Washington's table from time to time, the Paymaster General undoubtedly was in a position to verify the high cost of living at the front.

Mr. Youkin's account (item No. 30) is interesting because the bill is missing from Washington's papers. The principle here goes under the name of the *Vanishing Voucher* or the *Mislaid Manifest.* It works only when the item is included with a series of non-specific charges, like Mr. Campbell's.

"Severals," in item No. 32, is a new word in the basic expense account vocabulary. It is a synonym for "miscellaneous." Here it is used as a proper noun, in place of "the military-industrial complex of Boston."

1775 — September 1

No 33

*To cash for recovering my Pistols which had
been stolen, & for repairing them afterwards* . . . *$39*

This gives the lie to his critics who by now must be thinking that Washington bought everything on the expense account. There is no record of his having bought a gun for the war. All the expense account says is that he sold a gun (see page 2 of facsimile version).

Fitzgerald says, "The particulars of this theft of the Commander-in-chief's pistol do not appear to be available." Still I cling to the view that this was not the same gun he had sold to the Massachusetts militia man. The poor fellow whose foot locker it turned up in might have been flogged. His cries that he was innocent, that a militia captain had given it to him to shoot the British, would have cut little ice in an army where a boy named James Whaling who attempted to run away was given thirty lashes "in consideration of his youth." His defense was that he had to cut hay so his widowed mother wouldn't starve that winter.

There is no record, either, of Washington's having received a reprimand for not minding his gun. When I was in the army, my commanding officer made me sleep with my gun for two weeks for not cleaning it properly.

John M'Murty, who was cleaning a gun in the camp, put in the priming and pulled the trigger, not knowing that it carried a load. The shot went through a double partition of inch boards, through one board of a berth, through the breast of a man named Penn, and a chimney, leaving its mark there.* Guns were dangerous in those days. But that hardly explains the General's laxness.

---

* "A. Wright's Journal"; in *Historical Magazine,* July, 1862, p. 211.

1775 — September 7

No 34

To Mr. Sparhawks . . . *Acc*[*ount*] . . . *$573.30*

We might as well discuss General Washington's drinking, since these trips to stores like Mr. Sparhawk's recur so frequently in the expense account.

The General may have taken an occasional drink or two. But in wartime that is understandable.

Washington never drank more than a bottle of Madeira a night, as all the historians say, besides rum, punch and beer. He preferred Madeira to all other beverages, as previously noted, but he was catholic—not presbyterian, episcopalian or hard-shell baptist—in his drinking habits. He often drank cider, champagne and brandy, especially after the French alliance when surplus wine flowed into this country as tea had under British mercantilism.

Mixing liquors wasn't considered as dangerous then as it is today. In her amusing *Stage Coach and Tavern Days,* Mrs. Alice Morse Earle gives a recipe for Flip, a drink as common amongst the stagecoach set as martinis are in the jet set:

★ Take one pitcher of beer, only two thirds full.
★ Add enough sugar or molasses, until sweet.
★ Add about a gill of New England rum.
★ Take one hot poker—with a large head on it. Heat until red hot. Then plunge into the pitcher, and stir.

The red-hot iron, which was called "a loggerhead," brought the mess to a boil and gave it a burnt bitter taste. It would still give an expense account drinker today a nice high.

A loggerhead was a standard piece of equipment at every colonial fireside. Its role in the conduct of the Revolutionary War has never fully been explained by military historians. While the extremists on Washington's staff would argue when the moment was propitious to attack the British, they would often seize loggerheads to make their debating points. This is the etymology of the expression "to be at loggerheads." Washington apparently believed the rebels should never strike while the iron was hot.

If General Washington was ever intoxicated, I have never read of it. That is not so surprising. Have you ever seen a man on an expense account today drunk while on the job? He may have had three martinis and be in a stupor, but he can always function well enough to hang on to his job like an outclassed boxer in the eighth round.

Drinking had more stature in the colonial period than it does today among the Daughters of the American Revolution. It was neither a furtive sin nor a pastime. "It was sort of an athletic sport," as one historian put it. Private David How told the story of two men at Cambridge who fell to joshing one another as to who could drink the most. This led to excessive drinking, from which one of the men died in an hour or two.* He must have been otherwise in poor health. Our forefathers were rated as one-bottle men or two-bottle men. Three-bottle men were looked up to with the reverence we show these days for astronauts and Billy Graham. As a one-bottle man, Washington obviously wasn't first in drinking in the Continental Army. He was only first in saying, "See what the boys in the back room will have."

The honor of being the Dean Martin of the Revolution fell to Maj. Gen. William Alexander of New Jersey, better known by the title Lord Sterling. Alexander-Sterling spent a fortune lobbying for a peerage, which was finally rejected by the House of Lords in 1762. One of the patriotic songs of the day immortalized General Alexander-Lord Sterling's feats:

> What matters what of Sterling may become?
> The quintessence of whiskey, soul of rum;
> Fractious at nine, quite gay at twelve o'clock;
> From thence til bed-time stupid as a block.

It never reached the top of the hit parade, like "Yankee Doodle Dandy," but was quite popular with the Tories. General Alexander-Lord Sterling wasn't widely respected by the rebels either, especially by the enlisted men. When Washington gave the command, "Fall out," Sterling could hit the ground harder and faster than the best of them. Michael Nash, according to Washington's *Orderly Books,* got drunk and received fifty lashes. Lord Sterling received only Washington's disappointed glance. The lash may have sobered him up.

Although all historians agree he was the only one of our forefathers who might have been drunk every day during the war, Lord Sterling managed to hang on at headquarters. It may have been Washington's traditional deference for aristocracy. Stephen Hess in *America's Political Dynasties* explains the mystery in another way: "If his record was for the most part one of failures and misadventures, his devotion earned the sincere gratitude of the Commander-in-Chief."

Of the cost of the habit in Revolutionary times, Jackson Turner Main reports, "If only the head of the family kept himself in liquor, he could spend £5 on rum." That's for a year, not a day.

Washington's bar bill, as reported so discreetly in these pages, may have exceeded that figure by roughly 1,000 percent. Nevertheless, alcohol was a "household necessarie." It was good for his

---

* *Diary of David How,* ed. G. W. Chase and H. B. Dawson, p. 5.

health. Washington went through the entire war without getting scathed. Nor have I ever read of his falling off a horse while intoxicated. The time he fell out of the boat while crossing the Delaware was an accident. "When taken early in the morning, unmixed with water, it [liquor] impaired the health of men," Colonel Hutchinson wrote in his *Orderly Book* (p. 15). "And in long marches the hard drinker was most apt to suffer," another authority said.* Medical science was not as advanced then as it is today; it was drinking on an empty stomach that was the ruin of those malingerers. Much of Washington's continuing good cheer and famed fortitude during the long years of the war, caused to some extent by his overly cautious military tactics, may have come from the bottle.

1775 — September 7

No 35

To Mr. Pierce Adj. to Gen. Gates—Wages . . . *$104*

In this direct manner, Washington was commenting on a major problem which had plagued the army since he took command: the shortage of money. The payrolls were slow in coming and didn't go far enough once they came. General Washington was not above this battle.

In September, subalterns in the Massachusetts regiments united to petition the Commander in Chief for an increase in pay. He could have thrown these guardhouse lawyers in jail for insolence. Instead he passed the petition along to the proper higher authorities. The Continental Congress appointed a ways and means subcommittee to look into the army grievances. A report was handed up whose general conclusions were that privates were paid too much and officers too little. A pay raise of one third was granted to junior officers.

1775 — September 7

No 36

To Reuben Colburn *$426.40*

This is the already mentioned charge for sending Col. Benedict Arnold, bateaux-and-baggage, to Canada. (See my comment on item no. 25.) In light of later events, this showed poor judgment on

* Dr. E. Elmer's "Journal"; in *New Jersey Historical Society Proceedings,* Vol. 2. (1846), p. 48.

Washington's part. But the same thing could be said of General Eisenhower's making Sherman Adams part of his family, of L.B.J. for Walter Jenkins and of J.F.K. for Teddy. Washington had a fatherly affection for Colonel Arnold in this sordid chapter of the expense account.

1775 — September 7

No 37

> *To S. B. Webb Esq. for Maj. French*
> *(a prisoner) his expenses to Hartford* *$312*

Samuel Blatchley Webb was a lieutenant in the 2nd Connecticut Regiment who rose to lieutenant-colonel and aide to Washington. Maj. Christopher French of the 22nd Foot, British Army, had been seized by Pennsylvania civil authorities in 1775 while on his way to join General Gage at Boston.

Why Washington would put a prisoner of war on his expense account is a puzzle to me, especially when there were so many more qualified rebel troops. Major French of the 22nd Foot became something of a pain. During the first months of his imprisonment, Fitzpatrick says, he addressed a constant stream of letters to Washington complaining of ill-treatment received by himself and other British prisoners. Freeman says French demanded the right to wear his sword in jail. There was a limit to even Washington's patience. He stopped writing to French. To the end of his days, French referred to his former pen pal in language usually reserved for war criminals.

1775 — September 18

No 38

> *To Mr. Austin* . . . *Hd. Exps* *$156*

A story is told of two soldiers at Cambridge who, being temporarily out of provisions, put a stone in their camp kettle when a Colonel Winds was expected for an inspection. The colonel soon stopped before the men who snapped to attention. "Well, men," the colonel inquired, "anything to eat?"

"Not much," they replied.

"What have you in that kettle?"

"A stone, colonel," one of the patriots replied. "For they say there is strength in stones, if you can only get it out."*

* Dr. J. Campfield's Diary, p. 133.

"This guileless conversation," Bolton observes, "had the desired effect, for the officer declared that they must have something better to eat."*

During the siege of Boston all food rations for the week were delivered on Wednesday, unless the number of regiments eating made it necessary to serve part of the army on other days.† Feeding the men, so simple an undertaking on paper, developed endless complications. Some weeks the army's cupboards were bare.

The lack of food at Cambridge, in Washington's opinion, was a disgrace, the result of Yankee slovenliness and dishonesty.‡ More than any other word in the salty army language of the day, *Food* was an unmentionable. That the word never mars these pages is further evidence of Washington's good taste.

1775 — September 18

No 39

To the Exp. of myself and Party in
Reconnoitring [sic] the South & West Shore of
Boston Harbor **$423.20**

On the road the General probably advanced at what he described elsewhere as his "usual travelling gait of five miles an hour."§ In a letter to his half-brother, Washington revealed that "We have a Cemi Circle of Eight or Nine Miles to guard to every part of which we are obliged to be equally attentive."||

It would seem that he charged the government a little more than ten cents a mile, as well as ten cents an hour, for his attention to the perimeter of the Cemi Circle. That is about what the average drummer is allowed to charge when out beating the bushes for sales. It could be argued he should have charged more, on the grounds that this was war. A salesman also runs risks. (See Arthur Miller's *Death of a Salesman.*)

1775 — September 28

No 40

　　To Mr. Austin . . . *Hd. Exps.* **$312**

No 41

　　. . . . *Ditto* . . . . . *Ditto* **$156**

---

* Bolton, *The Private Under Washington,* p. 85.
† Col. William Henshaw's *Orderly Books,* August 8, 1775, p. 66.
‡ Cunliffe, *George Washington,* p. 73.
§ *The Diaries of George Washington,* ed. Fitzpatrick, II, p. 289.
|| *Writings of Washington,* ed. Fitzpatrick, III, pp. 371–73.

Washington cannot be credited with coining the phrase "Ditto
. . . Ditto" (also abbreviated "Do. to Do."). Few have used it to
cover so much, as Washington struggled to entertain his hungry
public.

One of the men who joined the expense account crowd about now
was the former Boston bookseller, Henry Knox. Washington met
him on his first trip around the lines at Roxbury in July. An amateur
soldier who had learned everything he knew about artillery from the
books in his store, Knox was a professional in applying the theories.
The 25-year-old Knox was a round, fat, convivial man with merry
gray eyes in a face already acquiring its second chin. It has been
said that he was probably the closest thing Washington had to a
friend during the war. The General frequently leaned on the stout
patriot for advice on military problems. Knox was well-read in other
subjects, too. Books did not sell as profitably as shoes, "goloshes,"
dry goods, utensils and linens, so his store stocked a variety of
merchandise during the prewar days. The high esteem Washington
had for the man can be measured by the fact that after the war he
consulted with Knox about gravel walks for Mount Vernon. He
asked Knox if he knew of anything better, or should he just stick to
solid paving for his serpentine drive?

Knox and his bombardiers performed miracles at Dorchester
Heights, Trenton, and elsewhere during the war. But his feats at the
General's table have never been widely hailed. He weighed 230
pounds as a civilian, and was growing. In a uniform, he reminded
one observer of an ox in a uniform. The main thrust of the army's
commissary department policies seemed to be an emphasis on losing
weight, rather than maintaining it. Yet Knox managed not only to
hold his own, but gain 50 pounds. Compliments may be due the
family's chef.

Eventually Knox went on to become our first Secretary of War
and bankrupt himself trying to live in the style he became accustomed to in the army. He died, according to historian North
Callaghan, "unexpectedly at the age of fifty-six as the result of swal-
lowing a chicken bone." (*George Washington's Generals,* p. 257.)
In the annals of patriotism Knox will live as the nation's first true
gourmand.

I mention him now as a warning to modern expense account
writers: *Choose your friends wisely.* Otherwise your meal expenses
will cover only meals.

1775 — September 28

No 42

To Eben. Grey *$156*

Lieutenant Ebenezer *Gray* (a proper name and a color put the General in double jeopardy in spelling tests) was of the 3rd Connecticut Regiment and later Lieutenant Colonel of the 6th Connecticut Regiment. At this time, however, he was serving as a glorified messenger boy, delivering copies of a handbill to Colonel Arnold, prior to the start of the invasion of Canada. This was Washington's memorable *Address to the Canadians,* the words of which escape me now. Colonel Reed wrote them anyway.

Historians don't tell us how many copies of the broadside were printed for distribution to the people of Canada, but $156 makes it sound like a sizable bundle. The bateaux fell apart at the seams, and if the rebels were not able to save their food from the Kennebec River, it's not likely that they tried very hard to rescue publicity releases. We do know that Arnold's men were issued only five rounds of ammunition apiece for taking Canada.*

1775 — September 28

No *43*

> To Willm. Van $918.99

No *44*

> To Captn. Oswald—per [illegible] [*] $87.65

* *Perhaps: Con[signment]: Stand. Harts—rec't.*

William Van's account was for Madeira wine.

I think I ought to emphasize again that the amount of drinking done by people on and off the expense account during the early days of our history is almost beyond belief. A visitor in pre-Revolutionary War Philadelphia, which still has blue laws, kept a record in his diary of an average day's alcoholic consumption:

"Given cider and punch for lunch; rum and brandy before dinner; punch, Madeira, port and sherry at dinner; punch and liqueurs with the ladies; and wine, spirit and punch till bedtime, all in punch bowls big enough for a goose to swim in."†

One may question the propriety of Washington's putting his liquor bill on the expense account in such a diffident manner as item No. 43, but not the inalienable American right to drink day and night. It's our birthright, and the mark of a true patriot, to be a little stoned.

* *American Historical Review,* Vol. I, p. 296.
† Woodward, *G. Washington: The Image and the Man,* pp. 153–54.

Prigs today may assume that liquor appeals to man's baser instincts, especially in an army. The records of the Revolutionary War show that much alcohol was consumed in the drinking of high-minded toasts. "To the health and success of the ladies," according to *The Military Journals of Two Private Soldiers,* is typical of the noble sentiments expressed by the liquored-up rebels. The military science of the day prescribed its use for celebrating victories (a rare usage); encouraging enlisting; by fatigue parties to counteract the strain of hard work in bad weather, and even more liberally when there was no object in view.*

Into the alcoholic haze that must have hovered over the plains of Cambridge like a pink elephant, General Washington rode on his white horse. On August 19, 1775, E. Clarke's *Diary* reports, the General proclaimed to the men that he planned to discourage "vice in every shape." High on his list of reforms was the reduction of the use of liquor by the patriots.

Judging by the bill for Madeira, this would seem to be evidence that Washington invented the double standard. Nothing could be further from the truth. He may have practiced it from time to time, but he didn't invent it.

His general orders made clear that he hadn't suddenly become a member of a society for the advancement for temperance. The imbibing of certain alcoholic beverages, he explained, caused stomach-aches and diarrhea. "Nothing is more pernicous to the health of soldiers, nor more certainly productive of the bloody flux," he reported, "than new cider."†

The hippie army was also warned that the General expected them henceforth to respect property, particularly gardens. They were to take baths. But outdoor bathing was forbidden, as the General ordered, "at or near the bridge in Cambridge, where it has been observed and complained of, that many men, lost to all sense of decency and common modesty, are running about naked upon the bridge, whilst passengers, and even ladies of the first fashion in the neighborhood are passing over it, as if they meant to glory in their shame. . . ."‡

Some of the rebels probably raised a glass or two in praise of decency. Others gave up bathing for the duration.

Captain Oswald's account, in item No. 44, was for part of his expenses to Ticonderoga. The heavy run on William Vans' Madeira supplies may have been for a going-away party.

---

* Bolton, *Private Soldier Under Washington,* p. 228.
† Freeman, *George Washington,* p. 525.
‡ *George Washington's Writings,* ed. Fitzpatrick, Vol. 3, p. 440.

1775 — October 1

No 45

> To Blacksmith's acc[ount] at Sundry times to
> the date $86.23

No 46

> To Servants . . . . Do . . . . Do . . . $20.80

No 47

> To Washing . . . . Do . . . . Do . . $170.73

Like many wealthy men, Washington sometimes was inconsistent in his tipping, which in my opinion is what the General was talking about here. (See item No. 48, where he is more specific about the costs of taking one's servants to the barricades.)

During a previous trip through the same territory in peace time, Washington also listed his expenses in a ledger book. Between New York and Boston, he put down "servants, ten shillings." Yet in Boston he gave one chambermaid £ 1 2s. 6d.

As I have already mentioned, the General admired, and was willing to pay for, neatness.

1775 — October 1

No 48

> To Servants Wages in part—74. dollars . . . $473.20

October 2

No 49

> To Expens. at Mystick $60.23
> Ditto for Servants $37.69

One of the ploys the British War Office used during this period of the war to weaken the patriot cause was the generous counterfeiting of Continental dollars. Fitzgerald says they indulged their humor at times by furnishing the Loyalists with counterfeit notes with which they could pay their Continental taxes. This is an example of British understatement in humor, and showed an awareness of the enemy's weakness. Nothing was calculated to break the spirit of the American people more quickly than funny money.

The paper dollar was *persona non grata* at reputable banking houses. Even George Washington instructed his manager at Mount Vernon not to accept any more Continental paper in payment of maturing obligations. The only mention of it in the expense accounts appears in entries for his employees, both domestic and foreign (spies).

I do not know whether it is true that he paid his servants in worthless or counterfeit dollars. The evidence is confused. There is no doubt, however, that he listed the wages of his servants as expenses in lawful money. If he did pay in unlawful, I am sure it only could have happened while the General was under the influence of alcohol.

Whatever the case, Washington at least gave his servants a free ride to the shores of the Mystick (item no. 49), where doubtlessly they had little free time to squander their wages. Though "To Expens. at Mystick" is hardly more than a bravura piece, it displays the virtuosity of the writer. One would suspect that it was a pure pleasure trip, since it omits the thought "reconnoiterring." All the evidence suggests that it was a no-nonsense routine military action: inspecting the left wing of the army under the command of Lee, which reached from the center at Cambridge to the Mystic, or Medford, River. The relatively low cost of the mission seems to confirm its real nature.

From here on in, we will never know the difference between a routine patrol and a fox-hunt.

1775 — October 2

No 50

To a Field Bedstead & Curtains, Mattrass,
Blankets &c.&c. had of different Persons $546

There is nothing unusual about George Washington charging the government for the costs of decorating his house in Cambridge. He did the same thing for most of the places he slept at during the war.

Fortunately his hobby was interior decorating. As a bachelor, even while sitting around the campfire during the French and Indian War, his thoughts always turned to home. "The Floor of my Passage is really an Eye sore to me," he wrote to John Augustine Washington, then employed as caretaker of Mount Vernon. "I would therefore take it up if good and Season'd Plank could be laid in its place."

His taste was impeccable, always *à la mode*. In 1757, months ahead of the other Virginia planters, he was ordering wallpaper,

Papier Machée, for the ceiling of two rooms. He redecorated as regularly as any Daughter of the American Revolution. "I incline to do it in stucco (which if I understood you right, is the present taste in England)," he wrote to a Samuel Vaughan. "Permit me to ask if the rooms with which it is encrusted are painted generally; or are they left of the natural color, which is given of the cement . . . And also whether the rooms thus finished are stuccoed below the surbase (chair high) or from thence upwards only?"

In the gallery of great American stereotypes, he reminds one most of the average suburbanite who is conservative in politics and morality, but progressive in home remodeling. He even complained bitterly about repairmen while he fought another form of tyranny during the war. "He must be a miserable artozan [sic] or a very great rascal indeed who after one experim't could not tell what kind of shingles were necessary to prevent a common roof from leaking," Washington wrote from his field headquarters at Newburgh, New York.

While this facet of his personality may make a red-blooded American's blood boil, it undoubtedly helped keep costs down during the Revolution. Without this useful skill, Washington might have hired one of those fops in velvet pants, silk tunic, and ruffled shirts wearing a silver-tinted wig to do the decorating.

For those who are reading these comments only to check on comparative prices, Jackson Turner Main reports that after a study of newspaper advertisements in the 1770 to 1780 period good blankets averaged a guinea ($27.30, by our reckoning). The blanket Washington bought on the expense account here could have been the same one he gave away to the troops at Valley Forge in the legendary story. (But then again it may not have been.)

The vouchers for the field bedstead, curtains, etc., are not among the Washington Papers.

1775 — October 3

No 51

    To Walton White Esq. for a Riding Mare . . . *$1,248*

October 5

No 52

    To Mr. Austin—Hd. Exps. *$156*

No 53

    To Halters—&C. *$57.50*

The mare was a bay. Washington didn't have one like this yet.

It was sold to him by a soldier, "Anthony West Outerbridge White." (That's how he signed the receipt; my guess is this was *the* Anthony White from West Outerbridge, New Jersey, who rose to the rank of lieutenant-colonel in the 3rd New Jersey Regiment.) Washington seemed to do business frequently with the troops, which was something of a disadvantage to the seller. A horse thief in the patriot army, according to the *Orderly Books,* got 200 lashes.

Fine horses to Washington were like sportscars to today's businessmen on an expense account. They provided basic transportation, as well as the mystique value. This one was no nag, as the price may suggest. (It is roughly what a Jaguar XKE, a Ferrari GTO, and several MG runabouts would cost with today's inflated prices.)

Washington knew his horses. "The Compleat Horseman or, Perfect Farrier. In Two parts. Part I, Discovering the surest marks of the Beauty Goodness, Faults and Imperfections of Horses; the best Method of Breeding and Backing of Colts . . . the Art of Shoeing, with the Several sorts of Shoes . . . The Art of Riding and managing the great Horse . . . Part II. Contains the Signs and Causes of their Diseases, with the True Method of Curing Them"— the Jacques de Solleysell best-seller of 1757—was in the Mount Vernon library.

He raced horses as a young man and served as a steward at the track in Alexandria in 1761. And he bet on the horses. Washington wasn't first as a handicapper: His diaries reveal frequent losses and few gains from a day spent at the races.

A random look at any month in his diaries demonstrates the role horses played in his life. Take January 1770:

Jan 4.   Went a hunting with Jno. Custis and Lund Washington. Started a Deer and then a Fox, but got neither.

Jan 5.   Rid to Muddy hole and Dock Run [two of the Washington plantations]. Carrd. the Dogs with me, but found nothing.

Jan. 8:   Went a huntg. with Mr. Alexander, J. P. Custis and Ld. W———n [abbrev. for Lund Washington]. Killd. a fox (a dog one) after 3 hours chase.

Jan. 9:   Went a ducking, but got nothing.

Jan. 20:   Went a hunting with Jacky Custis and catched a bitch fox after three hours chace—founded it on ye. Ck. by J. Soals.

From January 1768 to March 1774, according to historian Rupert Hughes, who must have shared Washington's passion for counting, the General went fox hunting 155 times. He "got nothing" 85 times; killed 11 foxes and one "Rakoon." In the same period, he went a gunning 31 times, with no results; went a ducking nine times, with a total bag of 26; went a deering 6 times and killed 3, and hunted pheasants once without flushing any.

He hunted as often as General Eisenhower played golf. When he was away from Mount Vernon on government business, it has been said in error, Fairfax County was overrun by foxes. Washington undoubtedly found it difficult to pass a horse dealer's corral without at least checking the prices. Horses were his strength and his weakness.

In the opinion of an English authority, Peter Weld, who after the war wrote *Weld's Travels,* "Virginians are wretched horsemen. They sit with their toes right under the horse's nose, their stirrups being left extremely long and the saddle put about three or four inches forward on the raner. As for the management of the reins, it is what they have no conception of. A trot is odious to them and they express the utmost astonishment at a person who can like that uneasy gait, as they call it. The favorite gaits which all their horses are taught are a pace and a *wrack.* In the first the animal moves his two feet on one side at the same time, and gets on with a sort of shuffling motion, being unable to spring from the ground on these two feet, as in a trot. We should call this as an unnatural gait, as none of our horses would ever move in this manner without being taught. In the *wrack,* the horse gallops with his forefeet and trots with those behind; this is a gait equally devoid of grace, and equally contrary to nature; it is very fatiguing also to the horse; but the Virginian finds it more conducive to his ease than a fair gallop, and this circumstance banishes every other consideration."

I don't want to get involved in a battle of ideas with the horsey set, or question Washington's horsemanship. Weld's opinion is only mentioned here by way of introducing the possibility that Washington was hard on his horses, which may explain the purchase of six even before the first battle. As taxpayers, we should be thankful that he didn't throw in a few dogs under "household necessaries." As expense account writers, we can't be sure he didn't. The investigation continues.

1775 — October 6

No 54

> *To Mr. Ritchie* *$728*

William Ritchie was a Cambridge merchant. The account was for Madeira wine.

On behalf of my coauthor, in defense of this expense, I only want to say two words:

"No comment."

1775 — October 6

No 55

> *To Expenses of myself & Party visiting the*
> *shores about Chelsea* $215.50

There have been daring people who claim that reconnoitering has no place on a soldier's expense account. But they are mostly dead now. I'm sure nobody at the Pentagon would say General Washington didn't know what he was doing.

The only loyal position the Pentagon can take on these items, which continue like a drumbeat in the text, is to judge them by how the battle turned out. If the reconnaisance resulted in a well-formulated plan, the money was well spent. If the plan was faulty, it was more taxpayers' money down the drain.

The scouting of the Boston Harbor mentioned briefly here paid off. Washington studied the Roxbury lines, through which the much-beaten and still relatively untrained, stumbling hippie army would soon seize Dorchester Heights, compelling the British to evacuate.

The basic principle for expense account writers illustrated here is: *Make a sale occasionally.*

1775 — October 10

No 56

> *To Mr. Austin* . . . *Hd. Exps.* $156

No 57

> *To Wm. Ryan's Acct.* $72.80

October 16

No 58

> *To Mr. Austin* . . . *Hd. Exps.* $429

October 23

No 59

> *Ditto* . . . . *Ditto* $156

Household expenses are limping along nicely averaging two hundred sixty dollars per week. Washington establishes his credibility by being draconian in finance, as well as military justice. They have more than doubled already, showing that the General discovered the principle of escalation early in his work.

Since these household expenses are mostly for food, it may be of value to learn what Washington's breakfast consisted of in the prewar days at Mount Vernon. According to a handbook published by the Mount Vernon Ladies Association of the Union, an unimpeachable authority on kitchen matters, Washington breakfasted at about seven o'clock "on three small Indian hoe cakes and as many dishes of tea."

With an appetite like that, Washington had ample opportunity to practice another basic principle of expense account writing, which we know today as the *hidden pair of pants trick*. It works this way: a man on an expense account lunch orders a tuna fish sandwich and Coke, which may cost $1.50, instead of his usual minute steak, which costs $7. He charges for the latter, and pockets the difference. At the end of a week, he has saved enough money to buy a pair of pants. There is nothing illegal about this. If he hadn't been saving for the pants (or shoes or a new golf club), he would have eaten the steak, so his corporation's overall cash picture is unchanged.

William Ryan's account was for gelding a pair of stallions, the first news that these were in the General's collection of fine horses.

1775 — October 27

No 60

Ditto . . . . Ditto $54.60

No 61

Ditto . . . . Ditto $312

Like many of the dollar-a-year men who served the government in later wars, Washington could play, and play hard. As the captains of industry today make something of a religion of their 18 holes of golf and relax at the 19th hole, so Washington hunted incessantly as a civilian and used to linger over the liquor and shop talk at the 19th. A biographer estimated that Washington gave thousands of hours to spirits. The foxes were few in the Boston area in 1775. They either were caught by the hippie army after a long chase on foot, or managed to go further into the country, where they could enjoy the sport of slyly evading the fox hunting crowd. Without the pleasures of talking about the ones that got away, how did the General relax in the foxholes of Cambridge?

I would imagine that he threw silver dollars across the Charles River, the costs of which may be included in items No. 60 and No.

61. Like many soldiers in a lull at the front, he also may have tried to improve his mind with study courses. Chippendale's "The Gentlemen & Cabinetmaker's Directory" and "Observations on the Nature and Use of Paper Credit" were in his footlocker.

More than likely he simply passed the time away during the siege of Boston playing cards with the other fellows on the expense account. Next to social climbing and dancing, cards were his favorite indoor sport. Like baseball fans today who keep statistics, Washington had a page in his *Ledger B,* titled "Cards & Other Play." The games are listed like a baseball team's schedule, with entries for Mount Vernon ("home") and on the road ("away") at Williamsburg, Fredericksburg, Annapolis, Alexandria, and so forth. He had a disastrous season at Williamsburg in March 1772, when he won a total of £17 17s. 6d. in five games, while losing £39 11s. 3d. in twelve games. The end of the ledger, however, gives a truer picture of the man's skill at the card table:

1775. January 1 . . . By Bal[ance]against Play
From Jan. 1772 to this
date . . . . £6 3s. 3d.

Analysis of the General's record at cards shows that he won 27 times and lost 36 times. With that losing record in games, he did well to come out ahead in the profit and loss column, which is where it counts in gambling. At home his record was 5–13; away 22–23. The General played better out of town.

Not that any of this matters in the way games of chance work out in the army. Junior officers who make a practice of whipping the old man at cards don't go far in the army. So it is not likely that the General had to put his losings on the expense account during the war, as modern expense account writers sometimes do under "entertainment." It is enough to say here that George Washington may have been first in card-playing during the Revolutionary War.

1775 — October 30

No 62

To cash gave servants at different times *$62.40*

What a responsibility owning slaves must have been in the old days. So many mouths to feed every day. So many orders to issue to get your money's worth out of them. A plantation was no business for a forgetful man to get into.

No historian seems to know exactly how many slaves Washington owned. The number apparently varied according to economic conditions. It can safely be said, however, that he owned more than his share of slaves. He also owned white slaves, or indentured servants.

General Washington was kind to his slaves, regardless of race, creed, or color. He believed that all workingmen were created equal. This may seem like faint praise, until you compare Washington's civil rights theories with that of another famous Virginia planter.

Nobody could write a better declaration of independence than Thomas Jefferson. The glittering generalities about all men being created equal, which captured the public's fancy in 1776 and since, were misinterpreted. It did not occur to him that anyone could suppose the statement was applicable to blacks.

Jefferson was also a leading anthropologist of the day, and he had scientific facts backing his theories of racial inferiority. "They secrete less by the kidneys," he writes in *Notes on the State of Virginia,* "and more by the glands of the skin, which gives them a very strong and disagreeable odor . . . They seem to require less sleep. A black after hard labor through the day, will be induced by the slightest amusements to sit up till midnight or later, though knowing he must be out with the first dawn of the morning . . . They are more ardent after their female; but love seems with them to be more an eager desire, than a tender delicate mixture of sentiment and sensation. Their griefs are transient . . . In general, their existence appears to participate more of sensation than reflection. To this must be ascribed their disposition to sleep when abstracted from their diversions and unemployed in labor. An animal whose body is at rest, and who does not reflect, must be disposed to sleep of course."

These notions are perhaps still widely respected today in the anthropology department at the University of Mississippi. However, most anthropologists think as little of them as Jefferson did of those who were taking seriously the moonshine philosophy about equality he spouted in the Declaration of Independence. It must have given him a good laugh, as he slept with his black mistress at Monticello. The black historian Pearl M. Graham says there was nothing unusual about Jefferson being involved with Sally Hemmings (known in the Federalist papers from Richmond to Boston as "Black Sal" or "Dusky Sal"). In public, the subject of sleeping with slaves was taboo; and no southerner of any standing willingly tolerated such discussion. However clean his own record, the southern white man was sure to have friends or kinsmen who stooped to such a practice. But Jefferson's affair was well-known. It even was immortalized in a William Cullen Bryant poem.*

Jefferson had the facts to prove that the black was not only racially inferior to whites, but to the American Indian. He was in favor of freeing the slaves, and giving them a separate-but-not-equal (presumably) nation out west, so there would not be intermingling

* "Thomas Jefferson and Sally Hemmings"; in *Journal of Negro History,* Vol. XLVI (April 1961) No. 2, pp. 90–103.

between the races. He may have been on sounder ground here. Miss Hemmings had four children by the third president during a courtship that lasted twenty years—according to Pearl Graham. It was one of the great interracial romance stories in American history.

General Washington, as I have mentioned, was also against slavery in theory. It was bad economics. Buying a slave tied up investment capital. His high standard of living at Mount Vernon always left him in a poor hard cash position. He could charge the newest fashions he purchased in London, but it was cash on the auction block at the slave markets.

By an actuarial estimate, which historian Albert Jay Nock certifies as "well worked out and doubtless accurate," the life of a laborer in the ricefields would last eight years. "In reckoning depreciation of capital, therefore, the planter calculated that his investment in a slave would evaporate in that period, and he managed accordingly." A man like Washington, who never tired of measuring and re-measuring the dimensions of his piazza at Mount Vernon (95′3″ × 14′6″—always), probably had it down to the day when a slave should be traded in.

"With this letter comes a negro (Tom)," he wrote to a trader, Captain John Thompson, on July 2, 1766, "which I beg the favor of you to sell in any of the Islands you may go to, for whatever he will fetch, and bring me in return from him

> One hhd [hogshead: a cask containing from sixty-three to one hundred forty gallons]
> One ditto of best rum
> One barrel of lymes, if good and cheap
> One pot of tamarinds, containing about 10 lbs.
> Two small ditto of mixed sweetmeats, about 5 lbs each

And the residue, much or little, in good old spirits. That this fellow is both a rogue and a runaway (tho' he was by no means remarkable for the former, and never practised the latter till of late) I shall not pretend to deny. But that he is exceeding healthy, strong and good at the hoe, the whole neiborhood can testify, and particularly Mr. Johnson and his son, who have both had him under them as foreman of the gang; which gives me reason to hope he may with your good management sell well, if kept clean and trim'd up a little when offered for sale."* It's no wonder the man has gone down in American history as "Honest George."

Next to horses, buying and selling slaves must have given Washington the greatest pleasure. What a sense of power it gives a man to deal in human flesh. For businessmen who feel they are missing something in this age of industrial democracy, it might be diverting to catch up on some early slave market bids and asked. The average

* *The Washington Papers*, ed. Padover, pp. 69–70.

price of a new slave including women and children, Main says, was perhaps £36 ($936) before the war and £50 ($1,300) after it. That is in the range of what Washington paid for a good horse (see item No. 51). His diaries and ledgers indicate, however, that he often paid more than the going rate, especially after his merger with Martha. In 1759, he bought a "Will" for £50, another unidentified one for £60, nine for £406, and a woman ("Hannah") with child for £80.

Although he was revolted by the white slaves' pretensions to being as good as anybody, still these indentured servants were a better deal for an over-extended businessman like Washington. His diaries say he bought an Irish shoemaker and a tailor, to serve for three years, for only £12 each. A German family—the man a miller and a good farmer; the woman healthy and strong with four-and-a-half years to serve—was purchased for £35 from an advertisement in a newspaper. A four-year-old daughter, bound till of age, was thrown into the bargain.

The upkeep for an indentured servant was as reasonable as a slave. Main says it cost from £3 to £8 a year to keep a slave alive. A reporter for the *State Gazette of Georgia* estimates that £1 annually was sufficient to clothe them. The usual practice in the south was not to spend any extra money on clothing. Young slaves were sometimes allowed, or required, to run around the plantation naked.

Indentured servants were preferred over free laborers for another sound business reason: Their salary scale was lower. Free laborers, according to Main, had to be paid £15 a year or more. Still, one was buying a pig in a poke.

General Washington called his employees, black and white, "my people," which added his dignity to their labor. He was strict with his people who worked at Mount Vernon, but treated them well—if not like humans, then like valuable horses. As the historians say, they were happy. The only thing I have read about working conditions under Washington which might have contributed to their sadness was his insistence that they go to church on Sunday. He also is recorded as having tried to encourage chastity and marriage among them. These were not cruel and unusual punishments in the Virginia of his day; all the planters were amateur missionaries. If he ever whipped a servant, I have not read about it. This kind of discipline was reserved for the troops under his command. No sound businessman abused his workers. They were too valuable an investment.

We have no way of knowing how many servants Washington bought on his expense account. It is disturbing enough, for anybody who thought the General was a real red-neck on slavery, to find that by the next year (1776) he was putting in the daily expense memo book things like:

July 16	....	Cash Paid Negro Hannah
25	....	Cash Paid Sailor Jack
August 14	....	Cash Paid Servant Lydia, Mulatto
September 3	.....	Cash Paid Negro Isaac
13	.....	Cash Paid Servant Jenny

These are the same names on the list of his slaves at Mount Vernon. He appears to have brought a goodly portion of the staff to the front, and begun the undermining process of paying them. In the General's defense, I will say that he didn't squander taxpayers' money in meeting his household's payroll (see item No. 151).

1775 — October 30

No 63

To Josiah Fessenden *$156*

No 64

To Moses Fessenden *$135.20*

The Fessendens, Moses and Josiah, were private express riders.

Rain, snow, &C, &C., do not delay the mails. The post office delays them. Like many businessmen today, Washington recognized this principle. Whenever something important had to be mailed, he hired private messengers like the Fessendens or used free junior officers.

At this time, Benjamin Franklin was postmaster general of the United States. The politician-inventor was testing the delivery of mail. His pet theory was that the service could be improved.

1775 — November 5

No 65

To Geo. Baylor Esq. pr. Acct. *$90.13*

November 7

No 66

To Mr. Austin . . . *Hd. Exps.* *$234*

November 10

No 67

Ditto . . . . *Do.* *$234*

November 20
―――――――――――
No 68

> *Ditto* . . . . *Do.* *$312*

George Baylor is a new character. He won appointment to the expense account crowd as an aide to the General through the recommendation of Edmund Pendleton.* A lawyer, speechwriter and a personal friend, Pendleton had worked behind the scenes in Congress to block Washington's election as Commander in Chief. But Washington didn't bear any grudges and used his influence to get this staff plum for young Baylor. Washington also knew Baylor's father well enough to order shoes from his last (see item No. 24). Young Baylor was a member of the upper stratum of Virginia society, which was almost always recommendation enough for the General.

George Baylor served with distinction on Washington's staff until appointed Colonel of the 3rd Continental Dragoons (January 9, 1777). As a reward for his bravery at Trenton, Fitzpatrick says, he was allowed to carry the news of that victory to Congress. General Washington used Baylor this time to buy silk thread, buckram, and stamps. Every office boy who slips a personal errand or two in for his boss may be following in the footsteps of Colonel Baylor.

Somehow General Washington discovered that great numbers of soldiers absented themselves from their posts to work on the farms of their officers, or on their own plantations, or for hire while drawing public pay. He called this "base and pernicious" and the men "infamous deserters and defrauders." The handling of this military problem required all of Washington's skill as a diplomat. He issued an order saying that he was "unwilling to believe the insinuations that any officer can be so lost to all sense of honor as to defraud the public in so scandalous a manner." He also promised to pay no further regard to the "insinuation." If the practice was not checked, however, he would show no favor to any officer guilty of such an iniquitous practice.†

The practice declined, I am happy to say, only below the level of headquarters. For this is a violation of all that is sacred in expense account writing.

There is no room for muckrakers in this genre of journalism. If Washington wrote those orders—it has the high moral tone of an Alexander Hamilton—I'm sure he must have been under the influence of Madeira. The basic principle, of which there are numerous examples in these pages, is: *Live and let live.*

---

* See letter from Pendleton to Washington, July 12, 1775; 16 *Papers of George Washington,* 86, LC.

† *The Writings of Washington,* ed. Ford, III, p. 73 and n.

1775 — November 20

No 69

To Exps. at Roxbury $160.55

Here we are back on the high moral plain, at Roxbury and Dorchester Heights, looking down at the British fleet.

Though the ideas behind these repeated business trips—the principle is: *For best results, you've got to know the territory*—have become so familiar as to be no longer important in themselves, they suggest how a man less dedicated to duty might have abused this expense account privilege.

Some night a member of the congressional armed services committee conceivably could have ridden up to field headquarters, quite out of breath, and ordered Washington to attack, say, Trenton.

"Trenton," the General might have whistled through his clenched false teeth, "that will cost you."

"How much?"

"Five hundred forty-two dollars. But I could do Hackensack for $180."

There is no record of Washington ever having allowed such considerations as cost to interfere with his strategy or tactics.

1775 — November 20

No 70

To Mr. Austin . . . *Hd. Exps.* $335.40

I have already mentioned that the family loved pears and hurtleberries. They also had a fascination for eggs. As Mr. Austin explained it in his book:

Sept.	27	2 doz eggs
Oct.	10	2 doz eggs
	11	2 doz eggs
	15	4 doz eggs
	16	3½ doz eggs
	18	[?] doz eggs
	19	1½ doz eggs
		2 doz eggs
	21	3 doz eggs
	24	2 doz eggs
		4 doz & 9 eggs
	25	2 doz eggs
	28	3½ doz eggs
	29	2 doz eggs
	30	[?] doz eggs

1775 — November 22

No 71

Ditto . . . . *Do.* *$312*

These "Ditto. . . . Do." remarks in the General's expense account tell less than meets the eye. For a greater understanding of how crucial supplies were in what must have seemed like the real Battle of Boston to the men in the field, we should read the General's *Orderly Books.*

The first court-martial sat to investigate the charge that the quartermaster of the Massachusetts regiment had drawn "more provisions for men than the regiment consisted of." A captain was found guilty of taking home large quantities of food issued for his troops.

A basic principle in items like No. 71 for modern expense account writers is: *In lean years, only the fittest survive.*

The food problem undoubtedly put the men on edge. General Lee, who as we will see was dropped from the expense account crowd, was mentioned in a Lt. Benjamin Craft's journal: "Stephen Stanwood for saucy talk to Gen. Lee had his head broke. The general gave him a dollar and sent for the doctor."

As a French army chef probably first said, "You can't make an omelette without cracking some eggs."

1775 — November 30

No 72

To Elijah Bennett *$23.40*

Elijah Bennett was an express rider who undoubtedly was paid by the method of charging established by his profession: get whatever the traffic will bear.

1775 — December 1

No 73

To Otway Byrd Esq. per Rec.—& by Order . . . *$800*

Otway Byrd is another one of those schemers who managed to get paid during the war. This charge, Fitzpatrick says, is for wages due him as aide-de-camp to Maj. Gen. Charles Lee. He must have been performing some invaluable service for Washington. Otherwise the General might have considered putting the remainder of his 16,000 troops on the expense account.

One of the reasons pay was scarce the first eight years of the war is that the founding fathers, who were to think of everything in drawing up a constitution a few years later, overlooked one important detail in drawing up the military budget.* This document calculates the salaries per diem of the standing army: "4 Aides-de-camp 4s. 6d [$5.85] each," "540 Drums 1s. 1d. and 540 fifes 1s. 1d. [$1.41]," "30600 Privates 1s. [$1.30]." Congress unfortunately did not specify sources of revenue to meet the modest budget. Every pay day, as a result, was a major financial crisis.

The troops were told to be cheerful: The army's pay scale was higher than in any other war.† Another blessing of war came their way when the colonies, at the request of Congress, prohibited the arrest of Continental soldiers for debts under $35, or attachment of property under $150.‡ Still the troops grumbled about wanting their pay.

It must have been this attitude that led Washington to complain about "a dirty mercenary spirit" he discovered in the trenches around Boston. "Stock-jobbing and fertility in all low arts to obtain advantages of one kind and another" pervaded the whole of his forces.§

If George Washington had one major shortcoming as a military leader, it may have been that he didn't understand his men. The General had an independent income; poorer officers and the rank and file depended for their subsistence and the support of their families upon their meager and uncertain pay. This difference in condition, it appears, was the cause of the misunderstanding.

Since Bunker Hill, the most heated battles in the war had been over money. "I am wearied to death with the wrangles between military officers, high and low," John Adams wrote.‖ "They quarrel like cats and dogs. They worry one another like mastiffs, scrambling for rank and pay like apes for nuts." The congressman couldn't have been referring to Washington. As far as I know, he was the one officer who never complained about his financial arrangements during the long war.

A standing army needs action to take its mind off the petty details of administration. But this was a sitting army which hadn't had a major battle since the expense account started, and the troops were growing tired of the degrading nature of army life. In September

---

* *Chronicles of the American Revolution*, ed. Vaughan, pp. 191–194.

† *Orderly Books*, October 31, November 12, 1775; in *George Washington's Writings*, ed. Ford, III, pp. 191, 221.

‡ *Journals of Congress*, December 26, 1775.

§ *The Writings of Washington*, ed. Ford, I, p. 81; III, p. 247.

‖ See *Familiar Letters of John Adams to His Wife*, p. 276.

1775, for example, a sergeant was tried for "disrespectful reference to the Continental association" (Congress) "and drinking General Gage's health." He was put in a cart with a rope around his neck and drummed out of the army for life.

Most of the freedom-fighters weren't due to go home until the end of the year. The terms of the Connecticut militia ran out earlier, on December 10, 1775. "Some of the soldiers sought to anticipate their freedom by going home early," Commager and Morris write in *The Spirit of Seventy Six*.

This was the origin of what is known today as *bugging out*. The Connecticut patriots who pioneered in this form of questioning the wisdom of leaders were anxious to get home to take care of their starving families before winter set in. Nothing was happening in Boston anyway. Bugging out was to grow in popularity in later years. "Hundreds would march off the field at once, and on the eve of great battles," Rupert Hughes writes in his biography of Washington, "giving the dastardly excuse that enlistments had expired." As late as January 31, 1777, Washington was complaining that unless people gave him help in returning deserters "we shall be obliged to detach half the army to bring back the other."

Faced with a sharp reduction in his forces now—7,000 Connecticut militiamen alone were due to phase out in December—the high command addressed a number of emotional appeals to the troops to re-up. "We was ordered to parade before the general's door, the whole regiment, and General Lee and General Solivan came out," recalls the Connecticut soldier Simeon Lyman in his diary entry for December 1.* "General Lee made a speech to the men. The first words was, 'Men I do not know what to call you; [you] are the worst of all creatures,' and flung and curst at us, and said if we would not stay he would order us to go on Bunker Hill and if we would not go he would order the riflemen to fire at us, and they talked they would take our guns and take our names down . . ." One of Lyman's buddies was explaining the advantages of not re-upping. "The general sees him and he catched the gun out of his hands and struck him on the head and ordered him to be put under guard."

Things took a turn for the better in January 1776. "Of the 7,000 due to go home," Commager and Morris write, "almost half finally re-enlisted, an example of patriotism which it would have been difficult to match in Britain at the time." The enlistment rate might have gone up further if one of Washington's "family," like Byrd, had read the troops excerpts from the expense account.

Frankly, I don't know what Washington meant by putting something like a family member's salary on his expense account. Ask your Congressman.

* "Journal," *Connecticut Historical Society Collection*, VII, pp. 128–131.

1775 — December 1

No 74

  To Servants wages $234

December 5

No 75

  To Mr. Austin . . . . *Hd. Exp.* . . . $1,726.40

No 76

  To Mr. John Dunlap $300.95

Throwing John Dunlap's name into the expense account with servants' wages and the family's expenses is an example of Washington's wit and wisdom. John Dunlap was one of the country's first press lords. His activities included book printing, stationery selling and publishing the *Pennsylvania Packet* of Philadelphia, the Revolution's *New York Times.* As Arthur Schlesinger reports in *Prelude to Revolution,* "doubtless its most illustrious subscriber was George Washington of Mount Vernon." Nevertheless, this item is as interesting as finding the name of Walter Annenberg on President Nixon's expense account before the ambassador became a civil servant.

A big issue in the press of the 1770s was tea. In the Boston *Evening Post,* a Dr. Thomas Young cited eminent Old World medical authorities to prove that the introduction of tea drinking into Europe had caused "spasms, vapors, dropsies, rheumatisms, consumptions, low, nervous, military and petechial fevers." A Connecticut *Courant* writer said the "herb bred fleas," and that Chinese coolies trampled it with "their nasty feet." This may have been the origin of yellow journalism, as we know it. The *Packet* was against tea, too, but in a lukewarm way.

Washington took the *Packet* because it was in good taste, at a time when the American press regularly printed slander, libel, and foul gossip. "He never inserted a paragraph which wounded the feelings of an individual," writes Isaiah Thomas in *The History of Printing in America* of Dunlap. The *Packet's* pieces in the 1770s ran to moralistic essays on themes like "Fatal Effects of Luxury and Idleness," which Washington must have meditated on in Boston.

In 1776, Dunlap came out for the Revolution. He was to stun the nation's other press lords by actually joining the army. It was as if William Randolph Hearst, after editorially endorsing the fight for freedom in Vietnam today, were to show up in the front lines at

Danang. But this was to happen in 1780 after the British occupied Philadelphia.

General Washington well appreciated the value of having the press on his side during the war. After the Fort Necessity affair, he had written to his brother Jack (John Augustine), "I have heard the bullets whistle; and, believe me, there is something charming in the sound." In some way the remark made the colonial papers, and was widely reprinted even in London, where it created much talk, not all of it favorable. "He has not heard many," King George II said, "or he would not think them very charming."*

Nevertheless, the press helped build Washington's reputation as a soldier. The inclusion of Dunlap's name in the expense account is probably the earliest concrete example of what is known today in government as news management. The *Packet* was the paper of record during the war and postwar years. Whenever Washington wanted the public to read one of his letters, or, as they are called today, press releases, a copy went to Dunlap. Anything the General had to say was considered hard news, as indeed it was.

Washington didn't buy newspapers on the expense account. Dunlap is listed for $300.95 worth of stationery supplies.

The possibility of this being a potential conflict of interest never entered George Washington's head, I am sure, just as borrowing money from an Alexandria businessman to attend his own inaugural in 1789 didn't.†

1775 — December 5

No 77

To Washing *$16.90*

No 78

To Barber at sundry times *$169*

Washington went to a barber more frequently than the average soldier during the Revolutionary War, which suggests some of these barbering items may have been a euphemism for dental work. Dentistry, such as it was in this period, was performed at tonsorial parlors. The General's wooden teeth fitted poorly—the reason he is rarely shown smiling in war pictures—and there are no expenditures for "carpenter."

* Woodward, *George Washington*, p. 67.

† Letters to Richard Conway, 30, *George Washington's Writings*, ed. Fitzpatrick, pp. 220–23.

1775 — December 12

No 79

To Mr. Austin—Hd. Exps. $936

December 19

No 80

To Mr. Van $986.48

December 28

No 81

To Sam B. Webb Esq. for Sundries—
House use $267.80

1776 — January 9

No 82

To Mr. Austin—Hd. Exps. $842.40

For George Washington, I will say re Mr. Vans's account, "No comment."

For myself, I would like to add only that the account was for Madeira: 108 bottles, bought October 11, and 109 bottles bought October 22. Madeira, then as now, is an imported wine, from the island of Madeira, off the Moroccan coast in the Atlantic. It has been replaced as a status symbol in American army posts today by another wine, champagne.

It is not clear whether this supply was laid in for the Christmas and New Year which occurred as regularly in the rebel army as in the office today, or for Thanksgiving Day. The escalation of Mr. Austin's household expenses (item No. 79) would indicate some kind of sundry action was being planned at headquarters.

Lieutenant Webb of the 2nd Connecticut Regiment seems to have returned from the prisoner of war camp at Hartford, where he had been sent on the expense account with that British army POW who wanted to wear his sword in jail, in time to participate in this engagement.

Austin's household accounts also contain the good news that from August to December 1775 milk was furnished to headquarters by a Joseph Smith. Bolton says that milk was brought in from the country for the sick whenever it could be had, but exorbitant sums asked by the shrewd Yankee farmers were frequent sources of vexation and worry. It is not known whether the family's major

health problem was liver or ulcers. My guess is that the rich diet at
headquarters gave the family gallbladder troubles. As the old medical saying goes, "Fair, fat, and forty."

1776 — January 9

No 83

    To the Farrier—attending my Sick Horses . . . *$235*

No 84

    To the Relief of the distressed sad Wives &
Children of the Soldiers from Marblehead *$390*

No 85

    To Ditto of Ditto—Cape Ann *$260*

Nowhere is Washington's open-handed charity so well shown as in
this expense account. Items No. 84 and No. 85 illustrate the basic
principle called: *I gave at the office.*

Washington was not as solidly in favor of the welfare state as
Lincoln, who said "charity for all." "Let the hospitality of the house
in respect to the poor be kept up," he wrote during the war to Lund
Washington, the Mount Vernon manager. "Let no one go away
hungry. If any of this kind of people should be in want of corn,
supply their necessities, provided it does not encourage them in
idleness, and I have no objection to your giving my money in charity
to amount of £40 or £50 a year, when you think it well bestowed."

The distress of the wives and children of the Marblehead and
Cape Ann soldiers he mentions here may have been a result of the
wild enthusiasm for enlisting at the beginning of the war, which
Fitzpatrick says "oftentimes left families illy provided for when the
men remained away longer than had been expected." With the
handout, General Washington may have given the women and
children advice to the effect that it's better to give than receive.

I have no idea what ailed Washington's horses in item No. 83.
Perhaps the milk was for the sick horses.

1776 — January 17

No 86

    To Mr. Austin—Hd. Exps. *$722.40*

January 20
___

No 87

To Paschal Smith Esqr. $1,950

January 20 should be a national holiday for expense account writers. It marks the day when General Washington switched his wine account from William Vans to Paschal N. Smith, a Cambridge merchant. It is not known whether Mr. Vans's cellar ran dry, or whether Smith gave more for the dollar. It is known that Washington purchased one pipe of Madeira. A pipe is a cask. When used as a measure of volume, a pipe is reckoned at two hogsheads. For what Washington paid the piper, today he could have purchased the island of Madeira.

1776 — January 25
___

No 88

To Matthw. Irwin $367.03

January 29
___

No 89

To Barber $97.50

No 90

To Geo. Bayler Esqr.—Exp. to & from
Norwalk on busin. $554.03

February 1
___

No 91

To Otway Byrd Esqr.—per ord. $793

No 92

To Washing $99.23

February 5
___

No 93

To Geo. Bayler Esq. for Sundry articles purchased by him for the use of the Family $178.43

Colonel George Baylor, of the 3rd Continental Dragoons, fought valiantly during the war. His command was surprised at Tappan, New York in September 1778, and he was severely wounded by a bayonet thrust through the lungs. At this stage of the war, he was doing marketing for the family. After his return from Norwalk on unspecified business, the accounts show he was entrusted with the mission of buying cakepans, saucepans, candlesticks, and other such utensils of death from William Lowder of Cambridge.

Matthew Irwin, the central figure in the mystery of item No. 88, was a Cambridge merchant. The account was for furniture and cloth.

These purchases can be explained easily in terms of what goes on in many business enterprises today, under the principle: *The left hand doesn't know what the right hand is doing.* One of the materiel shortages the army faced in February 1776, according to General Washington's letters, was guns. Two thousand men in camp lacked one.* Colonel Ritzema's regiment in May possessed in all ninety-seven firelocks and seven bayonets.† In July of the critical summer of 1776, nearly one fourth of the army had no arms.‡ In calling up the militia that summer, the New York Congress ordered each man to report to duty with a shovel, spade, pick axe or a scythe straightened and made fast to a pole.§

Whether by design or accident, Washington's strategy here was brilliant. British intelligence never would have guessed the army was so low on the basics by the things Washington's agents were buying for the family. My theory is it was no accident. General Washington always knew, probably down to the last grain of gunpowder, the state of the arsenal.

"To maintain a post within musket shot of the enemy for six months together," he wrote, "without [powder]"—the word was omitted lest the letter, if it fell into the hands of the enemy, disclose Washington's precarious condition—"and at the same time to disband one army [*i.e.,* of 1775] and recruit another within that distance of 20 odd British Regiments is more probably than ever was attempted."‖ The general also may have been first in brinksmanship.

1776 — February 7

No 94

To Mr. Austin . . . . Hd. Exps. . . . $842.40

* *Washington's Writings,* ed. Ford, III, p. 406.
† *Washington's Writings,* ed. Ford, IV, p. 65.
‡ C. F. Adams, in *American Historical Review,* Vol. I, p. 651.
§ *Washington's Writings,* ed. Ford, IV, p. 338.
‖ *Washington's Writings,* ed. Ford, III, p. 313.

Here General Washington demonstrates his skill at understatement, a style popular in the symbolist school of expense account writing. Actually this may be the understatement of the year 1776. In this innocuous item for household expenses is hidden the first major turning point of the war. Martha Washington has arrived at the front, bundled up in silk and furs.

She arrived in state, observers reported, on December 11, the same day the Connecticut troops walked out of the Revolution. The splendid coach and its four horses, with the postillions in white and scarlet, the harness buckles engraved with Washington's arms, pulled up at the Craigie Mansion. Young officers in their finest buff and blue stood stiff and bareheaded under the cold sky, bowing and mumbling polite words. It made an impression on the troops, but Washington's bills and vouchers do not mention the great event until February.

Despite the enormous expense of the trip from Virginia the General had invited his wife to see for herself what his life was like. That was on October 13, 1775. Like many businessmen today who issue similar invitations to their wives, his letters seem dutiful. "If she cared to make the journey," he wrote, explaining the dangers and giving her an out. Freeman says he erred in thinking she would not do so because of the lateness of the season.

Young Baylor, the triple threat of the expense account crowd, had been sent down to Connecticut to serve as Mrs. Washington's escort. He was first out of the coach. "Now her vehicle poured out Virginians as if they had been apples from a barrel," Freeman reports. After Martha came Jacky Custis, the General's stepson, followed by his slender wife, who also knew nothing of war, Mrs. Horatio Gates and George Lewis, Virginia neighbors. Sam Webb, of the expense account crowd, had received a letter from Colonel Reed in Philadelphia, temporarily retired to tend his law business, telling him that the ladies "were not a bad supply, I think, in a country where wood is scarce."* As a member of the welcoming committee of officers, Webb was probably pleased to see that the letter hadn't been a secret code; the well-clad, rosy-cheeked ladies confirmed his friend's intelligence.

Later on in these pages, Washington deals with the reasoning behind his putting Mrs. Washington's trip on the expense account. (He makes no mention of why the government should have paid for his stepson and his wife, and the neighbors.) Faced with a *fait accompli,* the General made sure the visit wasn't a total loss. Since this is Mrs. Washington's debut as a character, it is the appropriate place for expense account writers to doff their three-cornered hats to the General. Every businessman who takes his wife on a sales trip,

* *Correspondence and Journals of Samuel Blachley Webb,* ed. Ford, I, p. 121.

every congressman who takes his three secretaries and female staff assistants on a junket (see the exploits of Representative Adam Clayton Powell) is in debt to General Washington for this courageous action, one of the most important victories in the fight for free expression in expense account writing.

The arrival of Mrs. Washington in camp sparked a burst of activity on the stagnating front. Next day Gen. Nathanael Greene wrote home to his wife Catherine, in Rhode Island, that Lady Washington had moved into headquarters—the General didn't put her and the kids up at a motel—to brighten the drabness of army life. Mrs. Greene was ordered to bring her best frocks and join the women's auxiliary corps.

Mrs. Greene, the former Catherine Littlefield of Block Island, turned out to be the life of any party she attended. Kitty, as she was called, played a major role later in the war. At a Valley Forge soiree, according to historian Theodore Thayer in *George Washington's Generals,* she danced with General Washington for three hours without stopping, which set the Continental Army record. General Greene himself says that Kitty danced with the Commander in Chief for three hours without stopping, at Morristown. Perhaps it happened at both places. (General Greene, a former iron-monger, had a limp, and probably didn't dance.)

There was nothing immoral or un-American about dancing at Valley Forge or Morristown. As the patriotic song goes:

> Yankee Doodle, keep it up
> Yankee Doodle dandy—
> Mind the music and the step
> And with the girls be handy.

Dancing, as Washington said of his gambling, was "an agreeable and innocent amusement," a welcome relief from the time he spent in the saddle on reconnoitering trips. Some historians try to conceal his skill on the dance floor, as if it was something scandalous. As a result, many people today think that of our presidents Lyndon Baines Johnson was first in dancing. He was second.

Austin's accounts for February 7 include items for slippers and mending shoes for Lady Washington. It has been said she had the tiniest feet in the colonies.

1776 — February 7

No 95

To Taylering[*] for my Serv. *$223.60*

* *Tailoring*

Some historians, like Thackeray, say that George Washington married Martha Custis for her money. Others say that is nonsense. Washington was always a very careful, far-seeing person with a clear idea of what constitutes desirable qualifications in marriage. I am in a third group of historians, the undecideds willing to go along with the majority.

When Colonel Daniel Parke Custis died in 1758, he left his widow—who had been described as a small dumpy young woman of twenty with dark eyes, a sharpish nose and those tiny feet—two children and a considerable estate. It consisted of about 7,500 acres of cleared land, 7,500 acres of timber land, 300 slaves and cash and securities (the interest alone on Martha's Bank of England stocks, according to Freeman, amounted to £4,168 in 1786) in excess of $100,000.

Much of the confusion on this matter was caused by Martha Washington's burning most of George Washington's love letters after his death. One that remains, written on May 1, 1759, begins:

> Gentln., The inclosed is the minister's certificate of my marriage with Mrs. Martha Custis, properly . . . authenticated. You will, therefore for the future please to address all your letters, which relate to the affairs of the late Daniel Parke Custis, Esqr., to me, as by marriage I am entitled to a third part of that estate, and invested likewise with the care of the other two thirds by a decree of our General Court, which I obtained in order to strengthen the power I before had in consequence of my wife's administration . . .

No, that is a letter to Robert Cary & Company, the department store people in London. This is the love letter, written on July 20, 1758, when the couple had been engaged a month:

> My dear: We have begun our March for the Ohio. A courier is starting for Williamsburg, and I embrace the opportunity to send a few words to one whose life is now inseparable from mine. Since that happy hour when we made our pledges to each other, my thoughts have been continually going to you as another Self. That an all powerful Providence may keep us both in safety is the prayer of your ever faithful and affectionate friend, Geo. Washington.

That doesn't sound too different from what we find in his Weather Bureau report style in these expense accounts, or the memorandums executives dictate to their secretaries today. It doesn't compare well with President Harding's love letters, or even Washington's letters to Mrs. Sally Fairfax, his best friend's wife:

> Tis true, I profess myself a votary of love. I acknowledge that a lady is in the case, and further I confess that this lady is known to you . . . I feel the force of her amiable beauties in the recollection of a thousand tender passages that I could wish to obliterate, till I am bid to revive them. But experience, alas! sadly reminds me how impossible this is, and evinces an opinion which I have long entertained, that there is a Destiny

which has the control of our actions, not to be resisted by the strongest efforts of Human Nature. You have drawn me, dear Madame, or rather I have drawn myself, into an honest confession of a simple Fact. Misconstrue not my meaning; doubt it not, nor expose it. The world has no business to know the object of my love, declared in this manner to you, when I want to conceal it . . . Adieu to this till happier times, if I ever shall see them. The hours at present are melancholy dull . . . I dare believe you are happy, as you say. I wish I was happy also.*

This was the bachelor's lament before he took the big step three months later.

There was nothing unusual about Washington marrying for money, if that's what he found so irresistible about Martha. As Clinton Rossiter points out in *1787: The Grand Convention,* some of the finest founding fathers of the country did the same thing (of the Framers who thus improved their station, he cites Hamilton, Dickinson, Rufus King, Jared Ingersoll, George Clymer, Thomas Fitzsimmons and Charles Pinckney). He was in good company, making such a fortunate union. Perhaps the memory of Colonel Custis deserves some recognition from our patriotic societies.

Marriage was the only occupation open to Virginia women, and they brought a correspondingly high professional skill to bear on managing themselves into it. Colonel Washington didn't have a chance once Martha decided to merge their fortunes to make one of the largest conglomerates in the colonies. Her life had been one of unbroken elegance, of rustling silks, of feather boas and belt knots, of tuckers and lace flounces, all ordered from London. Her *savoir faire* did much to convert her husband from the manners of field and camp to that of the drawing room. The only domestic skill that she had was sewing. She loved doing her needlework as much as General Washington loved shopping. Martha spent the year 1760 making pin cushions from her wedding dress. She also made place cards in form of tiny ladies, each skirt being made from a piece of wedding frock.

Bivouacking in the Craigie House in Cambridge, how Martha must have been tempted to turn her hand to sewing flags, like Betsy Ross and Francis Hopkinson, or at least doing her bit for the war effort by working on the servants' uniforms. But she didn't. Item No. 95 was for sewing done for the servants by a Margaret Thomas.

The important principle established here is: *A wife, or a secretary, does not have to go through the motions of doing business to qualify as a deduction.*

1776 — February 7

No 96

To Postage of Letters $93.60

* *The Washington Papers,* ed. Padover, pp. 63–64.

February 22
___

No 97

    To Mr. Austin . . . *Hd. Exps.* $1,053

Then, as now, February 22nd was George Washington's Birthday. The postage may have been for invitations to a party.

1776 — March 2
___

No 98

    To Thos. Patton $157.65

Thomas Patton's account was for a new saddle, cloth holster, and snaffle bridle.

The frequency of expense items for saddle repairs and new saddlery may indicate the General had bad habits. Fitzpatrick says they are "evidence both of the time spent in the saddle by the Commander-in-Chief and also of his fastidiousness in all matters of horsemanship."

British intelligence may have deduced the General was anticipating action. So many of these shopping trips, however, had turned out to be false alarums.

1776 — March 2
___

No 99

    To Exps. of Myself and Party Reccng.
    Dorchester Heights previous to our
    possessing them $279

Four score and nineteen items ago, when General Washington first went on the expense account, he warned Congress:

> I will enter upon the momentous duty and exert every power I posses for the support of the glorious cause. But lest some unlucky event should happen, unfavorable to my reputation, I beg it may be remembered by every gentleman in this room, that I this day declare with the utmost of sincerity, I do not think myself equal to the command I am honored with.

He had been overly pessimistic. On the evening of March 4, only 240 days after he began worrying about his reputation, the General finally went into action at Dorchester Heights. The men he had described in his letters back home as "exceeding and dirty nasty people" did a fantastic thing. Under the cover of darkness, the rebels led by General John Thomas climbed Dorchester Heights. The men would not be able to dig in as they had on Breed's Hill, the place where the battle of Bunker Hill took place; the ground was frozen. With characteristic Yankee ingenuity, the New Englanders prefabricated entrenchments. Portable timber frames had been constructed which could be filled with hay; they also built barrels to fill with dirt and stone. The troops dragged 350 oxcarts filled with these materials, no record of which is found in the expense account.

"Working feverishly through the night," Commager and Morris's communique on the battle reads, "the Americans threw up their timber wall, cut down fruit trees to form an abatis in front of the timber, and in front of these placed their stone filled barrels, useful in defense and dangerous on offense." Then the ragged Continentals dragged 43 cannon and 14 mortars up the heights.

It was, said the British engineer Archibald Robinson afterwards, "a most astonishing night's work and must have employed from 15 to 20,000 men."

Washington's expense account for this night's work could not have included a party large enough to have performed such a feat. General Thomas and his 2,000 men must have been part of the non-expense account part of the army.

"When the ministerialists discovered in the morning early what we had been after," wrote the Reverend William Gordon, a spectator, "they were astonished upon seeing what we had done. Gen'l How [sic] was seen to scratch his head and heard to say by those that were about him that he did not know what he should do, that the provincials (he likely called them by some other name) had done more work in one night than his whole army would have done in six months. In this strong manner did he express his surprise."*

By dawn's early light, General Howe called a Council of War. The officers were especially depressed by the sight of the cannon and mortars staring down at them. Where had the artillery come from? Rather than see the rockets' red glare, as they had at Breed's, the British high command decided Boston was not really worth fighting for. They packed up and sailed away to Halifax.

While Howe was a leading dove in British colonial politics, he was also acting consistently with the British War Office's view of war. It was a big chess game. When they saw the Americans had seized control of a position that gave them command of the Boston area, it was tantamount to checkmate.

The real hero of the redemption of Boston was the amiable, rotund Col. Henry Knox. At one of the expense account lunches, concealed earlier in these pages, Colonel Knox had talked the General into allowing him to go on a trip to Ticonderoga to bring

---

* Gordon, "Letter," *Massachusetts Historical Society Proceedings,* LX, pp. 361–64.

back some captured artillery with which to blast the British out of Boston. It sounded like one of those wild schemes that are still proposed at expense account lunches today.

Knox reached the former British fort at Ticonderoga in December 1775 and sorted out the abandoned equipment. The guns weighed more than 120,000 pounds, and they had to be hauled almost 300 miles through the snow and ice until they reached Dorchester Heights.

Knox was a genius of logistics. He put together a caravan of 43 sledges bearing 59 field pieces and inched his way across New England hills undetected by the British. "To prevent runaway sledges from crashing downhill upon the men in front," historian North Callahan writes, "drag chains and poles were thrust under the runners, and check ropes were fastened around the trees along the way to hold back the heavy cargo. As an early January thaw set in, some of the big guns broke through the ice on the rivers and lakes. But the 'drowned cannon' were recovered in almost every case."*

While Mrs. Washington was being entertained at Craigie House in January, Knox and his men continued their back-breaking journey down the Hudson, then eastward, through the Berkshires. At Springfield, however, the snow was almost gone and Knox was stuck with his guns. The weather turned cold again, the ground froze and the column finally lurched into Cambridge, where Knox delivered "a noble train of artillery."

Perhaps it was the jolly Colonel Knox who should have received the Doctor of Laws degree conferred on General Washington the third day of April 1776. It was really Knox, as Washington's degree read, "who by the most signal smiles of Divine Providence on his military operations, drove the Fleet and Troops of the enemy with disgraceful precipitation from the town of Boston." For without Knox's artillery, Washington wouldn't have risked a confrontation with the British. This wasn't the last time that the academicians at Harvard were to be confused by military affairs.

In the way of awards, Colonel Knox had to settle for promotion to the expense account crowd, the highest honor Washington could bestow on any officer.

It was a glorious battle. The only loss, except for a night's sleep for the hippie army, was noted in the General Orders of March 9:

His Excellency the General lost one of his pistols yesterday upon Dorchester Neck. Whoever will bring it to him or leave it with General Thomas shall receive two dollars reward and no questions asked; it is a screwed barreled pistol mounted with silver and a head resembling that of a pug dog at the butt.†

---

* North Callahan in *George Washington's Generals*, ed. George Athan Billias, p. 241.

† Henshaw, *Orderly Books*, p. 101.

1776 — March 4
_____
No 100

    To Sadlery *$52.86*

Washington was regular in his habits.

1776 — March 12
_____
No 101

    To Mr. Austin . . . . *Hd. Exps.* *$722.40*

March 19
_____
No 102

    To Mr. Wm. Bartlett *$1,003.60*

These two items show that General Washington didn't let success go to his head. They have the same breeziness, the same sure command of action sequences, the same gift for phrase-making as in his writing before the great victory at Dorchester Heights.

The British left Boston on St. Patrick's Day, March 17. Washington entered on March 20. A day earlier, he bought from William Bartlett, the Continental agent for Armed Vessels at Beverly, Massachusetts, the following materiels:

    ★ 1 cask of porter
    ★ 2 cases of claret
    ★ 32 gallons of spirits
    ★ 4 loaves of sugar.

There is no record of what he did with these things. I would imagined he stirred them, and served.

1776 — March 23
_____
No 103

    To cash advanced the Baron De Woodkte . . . *$93.60*

This may be one case where General Washington bordered on going too far, nearly violating a basic principle of expense account writing.

Friedrich Wilhelm, Baron Woedtke, was a major in the Prussian Army under Frederick the Great and one of the foreign officers who came to the aid of the colonies. To many Europeans the fighting in

America was a civil war, and idealists rushed to join what must have seemed to them a kind of George Washington Brigade. An unusually high percentage of the volunteers wanted to fight for democracy, as generals, against the dictatorship of King George. Eventually Congress learned how to say *nein*. At this stage of the war, the George Washington Brigade had as many accents as a United Nations police force, and was functioning about as effectively.

Having served with Frederick the Great, Washington's model, Baron Woedtke appeared to qualify as a prize addition to the general staff. He was appointed a brigadier general in March 1776 and ordered to the Northern Army. It is not known what mission the Baron was serving at Washington's headquarters. While many of these military adventurers served the country well, others were common free-loaders. The baron was on the expense account by name in this entry "to help defray the expenses of the journey thither" [to the Northern Army]. Woedtke died suddenly in July 1776 at Lake George, New York, Fitzpatrick says, "before he rendered any service of importance." A real deadbeat.

This entry could be classified as "foreign aid." The lively case of xenophobia Washington developed during the postwar years may have come from his foreign relations during the war. He was to warn against the danger of foreign entanglements in the Farewell Address of 1796. Perhaps this explains why so many of Washington's advocates today are against the United Nations and feeding starving children abroad.

1776 — March 25

No 104

To Mr. Wm. Hollingshead $963.63

No 105

To Mr. Austin—Hd. Exps. $468

March 28

No 106

To Mr. Jos. Stanbury $20.80

March 30

No 107

To Cash advanced Capts. Birmingham,
Wm. Burns & Timothy Feely Riflemen
from Quebec $156

Joseph Stanbury was a poet. This expense item makes Washington a patron of the arts. When a businessman encourages culture today, he always likes to get something else out of it. Washington was in this tradition. Stanbury sold him cut-glass vinegar cruets and salt-cellars. They must have been of low quality; this is the lowest expenditure on the expense account.

William Hollingshead was a Boston merchant. His account has no hidden meanings. It is for knives, forks, camp cups, and other utensils. There is no record of what happened to the utensils the expense account crowd was using previously; they may have worn out from use.

Birmingham and Feely belonged to Capt. Daniel Morgan's Virginia Riflemen and Burns to Capt. William Hendricks' company of Col. Thompson's Pennsylvania Rifle Battalion, veterans of Arnold's disastrous Canadian expedition. Morgan's and Thompson's Riflemen hold the distinction of being the first to mutiny in the patriot's ranks in September 1775. The cause, according to one of the riflemen's letters home, was boredom. These sharpshooters had been treated as the elite of the army by General Washington until the mutiny.

"You cannot conceive what disgrace we are all in," wrote Jesse Lukens of the sharpshooters, "and how much the general is chagrined that only one regiment should come from the South that set so infamous an example: and in order that idleness shall not be a further bane to us, the general orders on Monday were 'That Col. Thompson's Regiment shall be upon all parties of fatigue (working parties) and do all other camp duty with any other regiment.'" This seems to confirm the New England sentiment that General Washington was not above playing favorites in his early days in camp. When crossed, however, his sword was double-edged.

The money he lent to the riflemen had strings attached. The receipt specifies that it be repaid from money due them in back pay.

1776 — March 31

No 108

 To Washing $93.60

No 109

 To Barber $39

[*There is no No 110*]

April 1
_____

No 111

> To amount of Sundry Inst[ances] per
> Mem[orandum] for Secret Services
> to the date $5,232

This business of spying gives us further insight into how General Washington's mind worked.

The director of what was probably the ancestor of our Central Intelligence Agency was Elias Boudinot. By the end of the war Boudinot was to sit on the congressional committee which approved the expense account. When Washington wrote this letter, Boudinot was serving as commissary of prisoners, a convenient cover for spying.

It is a matter of great importance to have early and good intelligence of the Enemy's strength and motions as far as possible, designs and to obtain them through different channels. Do you think it practical to come at these by Means of Mr. P———d? . . . .

  If Mr. P———d? is enclined to engage in a business of this kind, I shall leave it to you and him to fix upon such a Mode of corresponding, as will convey intelligence, in the Most Speedy, safe and efficacious Manner to guard against possible evils. Your correspondence might be under fictitious names, by numbers (representing Men and things) in character or other wise, as you shall agree. It is in my power, I believe, to procure a Liquid, which nothing but a counter Liquor (rubbed over the Paper afterwards) can make legible. Fire, which will bring lime juice, Milk and other things of this kind to light, has no effect on it. A letter upon trivial Matters of business, written in common Ink, may be filled with important Intelligence which cannot be discovered without the counter part, or Liquid here mentioned.*

Good thinking on the part of the man who couldn't tell a lie.

"Mr. P———d," whom Washington cites in part, was Lewis Pintard, the husband of Mrs. Boudinot's sister. His greater claim to fame in the commercial history of the Revolution was that he was the chief importer of Madeira in the United States.

The soundness of burying espionage in a prosaic document like the General's expense account is attested to by the manner in which the Central Intelligence Agency is funded today.

The first monument to the fallibility of espionage is probably also buried in item No. 111. Freeman says Washington was poorly informed to have sent Colonel Arnold's small, ill-equipped and poorly provisioned force on the Canadian expedition. It turned out

_____
* *The Life, Public Services, Addresses and Letters of Elias Boudinot*, ed. J. J. Boudinot, I, p. 180.

to be "an extremely difficult wilderness route concerning which Washington's information was both inadequate and inaccurate."* The people of Canada, Washington had been told, would rise up. From the little we know of intelligence today, it sounds like a typical Central Intelligence Agency operation.

1776 — April 2
No 112

> To Capt. Oakley to bear his Exps.
> to Providence $31.20

No 113

> To Steacy Read—Sundries $84.50

No 114

> To Mr. Hastings Postage $84.50

Captain Oakley, Fitzpatrick says, "may possibly be Miles Oakley of the 4th Massachusetts Regiment, sent to Providence in connection with the reported British intention to invade Rhode Island." The rumormonger's trip is significant only in that it offers an index of the cost of travel from Boston to Providence, of which we will soon see richer prose.

Stacey Read's account was for making and mending halters.

Jonathan Hastings was the Continental postmaster for the district of Boston and Cambridge. Although it was founded in 1775 by Postmaster-General Benjamin Franklin, and is said to have been furnishing even better service than the old Royal Mail, this is only the second time Washington appears to have used ordinary mail.

1776 — April 2
No 115

> To Mr. Austin . . . . . Hd. Exps. . . . $921.70

Mr. Austin's accounts for March 1776 indicate that "the family" consumed 239 pounds of cod. A Cambridge baker, Zaccheus Mor-

---

* *George Washington*, IV, p. 66.

ton, supplied bread from February 26 to April 2 at a cost of £6 8s. ($166.40).

, The Rhode Island Regiment, previously mentioned, was the best housed (their tents were like those in the British Army, a visitor to the camp at Cambridge reported) and the best-fed, on paper, in the Continental Army. According to the rules and regulations, approved by the General Assembly in June 1775, "the allowance to each soldier in camp be as followeth, to wit:

It is voted and resolved that no soldier . . . be allowed to take up of the commissary any more than ⅓ of his monthly wages for his own use.

One pound of bread, one pound of beef or pork, a half penny for vegetables, ½ a gill of rice, one pint of milk, and one qt. of beer per day, and one pint of mollasses per week; that once a week, instead of meet [sic], they have a pound of fish, an ounce of butter and ½ a pint of sugar. The commissary to furnish them with the same quantity of soap as is allowed by the colony of the Massachsuetts Bay to their troops.

Similar sentiments on rations were expressed in the Continental Congress throughout the war period. They turned out to be typical politicians' promises.

I don't know whether Karl Marx came across George Washington's expense account in the British Museum while researching *Das Kapital*. The expense account may have influenced his thinking as much as *TB Incidence Among Child Labor in the Alsace Steel Industry 1830–1840* and the British Parliament's Corn Laws. Each according to his need, Washington was saying in advance of Marx, each according to his ability to pay.

The dietetical necessity is clearly expressed in General Washington's letters and petitions to Congress. He spoke passionately about the need for the government to feed its troops. The men couldn't eat the Congressmen's words. Like any executive he was concerned that his employees should be provided for. But he wasn't going to quit over this bread-and-butter issue.

The General, his future spending will show, must have grimly loosened his belt a notch as he marched on to greater triumphs in the field of expense account writing.

1776 — April [?]

No 116

To Exps. in visiting the Several Islands in Boston Harbor—after the Evacuation of the Town by the Enemy *$227.50*

April 4
_____
No 117

> To Mr. Austin for Bal[ance] of his acc[ounts]
> as Steward to the date—and my leaving
> Cambridge for New York $237.03

No 118

> To Barber—in full $160.40
> To Washing . . . . Do. $188.60

These lines are pure poetry, bank verse, as it is known in expense account writing.

The opening stanza is almost not like Washington. It tells the purpose of his visit to the off-shore islands in Boston Harbor, an expansiveness that can be explained as the excess of a conqueror.

By the second lines, he has regained the jewel-like touch. These celebrate the end of Mr. Austin's valiant struggle to take care of the family. When Washington first arrived, Boston was the third best expense account town in America (after Philadelphia and New York). The siege had reduced it to a grim army post town.

Mr. Austin's work here, in basic expense account language, is called *cleaning out the bottom of the drawer*. At the end of a trip, you throw in everything including the kitchen sink, if you happened to have purchased one. Nobody quibbles with expenses if the trip was successful. If you're being fired, you have nothing to lose.

"For Bal. of his acc." includes such luxuries as milk. From March 12 to April 3, he purchased for the family 113 quarts from Parsons Smith, the Cambridge milkman, for £1 5s. ½d. ($32.55). That works out to 29 cents a quart, or approximately what the produce of a Jersey cow would cost today. I have no idea why the General didn't buy a cow and a milk maid. It is economies like these that give thrift a bad name.

Then there are the necessities, listed in the Book of Household Expences, but not by name on the expense account. Richard Peacock of Cambridge did tailoring. Elisha Avery, the Commissary at Cambridge, is on the account for cider, red wine, candles, and soft soap.

At the back of the daily expense book, we find entries of purchases from Mrs. Ann Van Horne and Lloyd Danbury for wine; from John Clark, a New York merchant, for a mahogany case and ivory-handled and black-handled table knives; from Elizabeth Moore for table linen; from John Deas and Dorothy Shewcroft for furniture; and from a Mr. Rhinelander for crockery. Why these items weren't up front with the other necessities may puzzle some expense account authorities. Perhaps they are covered by the rule: *Let the chips fall where they may.*

Thus Ebenezer Austin, Steward, exits the scene. It is not known whether Mr. Austin went into business for himself, or retired. His place, however, is secure in the subcolumns of history for his pioneering work in the basic expense account theory that *the whole should always be greater than the sum of its parts.*

1776 — April 6

No 119

> *To Cash paid Gov. Cooke at Providence
> per Acct.* $390

No 120

> *To Mr. Jefferson Express Rider—twice* . . . $148.20

April 13

No 121

> *To Exps. on the Road from Cambridge to
> New Yk., by the way of Provid[enc]e &
> along the Sound—per Mr. Palfrey* $1,397.72

No 122

> *To Ditto paid by Myself in Providence
> &c. exclusive of the above* $325.97

No 123

> *To the Exps. of Majrs. Cary & Harrison—
> My Aids de Camp on the upper, or
> Common Post Road with Mrs. Washington* . . $1,177.80

April 15

No 124

> *To Mr. Philips for Riding Express to
> Commodore Hopkins at New London* $78

General Washington may have suffered from a neurosis common to the military mind: the man-on-the-white-horse complex. There is no doubt that at this time he controlled the only insurgent army in the country. He had all the young right-wing colonels with him (some on the expense account). His war record was impressive: 1–0. Many modern captains of industry in his boots might have assumed that to the victor should go the spoils.

As these expenses for the trip to the front at New York show, he didn't abuse his power. Only item No. 123, which covered the expenses of Martha and her private military entourage, broke new ground. This carried the basic principle of charging for going to a battlefield one step sideways. Taking one's wife along to war in a separate-but-equal column of troops is an example of horizontal rather than vertical development. But that was Washington's brilliant mind. One never ceases to wonder at how many different ways he found to express his message to all: It is the American thing to live it up on the expense account.

The movement of the American army began on March 18, the day after the British evacuated Boston. General Washington despatched, under the command of General Heath, five foot regiments and two artillery companies. Their orders were to walk from Cambridge to New London, where they were to catch a fleet of small boats under Commodore Ezek Hopkins. Washington's express to him (item No. 124) said the troops were coming. He also conveyed the rumor that the British were planning to blockade New London.

Washington stayed behind in Boston until April 4, as the historians say, "attending to business." This included straightening out his accounts and sifting the various intelligence reports he was buying, many of which, like the New London report, proved false. The British fleet, after being becalmed in its escape attempt in Boston Harbor, sailed to Halifax.

Hastening to New York, Washington appears to have stopped off in Providence, where expense account history was written (item No. 119). Governor Nicholas Cooke of Rhode Island was the first state official ever to make an expense account, but not the last. A generous entertainment by Governor Cooke and some of the gentlemen of the town was tendered General Washington, according to the *Providence Gazette* (April 6, 1776), to mark the occasion.

The two Washington columns—his wife took the upper road, while he traveled the low road along the Sound so he could watch for the British fleet, which he still believed was coming—made stops in Norwich, New London, and New Haven, arriving at New York on April 13. He easily beat Sir William Howe's expedition, which had detoured through Halifax, to the big apple. The Howe fleet didn't arrive off Sandy Hook until June 29.

Lt. Col. William Palfrey, who kept the expense account on the low road, was aide-de-camp from March 6 to April 27, 1776. His head for figures must have impressed General Washington because a few months later he became Paymaster General of the army, and held that post until 1780.

The messages Mr. Jefferson carried (item No. 120) presumably told the people of New York that Washington was coming.

The people of Boston wept when George Washington, LL.D., bade farewell to the scene of his first triumph, as well they might. Whenever the family left an area, it was a severe blow to the community's economy. But Boston's loss was to be New York's gain.

1776 — April 15

No *125*

To Exps. of a Party of Oneida Ind[ia]ns
on a visit to me—& for presents for them . . . *$395.85*

The little trinkets were an expression of Congress's Indian policy of 1776, which hasn't changed much in recent years. The measure adopted called for the chiefs to visit Headquarters, where they would not only be entertained with dignity, but have an opportunity to be impressed with a display of the army's strength. The British general Sir Guy Carlton, military governor of Canada, according to intelligence reports filtering back to Philadelphia, was "instigating the Indian nations to take up the hatchet against them."

"A Speech of the Chiefs and Warriors of the Oneida Tribe of Indians to the Four New England Provinces, Directed to Governor Trumbull and by him to be communicated," stated the Indians' position:

"Brothers! We have heard of the unhappy differences and great contention betwixt you and Old England. We wonder greatly and are troubled in our minds.

"Brothers! Possess your minds in peace respecting us Indians. We can not intermeddle in this dispute between two brothers. The quarrel seems to be un-natural; you are two brothers of one blood. We are unwilling to join on either side in such a contest; for we bear an equal affection to both you and Old England. Should the great King of England apply to us for our aid, we shall deny him. If the colonies apply, we will refuse. The situation of you two brothers is new and strange to us. We Indians can not find nor recollect in the traditions of our ancestors the like case or a similar instance.

"Brothers! for these reasons possess your minds in peace and take no umbrage that we Indians refuse joining in the contest; we are for peace.

"We the sachems, warriors and female governesses of Oneida, send our love to you, brother Governor, and all the other chiefs in New England."

The standard Indian pacifist position was signed by "William Sunohsis, William Kanaghquassa, Adam Ohonwana, Handerchiko

Tegahpreghdyen, Johnks Skenanender and Germine Tegayhvaher."*

If anybody could talk the Indians out of that un-American un-warlike policy, it was George Washington, whose Indian name may have been "Chief Little Hatchet," in honor of the cherry tree story. That Congress should be interested in wining and dining the Indians was a progressive step forward in aboriginal affairs. A few years earlier, the colonies had handled the Indian problem by sending clothes infected with smallpox to Indian territory. This was one of the earliest instances of germ warfare and may have led to the Indian policy now of a pox on both Houses.

"The King of the Injans with five of his Nobles to attend him come to Head Quarters to congrattulate with his exelency," David How wrote in his diary (p. 12), confirming the accuracy of this type of expense. Bolton says a steady stream of congressmen, Indian chiefs and other dignitaries trooping into headquarters for enter-tainments helped the men while away the hours. What must have especially impressed the Injans was the performance of the rebel soldier, Joseph Coleman. In a toast to solidarity with the Indian brothers, he "drinkt 3 pints of cyder at one draught."†

1776 — April 25

No 126

To the Exps. of myself & party reccng. the
Sea & Landing places down on Staten Island . . . *$429*

"The fair nymphs of this isle are in wonderful tribulation, as the fresh meat our men have got here has made them as riotous as satyrs. A girl cannot step into the bushes to pluck a rose without running the most imminent risk of being ravished, and they are so little accustomed to these vigorous methods that they don't bear them with the proper resignation, and of consequence we have most entertaining court martials every day."

These words were written to Francis, tenth Earl of Huntingdon, by Francis, Lord Rawdon, a British officer who landed on Staten Island August 5th.‡ They would seem to disprove the common notion that Staten Island is neither a nice place to visit or live.

General Washington and his party, Fitzpatrick says, undertook this visit to Staten Island to devise a plan to prevent the British from landing here and doing their dirty work.

---

* "Interpreted and wrote by Samuel Kirkland, missionary"; Force, *American Archives*, IV, pp. 1116–117.

† *Military Journals*, p. 70; in Bolton, *The Private Under Washington*.

‡ Great Britain Historical Manuscripts Commission, *Hastings Manuscripts* III, 179–180.

1776 — May 11

No 127

   To Robt. Porter . . . . ⎫
                                          ⎬ *$423.13*
No 128   ⎪

   To Benj. Harbeson . . . . ⎭

Boston had been a dead city when the patriots went in, picked clean by the British wretches. "From such a set of beings," the *Pennsylvania Evening Post* (March 30, 1776) reported, "the preservation of property was not expected. And it was found that a great part of the evacuated houses had been pillaged, the furniture broken and destroyed, and many of the buildings greatly damaged. It is worthy of notice, however, that the buildings belonging to the honorable John Hancock, Esq., particularly his elegant mansion house, are left in good order. All the linen and woolen goods, except some that may be secreted, are carried off, and all the salt and molasses is destroyed."

But New York with a swelling population of about 25,000 was still bustling and elegant, despite the curbs put upon its normal life by the tensions and shortages of wartime. It compared favorably, according to travel writers of the day, "with any metropolis in Europe."*

These first entries for General Washington's invasion of Manhattan Island are a sheet of ice. But that isn't surprising: His personal records rarely reveal emotion. After his election as Commander in Chief, Washington went back to his rooms in Philadelphia with the immortal honor, and wrote in his diary:

[June] 15 [1775]: Dined at Burns' in the Field. Spent the Eveng. on a committee.

He doesn't even mention that he ate with Congressman Lynch of South Carolina, the man who spread the rumor that Washington was planning to bring a private army to Boston. We have to go elsewhere than to the expense account to find what Washington may have been thinking about when he entered New York. According to the orderly books for the first day on Manhattan Island, Washington instructed the troops that the secret passwords were "New York." The countersign was "Prosperity."

The widely-traveled Washington had already seen Staten Island. But for the troops Manhattan Island must have been heaven.

"The army continues healthy," Colonel Loammi Baldwin wrote to his wife in Woburn, Massachusetts. "The inhabitants of the holy

* Scheer & Rankin, *Rebels and Redcoats*, p. 161.

ground has brought some of the officers and numbers of the soldiers into dificulty [sic]. The whores (by information) continue their imploy which is become very lucrative. Their unparalleled conduct is sufficient antidote against any desires that a person can have that has one spark of modesty or virtue left in him and the last attum [sic] must certainly be lost before he can associate himself with those bitchfoxly jades, jills, haggs, strums, prostitutes and these multiplyed into one another and then their full character not displayed.

"Perhaps you will call me censorious and exclaim too much upon bare reports when I say that I was never within doors of nor 'changed a word with any of them except in the execution of my duty as officer of the day, in going the grand round with my guard of escort, have broke up the knots of men and women fighting, pulling caps, swearing, crying 'Murder' etc—hurried them off to the Provost dungeon by half dozens—Hell's work."*

General Washington, at least, had documentary evidence that his mind was on the finer things in life, as these two items prove. Robert Porter's account was for kitchen bottles and a pair of leather-cover canteens. Benjamin Harbeson's was for a nest of camp kettles, canisters and tin dishes. Both of these men were members of the military-industrial complex of Philadelphia, whom he had not patronized during his first buying spree. It is not known whether these items were had by mail order, or whether they were actually purchased on the trip he took a few weeks later (May 21) to the City of Brotherly Love.

1776 — May 11

No 129

> To Exps. of a tour on, and Recong. of Long
> Island $687.05

No 130

> To Washing—&c. $212.33

Washington continues his sound policy of not giving anything more than the equivalent of his name, rank and serial number on these rides. He adds a wrinkle, though, by calling it "a tour." Commuters on the Long Island Railroad today may wonder whether the General also had to change at Jamaica. If this trip had been cancelled, the government could have used the General's expenses (adjusted by the acceleration rate) to subsidize the railroad.

* *Baldwin Papers,* Houghton Library, Harvard University.

It is not known whether this item for washing happened on the tour, or after. Why this is of any importance will soon become clear.

1776 — May 11

No 131

    To Mr. Plunkett Fleesons Acct. $1,333.80

May 28

No 132

    *To Mr. Jn. G. Fraser for a Trunk
to pack my Papers in* $72.80

June 4

No 133

    *To Mr. Sparhawk for a collection of
Maps & cover to the Book* $441.05

No 134

    *To the Exps. of myself a Suit[e] to,
at, & from Phila. per Mr. Harrison* $2,287.26

In the technical language of political science, this package of items constitutes "a junket." Washington couldn't have known what a fringe benefit to democracy he was starting here.

The General left on this precedent-making trip on May 21 and arrived in the nation's capital on May 23 at two o'clock in the afternoon.* He passed through Paulus Hook, Brown's Ferry, Elizabethtown, Newark, Woodbridge, Hicks Tavern, Brunswick Ferry, Princeton, Red Lion Tavern, and Philadelphia. The visit to Amboy was of military importance. As he wrote to General Schuyler, he stopped "to view the ground and such places on Staten Island contiguous to it, as may be proper for works of defence."

We already know about Staten Island. The General seems to have had a fixation on this place, which as previously mentioned was especially vulnerable to attack.

Viewing Staten Island alone would have made the whole trip deductible. However, he also had congressional business to attend to in Philadelphia: a date to discuss the state of the nation with the military affairs committee.

* *Pennsylvania Journal,* May 29, 1776.

One of Washington's great strengths as a general was his ability to play military politics with Congress. We may have had better minds on the general staff—Benedict Arnold, Charles Lee, Horatio Gates, Nathanael Greene, the list goes on and on—but they were driven to irrational actions by the frustrations of dealing with the armchair generals of Congress. Washington was the only general in the Revolution who never grew tired of talking their language. His letters reveal his skill as a politician; reading them, one feels he spent most of his time during the war writing "Dear John" letters to his admirer, John Adams. Washington had what it takes to hold his own in the red tape factory that was the Continental Congress. "Resolved that he be directed to attend again tomorrow," the *Journal of Congress* reports after his appearance on May 24. "A Committee appointed to confer with his excellency the general to concert a plan of military operations for the ensuing campaign," the *Journal of Congress* reports for May 25. The General dug in for a long fight on the floor of Congress.

Philadelphia in the late 18th century was what we call today "a convention town." In 1787, for example, while the Constitutional Convention was in session, the Order of the Cincinnati, a veterans' organization for officers which may have inspired the founding fathers of the American Legion, was meeting down Walnut Street. So was the eleventh General Assembly of the Pennsylvania Society for the Abolition of Slavery, the Presbyterian Synod and a convention of Baptists, not further identified in the Pennsylvania *Packet* (May 18, 1787, p. 2) and the Pennsylvania *Mercury* (May 25, 1787, p. 3). It may be hard to imagine it now, but Philadelphia was a lively town in the 18th century.

The General's favorite mess hall during the war was the City Tavern on Walnut Street. Dinner was usually eaten at four o'clock. The candles were already lighted in the darkened wainscoted room, its walls decorated with brass wall sconces in which the General could check his reflection to see whether his wig was mussed. The baked oysters served hot in their shells were the specialty of the City Tavern and the piles of shells made mountains. The Madeira flowed like water, as did the colored waiters who it is said appeared like magic at the diner's least gesture. City Tavern was large enough to seat the whole Congress for a banquet. While General Washington attended these committee meetings, telling stories about the war in Boston, some of the Congressmen danced the quadrille. Like NCOs and BOQ Clubs of today, a small combo was provided for the entertainment of the troops. Undoubtedly the General won the fight for the check after the balls were over.

Those were the days when army meals were army meals. Philadelphia had always been proud of her banquets and her Madeira. Washington was never more at home, as we have seen, than when the Madeira was free and the toasts were numberless. But the days were not far off when food would be scarce and the tables lean, when his gaunt soldiers must quench their thirst with snowballs, and he himself would make the sacrifice that John Adams described to his wife after a visit to Valley Forge:

"Gen. Washington sets a fine example. He has banished wine from his table and entertained his friends with Rum and water."*

Many congressmen lived at Miss Jane Port's rooming house while in Philadelphia on government business. Miss Port's on Arch Street near Front, about five blocks from Carpenter's Hall, where the General had won his first national election, would not be recommended as an expense account place. Her dark halls smelled strongly of cabbage; in May, it was steamy and close. Miss Jane, the landlady, magnificent in side curls and a high starched cap with purple ribbons, was always darting from a doorway at a congressman and sinking to the floor before him in a curtsy. She rattled brave men.

General Washington usually stayed at Powel House, the home of Philadelphia's mayor, Samuel Powel, and one of his great admirers, Mrs. Powel (the former Elizabeth Willing). It is still standing on the west side of Third Street, between Walnut and Spruce streets, No. 244 (formerly No. 112). It was here that the General lifted the morale of the Philadelphia radicals by dancing with Mrs. Bache, the daughter of Benjamin Franklin.

His vouchers show that he *paid* for board and lodging at Benjamin Randall's and Daniel Smith's Tavern. Nothing is known of the advantages of these places.

Between sleeping, eating, dancing, and politicking on this junket, General Washington still found time to continue building the military-industrial complex of Philadelphia. The prose of these items (No. 131 to No. 134) does not capture the vigor of his spade work. He appears to have run amuck.

Punket Fleeson (item No. 131) was on the expense account for making a large dining *marquee* with a double front and another large *marquee* with an arched "chamber tent" of ticking. Other sundries included 52 yards of red striped Flanders ticking; a large baggage tent, with pins, cord, poles, etc.; 18 walnut camp-stools, studded with brass nails; 3 walnut camp-tables, and 3 iron clamped packing cases.

John G. Frazer was the Assistant Deputy Quartermaster. The traveling trunk (item No. 132) was made out of hair; we don't know what kind. It was originally purchased from John Head, a Boston merchant, and the government's property was soon on its way to Mount Vernon.

John Sparhawk was a Philadelphia bookseller. The maps were a series of "The Topography of North America and the West Indies."

* Adams, *Familiar Letters to His Wife,* p. 303.

This may have been an indication that even in the good days, when still undefeated in war, the General was expecting to do a lot of traveling. By the price, this atlas was either one of those big coffee table books or shorthand for a five-foot shelf of books. Much of the reading matter Washington purchased during the war eventually found safe repository in the Mount Vernon library.

From May 14 to June 4, according to Fitzpatrick, there are vouchers of John Brower of New York for making bed curtains and John Martin of Philadelphia for making a green baize bookcase. William Simmons, one of the Treasury clerks who audited Washington's accounts at the close of the war, said, "These vouchers we do not find charged in the Genl's account."

This criticism is justified. The General violated one of the basic principles which he had gone to great pains to establish: *Omit nothing.* Let the proper authorities decide what is trivial or frivolous.

Robert Hanson Harrison, who kept the expense account on the junket, was one of the General's secretaries during this period. It had been difficult for Washington to get adequate secretarial help after Joseph Reed had put his private interests before the nation's in October 1775. He had been indispensable to Washington, according to Freeman, yet the Philadelphia lawyer left the army to attend to cases pending in his law practice. Annoyed and distressed, Washington tried to pull strings through Richard Henry Lee and get Reed's cases postponed. Although Colonel Reed was only doing what so many of the so-called deserters (enlisted men and officers who went home to make a living) did, General Washington considered Reed's defection not as serious a crime. He rejoined the expense account crowd later in the war.

George Baylor, who has already been mentioned, and Harrison, a 30-year-old native of Maryland, were moved up to the General's table in place of Reed. "A fortnight sufficed to show that these arrangements would not be satisfactory for some time to come," Freeman writes in *George Washington* (IV, p. 18). "Mr. Baylor, contrary to my expectation, is not in the slightest degree a penman," Washington complained to Reed, "though spirited and willing; and . . . Mr. Harrison, though sensible, clever and perfectly confidential, has never yet moved upon so large a scale as to comprehend at one view the diversity of the matter which comes before me, so as to afford me that ready assistance which every man in my situation must stand more or less in need of."* Despite that lukewarm recommendation, Harrison resigned from the General's staff on March 5, 1781 to become Chief Justice of the State of Maryland. Like many in the business world today, secretaries went far in Washington's time.

Among the things Harrison put on the tab for the General in

* *Washington's Writings,* ed. Fitzpatrick, IV, p. 104.

Philadelphia (item No. 134) is an unspecified charge for Jacob Hiltzheimer (he later became Continental Agent for the purchase of wagons, and may have sold Washington a wagon to carry home his purchases), and 7s 6d. ($9.75) to a lame rifleman walking home to Virginia, another charitable deduction.

The details of Washington's return to New York are meager. He spent some money with Minnie Voorshies of Brunswick and William Graham at Elizabethtown. The concluding expense appears to have been a welcome home party at Samuel Fraunces Tavern in New York City, June 7.

1776 — June 4

No 135

To Washing & other Accts. paid by
myself am[ountin]g per bills to *$266.50*

By the date, this washing apears to have taken place on the junket. While we are discussing dirty linen, I might as well try and clear up the mystery behind one of the major scandals in the period covered by these accounts. It was known as "The Washerwoman Kate Affair."

Congressman Benjamin Harrison, a political crony of the General's in Virginia, is purported to have written him a letter shortly before a trip to Philadelphia. It opened with a brief discussion of local Virginia politics and wheeling and dealing in Congress and closed with Harrison asking that Washington find a job for a worthy captain of riflemen from their home state. A footnote mentioned a private affair:

As I was in the pleasing task of writing to you a little Noise occasioned to turn my Head around, and who should appear but pretty little Kate, the Washerwoman's daughter, over the way, clean, trim, and rosey as the Morning; I snatch'd the golden glorious Opportunity, and but for that cursed Antidote to Love, Sukey [Mrs. Harrison], I had fitted her for my General against his return. We were obliged to part, but not till we had contrived to meet again; if she keeps the Appointment I shall relish a week's longer stay—I give you now and then some of these adventures to amuse you, and unbend your mind from the Cares of War.

Some historians say this was obviously a forgery, British army propaganda designed to weaken the nation's moral fibre by revealing that Washington, the monument, was also Washington, the man. Especially in war time, sex makes strange bedfellows. The last passage from the letter was widely printed, from the *Boston Weekly News-Letter* (an anti-war, anti-Washington smut sheet) to the *Gentleman's Magazine* of London, a monarchist *Playboy*. The General, who was quick to take offense at anything negative the press had to say about him, let this issue go by.

Whatever the truth of the matter, the expense account shows that Washington certainly charged the government for thousands of dollars of washing. I prefer to think he had a cleanliness obsession.

Space limitations prevent me from giving a complete list of what the members of the family were doing while the General was in Philadelphia. Mrs. Washington, who had made the trip down a few days earlier, was indisposed. Freeman says Martha preceded her husband in order that she might undergo inoculation for smallpox. "Although John Hancock had invited the General and Mrs. Washington to stay at his residence while they were in Philadelphia," he explains, "and to have Martha inoculated there, Washington had been unwilling to subject a host to inconvenience and possible risk. The location of the General's quarters in Philadelphia at this time has not been ascertained." (*George Washington,* IV, p. 101, n.)

1776 — June 14

No 136

To George Bayler Esq. $913.90

No 137

To Ab. Duryee $195.65

This is not to say that Washington could not have buried the costs of being the *de facto,* as well as *de jure,* father of his country, elsewhere in the expense account. Any of the items No. 1 through No. 137 thus far may have been the military code words for sex. Every time an expense account writer today conceals an indiscretion with some far-fetched story about "secretarial services" or "massage," he may be following in George Washington's size 13 footsteps.

The bill for George Baylor was not for call girls. It was for a few additional expenses incurred by the General on that trip fom Boston to New York. Here we see a maturing of the idea first expressed on the Philadelphia–Boston run of 1775: *Hand in two bills for an expense when one will do.* This marks the fourth item for the trip to New York. The theory behind this kind of writing is that spread out over a number of different items the total will be less likely to give the controller a heart attack.

Baylor's account is especially admirable because he also includes a number of expenses incurred in New York City from April 4 to 18: stockings, tailoring work, and an inkstand.

Duryee's account was for Madeira wine. In defense of the General, I would like to add that the wine, according to his records, was for Gen. Charles Lee.

For June 27, Washington's *Papers* include a voucher from Samuel Fraunces, the Toots Shor of his day, for one dozen bottles of Madeira wine, which is not entered in the expense account. This may be the first instance of the General paying for wine out of his own pocket. I wouldn't recommend that modern expense account writers follow this outrageous precedent. There may have been extenuating circumstances.

Control of New York City and the Hudson River would give the British, according to Washington, "an easy pass to Canada." If the British overran the patriots here, they could split the nation in two, cutting off supplies from the south to the troops in the north. It had to be held at all costs. The manpower of the city was enrolled to build fortifications, the woodlands of the rich loyalists were leveled, and the city's mansions used as barracks. "Oh, the houses of New York," lamented a wealthy Greenwich Village resident, "if you could see the insides of them." The troops never had it so good.

As we have already seen, Washington was strong on law and order. Problems of discipline in the ranks became much more difficult than in Boston. The city, full of women, offered temptations that had not existed in the villages and camps of New England. Nothing was sacred to these bumpkins from the puritan hick towns. "An old time church property, and still called the holy ground," historians Scheer and Rankin report, "now supported quite unchurchly activity."

General Washington acted swiftly to restore law and order:

The gin shops and other houses where liquors have been heretofore retailed within or near the lines (except the house at the Two Ferries) are strictly forbidden to sell any for the future to any soldier in the army . . .

If any soldier of the army shall be found disguised with liquor, as has been too much the practice hertofore, the general is determined to have him punished with the utmost severity, as no other soldier in such situation can be either fit for defense or attack. The General orders that no sutler in the Army shall sell to any soldier more than one half pint of spirit per day.*

This worked as effectively as banning office parties as a means of preventing executives from showing their high regard for secretaries

* Henshaw, *Orderly Books*, p. 219.

during the Christmas season. Even General Washington didn't take it seriously.

The New York Provincial Congress met at Fraunces Tavern from May 18 to June 30, 1776. General Washington and his suite were invited to attend a closed door committee meeting the night of June 18. A bill submitted by Sam Fraunces to the Congress reveals the following business was conducted:*

	£	s.	d.
To an Entertainment	45	0s.	0d.
To 6 Dozn. & 6 Bottles of Madeira	23.	8	0
To 2 Dozn. & 6 Bottles Port	9.	0	0
To Porter 23/—Cyder 37/—Spruce 4/6	4.	9	6
To Sangary 66/—To Do. 18/—Punch 12/	4.	16	0
To Madeira 12/—Bitters 3/	0.	15	0
To Lights 8/—Wine Glasses broken 16/	1.	2	0
To 4 Wine Decanters 8/—2 Water Decanters 14/0	1	2	0
To a Chainie Pudding Dish 12/Tumblers 14/	1	6	0

"Many patriotic toasts were offered and drank with the greatest pleasure and decency," wrote Captain Caleb Gibbs of Washington's staff to his "Dear Penelope" regarding the events that took place on June 18. "After the toasts little Phil, of the Guard, was brought in to sing H————'s new campaign song, and was joined by all the under officers, who seemed much animated by the accompanying of Clute's drumsticks and Aaron's fife. Our good General Putnam got sick and went to his quarters before dinner was over, and we missed him a marvel, as there is not a chap in camp who can lead him in the *Maggie Lauder* song."†

This can be dismissed as the characteristic bravado of an army officer writing to his sweetheart. Some graduate student has probably done a dissertation on the illness General Israel Putnam suddenly came down with, but I would guess that it wasn't serious. "Old Put" recovered and is recorded as having participated in many other battles. Of the nature of the discussions which took palce behind the closed doors, we know nothing other than that they must have been heated, judging by Fraunces' charges for all the broken wine glasses, water and wine decanters, pudding dish and tumblers.

Boniface Fraunces made other sacrifices for the cause. One of his daughters served with Washington during the war. Phoebe Fraunces was his housekeeper at his office in downtown New York. Traditions are many, Freeman says of where Washington's headquarters was located in 1776, but facts are few. He may have worked and lived in William Smith's house on lower Broadway, at Abraham Mortier's house, across the street, or at Bayard's "Hill" near Grand and Mott streets. We ran into this confusion the last time the

* Henry R. Drowne, *The Story of Fraunces Tavern*, p. 17.
† *The Diary of the American Revolution*, ed. Moore, p. 117.

General visited New York. To avoid angering any of the real estate interests, we can safely say that the General slept in all of the houses downtown. This may be an exaggeration.

We do know that Phoebe Fraunces was the heroine in the plot to assassinate Washington. This foul scheme was contemplated not by some enraged husband, but by either the Mayor of New York, distinguished community leaders, or several of the General's trusted bodyguards, depending on which historian you read. The General never lacked opponents. The plot of June 1776 was probably the closest General Washington came to being killed during the war.

Since Thomas Hickey was hanged for the attempted assassination, I will assume that he was the guilty one. An Irishman who deserted the British army, he was Phoebe Fraunces's lover, say some historians. According to gossip, Hickey confessed his role in the plot to kill Washington. He blamed the beginning of his downfall on his dealings with lewd women, a shabby way to treat Miss Fraunces. Washington, Freeman says, passed on Hickey's admonition to the troops. Hickey, who sounds like a fictitious Irish-American bounder, also said he was innocent of the crime; if he had done anything wrong, it was to take money from the Tories. But he never meant harm to his general. From other, more reliable sources, we learn that he was planning to poison Washington as he ate and drank at Fraunces Tavern. Perhaps some of the unexplained money for secret services Washington lists later on was for the employment of a food-taster.

If the plot had thickened, Fraunces would have been justified in charging the government for loss of reputation and damages to his good name. His tavern was famous for its food—indeed one of General Washington's first acts as President in 1789 was to appoint Sam Fraunces steward of the first presidential mansion in New York. "[Fraunces] tossed off such a number of fine dishes," according to Tobias Lear, the President's secretary, "that we are distracted in our choice when we sit down to the table, and obliged to hold a long consultation on the subject before we can determine what to attack." The cuisine at Fraunces Tavern must have been mainly soul food, for as Samuel Fraunces's nickname, "Black Sam," would indicate, he was a Negro.

"I would like to suggest that the name of Samuel Fraunces be considered . . . for an appropriate honor in a Negro community or elsewhere in the city," historian Philip M. Jenkins wrote in a letter to the *New York Times* on October 31, 1966. "Whether by design or by accident, the fact that Fraunces was a Negro has not been publicized, and relatively few people in New York City are aware of it."

Let's have it for Black Sam! The next time you're in New York take a cab down to the Wall Street area and put one on the old expense account for Samuel Fraunces, a true son of the Revolution.

1776 — June 26

No 138

> *To Expens. in Recong. the Channel & landings*
> *on both sides of the No. [*] River as high as*
> *Tarry Town to fix the defenses thereof* . . . *$283.40*

* *North River, also the Hudson River.*

June [?]

No 139

> *To a Reconnoitre of the East River—&*
> *Along the Sound as far as Mameraneck[†]* . . . *$428.13*

† *Mamaroneck, in Westchester County.*

In 1771, Washington began to make cryptic symbols in his diaries. After his retirement as President they began again. This untranslatable record is in the margins of the printed almanac pages in which the diary is entered. They consisted of dots, and sometimes tally strokes and minute circles, sometimes followed by the names of various female slaves or vice versa. Some Washingtonologists feel these entries are a cipher, the secret of which has never been broken.

"My personal opinion," wrote Fitzpatrick on this issue, "is that the symbols are merely farm memoranda of some kind or another. . . . They could, of course, have been a record of card games, but for the fact that oftentimes the entries are on days that Washington was not at Mount Vernon. It is a puzzle but I take it to be so insignificant a one that there is no need of getting excited about it, especially as it can never be deciphered."

In my opinion, these markings strongly suggest the plantation work record. Although he was a painstaking person who wrote elsewhere voluminously of farming operations, it was not beyond Washington to make an additional note on the ploughing of the north forty. The number of them in any given period make it physically impossible to sustain an immoral reference.

I rake up this material from the past now only for those who may be puzzled by the strange markings and spellings in these reconnoitering items.

It is still too early to say what went on during the many visits to the suburbs of New York. We only know that Washington and his staff often dined at the mansions of the wealthy people who lived north of 14th Street. Alexander Hamilton decided to build the Hamilton Grange at 137th Street and Convent Avenue after one of these inspection tours. If Washington hadn't gone out of town on business so frequently, nobody would have believed what has gone down in history as the Mary Gibbons Affair.

It came to light in stories about the investigation of the previously mentioned assassination plot against the General in June 1776. A New York Assembly committee was ferreting out Tory conspiracies against the patriot cause. These were being directed by the Royal Governor, who had fled to a British warship in New York Bay. After the battle of Long Island and Kips Bay, the proceedings fell into British hands. A book titled *The Minutes of the Trial and Examination of Certain Persons in the Province of New York* was published in London about the affair and became an immediate bestseller.

The minutes stuck to the facts in retelling the conspiracy proceedings against the luckless Thomas Hickey (a crowd of 20,000 New Yorkers and visitors turned out for his hanging on June 28, 1776—a better crowd than Nathan Hale drew). Establishing credibility, the book then becomes a non-fiction novel with the story of George Washington dating Mary Gibbons.

William Cooper, a soldier, was said to have testified that he overheard John Clayford (another fictitious character) inform the Tory company at the Sergeant-Arms Inn "that Mary Gibbons was thoroughly in their [the Tory] interest . . . Mary Gibbons was a New Jersey girl of whom George Washington was very fond; that he maintained her genteely at a house near Mr. Skinner's at the North River; that he came there very often late at night in disguise." This woman, the story went, was very intimate with Clayford, and made him presents and told him what General Washington said. One of the pieces of military information Washington was reported to have said often as he slept with Miss Gibbons was that "he wished his hands were clear of the dirty New Englanders," or words to that effect.

A second witness, William Savage, testified: "Papers and letters were at different times shewn to the Society, which were taken from Gen. Washington's pockets by Mary Gibbons and given (as she pretended some occasion for going out) to Mr. Clayford, who always copied them and they were then put in his pockets again. These copies were sent to Gov. Tryon."

"No such persons were examined by the New York Assembly Committee," Fitzpatrick says. "No mention made in either Tryon or Howe's despatches of obtaining information from rebel commander-in-chief, things that would have been promptly reported to the home government in official confidential reports." There was no evidence either that General Washington ever carried important papers around in his pocket, either in 1776 or any other time—except his expense account. Nor was there evidence that George Washington ever was away from headquarters while in New York on secret or unexplained business. (See his expense account.)

Yet this obviously clumsy, British-attempted character assassination caught on sufficiently to become part of the folklore of the war. Mary Gibbons was as widely discussed as Molly Pitcher in the drawing rooms and taverns of the period. If only the gossips who read *The Minutes of the Trial* could have also read a book from the Mount Vernon Library: *Several Methods of Making Salt-Petre; Recommended by the Inhabitants of the United Colonies, by their Representative in Congress.* This was one of the first self-help pamphlets put out by the Government Printing Office.

1776 — June 26

No 140

    To Captn. Gibbs for Household Exps . . . .
    91 Dolls. [*] $709.80

July 8

No 141

      To—Ditto . . . *Do* . . . [*] $936

No 142

      To—Ditto . . . *Do* . . . [*] $1,560

No 143

      To Timothy Wood $123.50

No 144

    To Mrs. Smith the Ho. Keeper [*] *at*
different times, frm. Thos. Mifflin Esq., the
Q. M. Gen. as per contra—and [*] *by Myself*
thro' Captn. Gibbs—in all [*] $14,653.60

---

* Washington mentions dollars here, as in item No. 48. Since he once again doesn't specify what kind of dollars he paid in, but does list their equivalent in the usual form to the right, I continue using his standard conversion rate.

The events covered by these few entries include the proclamation of the Declaration of Independence, which really took place July 2. The only thing in the account which reflects the spirit of Jefferson is the liberty Capt. Caleb Gibbs exercised in keeping the household account. Item No. 144 borders on poetic license.

Gibbs was a secretary at Washington's headquarters. When Mrs. Mary Smith was discharged as housekeeper for some unknown reason, he took charge and exercised general supervision over domestic matters at headquarters. His first chit (item No. 140) is reminiscent of Ebenezer Austin at his best. But it was not good enough. Captain Gibbs makes a name for himself with his second essay (item No. 144).

This may seem a trifle high, when you remember what the Dutch spent for Manhattan Island. However, that isn't a reliable index. The Indians dealing with Peter Minuit are often thought to have been swindled in this sale. But they were the smart operators, not having title to what they sold. They took the money and ran.

Captain Gibbs is a hero in the annals of secretaries because of war conditions not reported in these pages.

According to the confessions of a Continental private, thought to be either James Sullivan Martin or Joseph Plum Martin:

The soldiers at New York had an idea that the enemy, when they took possession of the town, would make a general seizure of all property that could be of use to them as military or commissary stores. Hence they imagined that it was no injury to supply themselves when they thought they could do so with impunity . . .

I was stationed in Stone Street . . . Directly opposite to my quarters was a wine cellar; there were in the cellar at this time several pipes of Madeira wine. By some means the soldiers had "smelt it out." Some of them had, at mid-day taken the iron grating from a window in the back-yard, and one had entered the cellar and, by means of a powder-horn divested of its bottom, had supplied himself with wine, and was helping his comrades through the window with a "delicious draught" when the owner of the wine having discovered what they were about, very wisely, as it seemed, came into the street and opened an outer door to the cellar in open view of every passenger. The soldiers quickly filled the cellar, when he, to save his property, proposed to sell it at what he called a cheap rate—I think a dollar a gallon . . . While the owner was drawing for his purchasers on one side of the cellar, behind him on the other side another set of purchasers were drawing for themselves (with empty flasks found in the corner of the cellar). As it appeared to have a brisk sale, especially in the latter case, I concluded I would take a flask amongst the rest, which I accordingly did, and conveyed it in safety to my room, and went back in the street to see the end.

The owner of the wine soon found out what was going forward on his premises, and began remonstrating, but he preached to the wind. Finding that he could effect nothing with them, he went to Gen. Putnam's quarters, which was not more than three or four rods off. The General immediately repaired in person to the field of action. The soldiers getting word of his approach hurried out into the street when he, mounting himself upon the doorsteps of my quarters, began "harangueing the multitude," threatening to hang every mother's son of them. Whether he was to be the hangman or not, he did not say; but I took every word he said for gospel, and expected nothing else but to be hanged before the morrow night. I sincerely wished him hanged and out of the way, for fixing himself upon the steps of our door; but he soon ended his discourse and came down from his rostrum, and the soldiers dispersed, no doubt much edified.

I got home as soon as the General had left the coast clear, took a draught of the wine, and then flung the flask and the remainder of the wine out of my window, from the third story, into the water cistern in the back yard, where it remains to this day for aught I know. However I might have kept it if I had not been in too much haste to free myself from being hanged by General Putnam, or by his order. I never heard any thing further about the wine or being hanged about it; he doubtless forgot it.*

On the army's tour through the suburbs, which began in September after the failure of Washington's reconnaissance trips to come up with a viable defense plan, Americans continued showing disrespect for property rights, even those of the Declaration of Independence signers. "There is a regiment at Morrisania [the Bronx]," Lewis Morris, Jr., wrote to his father, Lewis Morris, one of the signers, "and your own house is made a barrack of, that is for the officers, and there are troops all about us which makes it impossible to prosecute the business of farming and besides they press your horses; the two coach horses were pressed this afternoon . . . and I believe unless speedily secured your breeding mares will come next. . . . Your fat cattle are in the hands of the Commissary . . . Colonel Hand's regiment plunder every body in Westchester County indiscriminately, even yourself have not escaped. Montrasseurs Island they plundered and committed the most unwarrantable destruction upon it; fifty dozen of bottles were broke in the cellar, the paper tore from the rooms and every pane of glass broke to pieces. His furniture and cloaths were brought over to Morrisania and sold at publick auction. Jimmy Delancey, Oliver and John . . . are gone off to the enemy and their house is plundered. Mrs. Wilkins is upon Long Island with her husband and her house is plundered and hers and Mrs. Moncriefe's clothes were sold at vendue. . . . Give my love to all."†

General Washington, it would appear, was one of the few who paid his bills in 1776.

Captain Gibbs, on an average summer day in New York (July 11, 1776), bought: ‡

> To 2 Bushells ½ of Salt . . .
> To a Side of Beef . . .
> To Lobsters & fish . . .
> To 1 Quarter of Mutton . . .
> To a Side of Bacon . . .

* Martin, *A Narrative of Some of the Adventures, Dangers and Sufferings of a Revolutionary Soldier*, pp. 15–18.

† Morris, Letters, *N.Y. Historical Society Collection*, VIII, pp. 440–43.

‡ Gibbs, daily expense book, Library of Congress.

To 6 Chickens . . .
To tripe & Cucumbers . . .
To Pieces Sallad & Milk . . .
To 3 pair of Ducks . . .
To 1 Quarter of Pork . . .
To Strawberries . . .
To 24 Butter . . .
To Eggs . . .
To Rum for the Indians . . .

No wonder the cost of living was so high in New York.

The Timothy Wood referred to in item No. 143 was a cobbler. His account was for half-soling a pair of boots for William Lee, Washington's body servant, and for making shoes for another servant.

1776 — July 15

No 145

> *To guns bought* *$351*

I will leave to the military experts to explain what a thing like this is doing on the expense account. To my mind, however, it is entirely proper. General Washington wouldn't have done it if he thought otherwise.

1776 — July 15

No 146

> *To Lieut. Lewis—for Sundries for ye use*
> *of the Ho [usehold]* *$62.40*

No 147

> *To my own & Parties expenses laying out Fort*
> *Lee—on the Jersey side of the No. River* . . . *$277.50*

Gen. Charles Lee, whom you will recall Washington could have arrested and broken for possession of liquor (See item No. 136), had not been part of the expense account crowd since the early days of this chronicle. When Washington moved into the spic and span, new headquarters at Craigie Mansion in Cambridge, Lee left for other quarters, probably under a cloud.

Lee did not exactly cut a royal figure. He was an unhealthily thin, ugly, spindly, short (5'8") man who wore dirty, ill-fitting uniforms. Judging by what the historians say of him, he must have looked like he was in a war. He had other bad qualities. "The General is a perfect original," wrote Jeremy Belknap, an 18th century minister and historian, "a good scholar and soldier; and an odd genius, full of fire and passion and but little good manners; a great sloven, wretchedly profane and a great admirer of dogs, of which he had two at dinner with him, one of them a native of Pomerania, which I should have taken for a bear."

Aside from dumb animals, Lee loved Shakespeare, talked dogmatically about Rousseau and the rights of man, and Swiss democracy. He also thought highly of the undisciplined patriot soldiers. Though he lost his temper frequently and hit them over the head—his Indian name was "Boiling Water"—he authored a biting pamphlet explaining why the raw American militiamen could fight more effectively than polished British regulars.

Lee's sense of humor alone would have been reason enough to send him packing to Medford, Massachusetts, off on the Americans' left wing. He moved into the former residence of the British General Royall, and renamed it "Hobgoblin Hall." A letter of introduction he wrote to the sober General Putnam for a church clergyman named Page, is an example of his odd mind:

Hobgoblin Hall . . .

Dear General: Mr. Page, the bearer of this, is a Mr. Page. He has the laudable ambition of seeing the great General Putnam. I, therefore, desire you would array yourself in all your majesty and terrors for his reception. Your blue and gold must be mounted, your pistols stuck in your girdle; and it would not be amiss if you should black one half of your face. I am, dear general, with fear and trembling, your humble servant,

Charles Lee*

If Washington had a sense of humor, I haven't uncovered any evidence of it. The closest he ever came to making a joke was on September 5, 1783, at Princeton, New Jersey, then the capital—Congress having fled Philadelphia when it was besieged by the patriot army trying to get paid after the war. When someone remarked at dinner, in honor of Congress, that the Superintendent of Finance had his hands full, General Washington remarked, "I wish he had his pockets full, too." This is what we call a private. joke today; you would have to know that he had already submitted his expense account, something the mutinous troops wouldn't have known.

The value of psychological testing in the modern corporation—he

---

* Belknap, *Journal of my Tour to the Camp,* Massachusetts Historical Society *Proceedings,* IV (1858–1860), pp. 82–83.

would have been spotted as a troublemaker—is proven by Lee's unwillingness to go along with company policy, as formulated by General Washington. Lee hated "Hyde Park tactics." Being presented with a gang of backwoodsmen and farm boys, he advocated guerrilla warfare. He saw the war as one long Lexington and Concord, of picking the enemy off one at a time. Lee's thinking is reminiscent of Mao Tse-tung, while Washington's was like that of General Braddock.

Washington had sponsored Lee in the election of major generals before Congress in 1775, but recognized his error. He later called Lee fickle. Certainly he was immature. The ease with which Lee let the British capture him in New Jersey in 1781 was the action of a small boy who doesn't want to play a game unless he is the leader. Although he borrowed Washington's money and drank his wine (or rather, the government's), he wasn't going to fight his way out of a trap just because the General was counting on his presence at the battles that soon followed.

I go into all of this now to demonstrate how General Washington could rise above the battle of personalities which plagued his command. He could have named this fort (which he mentions laying out in item No. 147) after a team-man like General Greene or a true-blue expense account crowd member, General Mifflin.

Fort Lee was located at the foot of what is now the George Washington Bridge. Across the river, on what is now called Washington Heights, stood Fort Washington.

After Fort Lee fell without a fight (see below), Lee told war correspondents there was significance in the way the General chose to defend Fort Washington and not Fort Lee. The debacle there—2,800 men captured—never would have happened, according to Lee, if not for Washington's ego. The patriots should have made their last stand in the New York area atop the grim, grey palisades, Lee said, and would have done so if not for the fort's name.

Lee didn't nurse his grudges privately. After being court-martialed for his retreat from the battlefield at Monmouth Court House, Lee charged Washington with cruelty to slaves and that he used them immorally, though with what historians call "Lee-like absurdity" he said it was done so very discreetly it was difficult to detect.

How absurd this is. Washington would not treat slaves cruelly. That would be like throwing money away.

1776 — July 23

No 148

To Capt. Gibbs Household Expenses *$1,560*

No 149

> *To the Exps. of Recong. the Country as*
> *far as Perth Amboy* $487

August 9

No 150

> *To Capt. Gibbs. Ho. Exp.* $3,900

Nobody told farmer's daughter stories about General Washington. They did tell Mary Gibbons stories. The original Mary Gibbons was mentioned during the New York assembly hearings on the assassination plot (see items No. 138 and No. 139). Unfortunately, Miss Gibbons never published her diary, and thus clear the General's name. Wherever Washington traveled during the war, a Mary Gibbons story would make the rounds of taverns.

A variation of the Mary Gibbons story may have been inspired by this trip (item No. 149). Mary was said to have lived in New Jersey, and Washington was rowed across the Hudson at night by a devoted aide-de-camp—to visit her in the suburbs. Another variation said it was the Passaic River. In both cases, the New Jersey Loyalists were to capture the Commander in Chief while he slept someplace.

All of this shows the credulity of scandalmongers. To cross the Hudson at night in a small boat—often—while the British warships were patrolling the river would have been a remarkable feat. As the Continental Army was soon to be rapidly retreating—despite this reconnoitering in Perth Amboy—the moment it crossed into Jersey, the Passaic River boat crossings become even more remarkable.

The series of Mary Gibbons stories were merely cheap propaganda manufactured for the purpose of sowing discord among the revolting colonies, Fitzpatrick explains. They always had the kicker about his telling his inamorata the New Englanders were a dirty lot. The immoralities of Washington were incidental. Still the American public seized on the incidentals, and missed the point of the stories.

If the General wasn't spending money on a Mary Gibbons, modern expense account writers might ask, what was he charging so much for? That's a good question. So many of his basic living expenses are already listed. Household items No. 148 and No. 150, for example, include payments to Thomas Marston for Madeira; John Osborne for furniture, and Andrew McAlpine and Alexander Milne for vegetables—the three staffs of life for the General. With such a well balanced diet, what remained to write off on a patrol to Perth Amboy?

Freeway tolls? Leasing canoes from the Indians? Every time he stopped and asked a farmer a question, he may have had to tip him. (Our ancestors were a lot like civil servants today: They seemed to be with both parties during a transition in government, waiting to see who will win.) Or maybe he charged for the wear and tear on his horses.

They were, after all, war horses, and entitled to special handling. The life span of an average horse during the 18th century was ten years; but a war horse, judging by the number Washington bought on the expense account, had a life expectancy of ten months. In view of the precarious nature of the business enterprise he was engaged in, Washington would have been justified to take an accelerated depreciation, or rapid write-off, for his horses.

The only loophole in this theory is that the government paid for them in the first place.

1776 — September 1
No 151

To Servants at Sundry times *$327.60*

There are no entries between August 9 and September 1, which isn't surprising because the rebel army was finally engaged in a number of battles. Sir William Howe's army had arrived in New York Bay from Halifax on July 3. Reinforced by Sir Henry Clinton's armada from South Carolina, His Majesty's American expeditionary force landed at Gravesend Bay on August 22.

The Battle of Long Island, some historians say, rattled General Washington. This item for servants' wages is evidence that the General didn't lose his head completely. It was paid the day after the rebel army extricated itself from the banks of Brooklyn Heights and moved to the banks of Wall Street in a daring night-time Dunkirk-like evacuation while the British slept.

As previously mentioned (see item No. 62), these servants employed at the New York headquarters sound suspiciously like the list of employees at Mount Vernon after the war. I may be wrong. All the names of servants, as recorded in Captain Gibbs's memo book in the Library of Congress, sound alike. My feeling that Washington may have imported slaves to New York is reinforced by the way Gibbs heads this page in the memo book: "Cash paid to Servants *Belonging* [italics mine] to General Washington." That doesn't sound like the standard office payroll. If this is as it seems, General Washington would appear to have written not just another prosaic expense account item but an emancipation proclamation. I wonder what the General's Virginia neighbors would have thought had they read that Negro Hannah earned £1 10s. ($39) on July

17, 1776, while the master was off fighting somewhere in darkest Long Island. George Washington probably would have been accused of undermining the Southern way of life.

1776 — October 2

No 152

> To Richd. Peacock $66.30

October 10

No 153

> To Captn. Gibbs Ho. Exps. $3,390

October 22

No 154

> To Exps. at Valentine's Mile Square $156

Some historians say the rebels lost the battle at Valentine's Mile Square (in the Bronx) because they didn't stop the British for more than a few hours. Washington managed to turn the loss into a clear moral victory by putting it on the expense account.

As the rebels fell back on White Plains, the General paid Richard Peacock (item No. 152) for tailoring work, mending clothes for his body servant, William, and the coachman. He also paid for furnishing linings and thread, as well as mending, for servant Peter's breeches.

1776 — October 25

No 155

> To Mr. Fleeson $89.51

No 156

> To Barber at Sundry times $131.11

No 157

> To Cash advanced Monsr. Imbart French
> Engr. $156

December 3
_____

No 158

> *To Household Expences paid by Maj. Cary*
> *and Bayler in Oct. & part of Nov. while*
> *Captn. Gibbs was absent with the Baggage—*
> *per acct. settled* *$5,658.90*

Item No. 158 appears to be somewhat out of line for moving a household from the city to the suburbs.

A modern expense account writer at the end of the week calculates that he has spent, say, $100 on out-of-pocket expenses. He sits down and creatively figures out whom to charge what for. Then his secretary forgets to include his memorandum in the year-end figures. So he still has to pay taxes. Perhaps in the confusion of Captain Gibbs's being away from the front with the General's baggage, something was omitted from the expense account.

Since there is no record of his having charged for the battles of Kips Bay, Harlem Heights, Knightsbridge and White Plains—a precedent he established at Valentine Hill (see item No. 154)—my guess is that they are included in item No. 158. Nobody likes to criticize General Washington's bookkeeping. What was needed here, however, was a crisp statement of principle, like:

To 1 battle at Kips Bay @ Time-and-a-half. See the attached voucher for explanation of the 20% extra charge for losing my temper.

Plunket Fleeson's account was for making a mattress of wool and hair (item No. 155).

Thus ends Washington's second year on the expense account. He sums up the experience with a footnote on page 20, the credit side of the ledger:

This Bal[anc]e. arises from the Expenditures of my private purse.— From which (as doth appear from the dates of the public debits against me) my outfit to take the Command of the Army at Cambridge—The Expences of the Journey Thither—and disbursements for sometime afterwards were borne.—It being money which I brought to, and rec[eive]d at Philadelphia while there as a Delegate to Congress, in May and June 1775.

Translated from the Washingtonese, the General has laid out mostly his own money for expenses so far. On the last page of the expense account we will see that General Washington charged the country for using his money. It's not the principle which will hurt some of his critics, but the interest.

1777 — January 1

No 1

> To Col. Josh. Reed pr. acct. rendered the
> Paymaster Gene. $975

No 2

> To Sundry Exps. paid by Myself—at different
> times & places in passing from the White plains
> by the Way of King's ferry to Fort Lee—and
> afterwards on the Retreat of the Army thro'
> the Jerseys into Pennsylvania—& while there   . $3,281.53

Things are looking up. The new country had a $2,000,000 net loss in its last fiscal year. Commodities are up. Taxes are at an all-time low. Profiteering is rampant and smuggling is booming. Wall Street is in the hands of the British. None of these indexes, however, affect the expense account.

At the start of the new year, the mood is optimistic in the family, if for no other reason than that Colonel Reed is back (item No. 1). Court must have been out.

On the battlefield, General Washington's strategy was clear by now. He planned to win the war by losing all the battles. But he is flexible. Some of the battles were lost by leaving his left flank exposed, as in the Battle of Long Island, where the British rode up an undefended Flatbush Avenue. Others were lost by leaving the right flank open. At White Plains, General Lee saw serious flaws in Washington's deployment of the troops, according to historian John Shy, in *George Washington's Generals,* "and recommended a movement northward to the next ridge line. Washington agreed, but immediately received a report that British troops were preparing for an attack. There was no time to deploy, and Washington could only alert his command and tell his generals, rather lamely, 'Do the best you can.' Their best was not good enough to hold a faulty position and the American army was again driven back." Still other battles were lost because Washington was weak in the center of the line.

His expense account, however, shows none of this inattention to detail. Item No. 2—the logical consequences of such a strategy as described above—reads like an American Automobile Association Triptyk. The stop-offs on the tour, we learn from other sources, were Hackensack, November 18; Newark, November 24; New Brunswick, November 29; Princeton and Trenton, December 3. No vouchers for these sundry expenses have been found among the Washington Papers. So we don't know the names of the places where Washington actually slept, if he was able to sleep under the conditions. The British were so close on Washington's heels after he abandoned Fort Lee without a fight that at Newark His Majesty's advance guard entered one side of the town as His Majesty's misguided subjects' rear left the other. The absence of the vouchers for the retreat prevents us from learning once and for all if General Washington charged for loss of pride and dignity.

1777 — January 1

No 3

> *To Secret Services since the Army left*
> *Cambridge in April—while it lay at New*
> *York and during its retreat as above* *$8,414*

Sir William Howe to Lord George Germain:

> York Island
> September 23, 1776.

My Lord: Between the 20th and 21st instant, at midnight, a most horrid attempt was made by a number of wretches to burn the town of New York, in which they succeeded too well, having set it on fire in several places with matches and combustibles that had been prepared with great art and ingenuity. Many were detected in the fact, and some killed upon the spot by the enraged troops in garrison. . . .

The destruction is computed to be about one quarter of the town; and we have reason to suspect there are villains still lurking there, ready to finish the work they had begun, one person escaping the pursuit of a sentinel the following night, having declared he would set fire to the town the first opportunity. The strictest search is making after these incendiaries, and the most effectual measures taken to guard against the perpetration of their villainous and wicked designs.*

By the one-quarter effectiveness, this sounds like another secret service job. With his usual humility, Washington denied it. If there was sabotage, he said, it was unauthorized by the American commander.

Whenever confronted by evidence of its spies' work, government officials are required to deny responsibility. In bureaucratese today, this is known as *lying*. General Eisenhower, during the U-2 incident of 1956, broke the tradition by suddenly telling the truth. The United States and Russia were on the verge of World War III because of Eisenhower's well-intentioned bungling. Had Ike been up on his American history, he might have quoted Washington's official disclaimer: "Providence, or some other honest fellow, has done more for us than we were disposed to do for ourselves."

New York has never been completely rebuilt since George the

---

* Force, *American Archives*, 5th Series, II, p. 462.

Torch's day. It wasn't insured in 1776. The city's fathers might have been justified in sending Washington a bill for fire damage, which as a matter of course he would have added to the expense account.

1777 — January 12

No 4

To Sundry Exps. paid on the March from
Trenton to Morris Town & during two days
halt at Pluckamim—Per Memm. Book *$1,021*

This is a charge that rivals the Charge of the Light Brigade. It is for a series of battles in which the poor Continental Army distinguished itself.

While in New York City Washington's tactics confused some of his critics. They are explainable if you suppose they were based on his belief that the British were on the verge of capitulating. Where he received this information is not known; likely it came from the spy network that he was stringing together at great cost (see item No. 3, above, and others). He believed in it to the extent that as late as August he was advising the custodial staff at Mount Vernon to finish the chimney-piece in the new dining room before his return.* The General miscalculated, by six years.

After the battle at White Plains his letters to Congress help explain the army's losing streak after Boston. He wrote to the president of Congress that as long as he was permitted to inflict only 39 lashes for any ordinary offense, discipline might as well be abandoned. "His idea of developing an *esprit de corps* appears to have been tied up exclusively with the mental picture of a whipping post," wrote one of his critics. "Napoleon, the greatest soldier in the world's history, depended on medals, promotion, and an imperial pat on the shoulder."

Lee was wrong that General Washington abandoned Fort Lee in spite. Washington's strategy in the battle of Fort Washington was to be hesitant. He had received conflicting reports from his spies about what was taking place on the upper west side of Manhattan. "This kept the General's mind in a state of suspense till the stroke was struck," wrote Joseph Reed, his secretary. "Oh! General—an indecisive mind is one of the greatest misfortunes that can befall an army. How often have I lamented it this campaign."†

After what has been called "Washington's greatest defeat" at Fort Washington, the Commander in Chief's new strategy at the battle of

---

* *Washington's Writings,* ed. Fitzpatrick, III, p. 435.

† Joseph Reed to Charles Lee, Nov. 21, 1776, Lee, *Lee Papers,* II, pp. 293–94.

Fort Lee was to act too fast. The night Cornwallis' men climbed up the Palisades undetected by the Secret Service, the patriots abandoned Fort Lee so quickly there was no time to bring the pickaxes and shovels, the secret of their success at Breed's Hill. This loss of equipment is not charged on the expense account.

The Continental Army's sneak attack at Trenton (December 26, 1776) was as successful as the Vietcong Tet offense in Vietnam some two hundred years later, and perhaps just as immoral. A religious holiday period, the night after Christmas was traditionally observed with an informal armistice. While certainly not "a dirty little atheist" like Tom Paine, Washington was a deist who gave only lip service to formal religion. That the God-fearing Hessians would not fight over the Christmas holiday was a gamble Washington took, and it paid off. The Battle of Trenton, in the annals of Anglo-Saxon military history, ranks in infamy with Pearl Harbor.

This isn't the only chronicle of the war to underplay the significance of the Battle of Trenton. Some of the privates who were there didn't realize what a success it was. As David How saw it:

26. This morning at 4 a Clock We set off with our Field Pieces Marchd 8 miles to Trenton Whare we ware Atacked by a Number of Hushing [Hessians] & we toock 1000 of them besides killed some. Then we marchd back And got to the River at Night and got over all the Hushing.
28. This Day we have been washing Our Things.*

Washington completely ignored the Battle of Trenton, the charges for it probably being included in item No. 2. In John Trumbull's combat picture, "The Capture of the Hessians at Trenton," the mortally wounded Col. Johann Rall is shown surrendering himself and 900 men to Washington, who is sitting on a sorrel charger. These pictures sometimes are unreliable source materials. Lt. Col. Robert Hanson Harrison, a member of the expense account crowd, was not actually present at the surrender even though in Trumbull's work he is shown next to Washington. Harrison happened to be a good friend of the artist, who took the liberty to paint him in. Nevertheless, historians seem to agree Washington rode a sorrel charger in the battle. Since there is no record for a sorrel charger in the expense account, this may be another example of the *hidden pants trick* (see comment on items No. 56 to No. 59, October 1775).

After a Victory Dinner at Trenton on the Hessians' supplies, which helped defray the costs of the retreat, the events described in item No. 4 began.

"Three or four days after the victory at Trenton," a Sergeant R——— also wrote on this period, "the American army recrossed

* How, *Diary*, p. 26.

the Delaware into New Jersey. At this time our troops were in a destitute and deplorable condition. The horses attached to our cannon were without shoes, and when passing over the ice they would slide in every direction and could advance only by the assistance of the soldiers. Our men, too were without shoes or other comfortable clothing; and as traces of our march towards Princeton, the ground was literally marked with the blood of the soldiers' feet. Though my own feet did not bleed they were so sore that their condition was little better.

"While we were at Trenton on the last of December, 1776, the time for which I and most of my regiment had enlisted expired. At this trying time General Washington, having now but a little handful of men and many of them new recruits in which he could place but little confidence, ordered our regiment to be paraded, and personally addressed us, urging that we should stay a month longer. He alluded to our recent victory at Trenton; told us that our services were greatly needed, and that we could now do more for our country than we ever could at any future period; and in the most affectionate manner entreated us to stay. The drums beat for volunteers, but not a man turned out. The soldiers, worn down with fatigue and privations, had their hearts fixed on home and the comforts of the domestic circle, and it was hard to forgo the anticipated pleasures of the society of our dearest friends.

"The General wheeled his horse about, rode in front of the regiment and addressing us again said, 'My brave fellows, you have done all I asked you to do, and more than could be reasonably expected; but your country is at stake, your wives, your houses and all that you hold dear. You have worn yourselves out with fatigues and hardships, but we know not how to spare you. If you will consent to stay only one month longer, you will render that service to the cause of liberty and to your country which you probably never can do under any other circumstances.' "* The men were won over by the General's sincerity.

On December 28, 1776, as Private How wrote in his diary, the rebel band washed clothes. Two days later, in fresh rags, the troops moved out to fight Cornwallis' slow-moving pursuers in the second battle of Trenton. In three columns totaling 8,000 men, the British ran into the Continentals' advance guard. The shoeless patriots fought so stubbornly, according to Trevelyan in his *American Revolution,* the British advanced only eight miles in eight hours. Three times Cornwallis attempted to cross the unfordable Assanpink at the bridge, and three times he was bloodily repulsed. Cornwallis rejected the advice of his officers to attack Washington again, observing that he could just as well "bag the fox" the next morning.

* R———, "Account of Princeton," *Pennsylvania Magazine of History and Biography,* XX, pp. 515–19.

Leaving their campfires kindled to deceive the enemy and muffling the artillery wheels with rags, Washington by a circuitous route marched around General Cornwallis' rear. By daylight he was in Princeton, attacking three British regiments on their way to join Cornwallis. Alexander Hamilton, the Columbia man, won fame in this battle. He gave the order to fire the cannons at Nassau Hall when the redcoats who sought refuge inside refused to surrender. A Princeton man, Aaron Burr, was to score a point for Old Nassau against Hamilton a decade later. Washington was in the thick of the battle, too. He halted a retreat at a critical moment by riding into the patriots, and reportedly exclaiming: "Parade with us, my brave fellows, there is but a handful of the enemy and we will have them directly."

Some historians say the Trenton-Princeton campaign revealed a military mind of high order. "It was nothing less than masterly in conception and execution," W. E. Woodward wrote. "In celerity, daring and vigour it reminds one of the astonishing 1862 campaign of Stonewall Jackson in the Shenendoah." Friends of Nathanael Greene claim it was his plan. Washington himself said to a committee of Congress, "I assure you, the other general officers who assisted me in the plan and execution have full as good a right to your encomiums as myself."

Nobody will argue that the General showed daring and vigor in his putting the work on the expense account. The Battle of Princeton lasted about an hour. Unfortunately the way Washington wrote up this item does not make it possible for us to arrive at an hourly rate for battles. The absence of the Memorandum Book from the Washington Papers in the Library of Congress also complicates the problem of finding out if he charged a differential for night work. At least we do know the portal to portal rates.

1777 — February [?]

No 5

To Col. Weeden—lent him for the use of his
Reg[imen]t *$500*

Col. George Weeden commanded the 3rd Virginia Regiment. At this time in the expense account, he was acting Adjutant General filling in for Joseph Reed, who had been promoted from secretary to a kind of executive vice-president of the army, and gone home again to his law business. It is not known which men Weeden gave the money to. Possibly it went to fulfill the promise the General made on December 30, 1776:

I have the pleasure to acquaint you that the Continental Regimentals from the Eastern Governments have to a man, agreed to stay six weeks beyond their term of enlistment; for this extraordinary mark of their attachment to their country, I have agreed to give them a bounty of ten dollars per man besides their pay.

It would appear that the General was finally beginning to understand his men. Actually he was of a mixed mind about the wisdom of giving the troops money. They deserved to get what was lawfully theirs; yet he feared that money was the root of all evil in his army.

Mrs. Esther Reed of Philadelphia ran a war relief drive for the aid of our boys in the trenches in 1780. Her ladies raised a considerable amount in paper, and Mrs. Reed proposed to General Washington that the Philadelphia relief organization convert the paper into specie and present to each soldier two "hard" dollars. The Commander replied he preferred the ladies give each man a shirt, as money would induce drinking and discord in the ranks.*

A father of his country knows his own sons. "Peace with our enemy," a soldier at Cambridge had written, "but disturbance enough with rum, for our men got money yesterday."† Still, it might have helped the situation if the General had openly explained to the troops how good it was not to have money.

Not knowing any better, Private David How was one of those who hadn't heeded the General's entreaties after the battle of Trenton to remain in the service for only six weeks longer. He turned his back on the $10 bonus and marched home, missing by only two days the opportunity to fight in the battle of Princeton and half a dozen others covertly listed on the General's expense account (see previous entry).

A massive troop reeducation program on the corrupting nature of money was needed. Mao Tse-tung appreciated this fact by assigning political cadres to his guerrilla units to correct errors in thought.

Tom Paine was with the General from Fort Lee to Princeton doing research for his *Crisis Papers* (soon to be published). The author of the best-selling pamphlet *Common Sense*—100,000 copies in 1775 and 1776, the equivalent of at least 5,000,000 copies today when you take into account the growth in population—Paine was the General's favorite war correspondent.

"These are the times that try men's souls," Paine was to write as his lead for the first of the *Crisis Papers,* as accurately as most correspondents too close to the action. Actually he was ahead of his time. The winters at Morristown and Valley Forge were much more

* *Life of Joseph Reed,* II, pp. 262–66.

† Aaron Wright's Revolutionary War Journal; in *Historical Magazine* (July 1862), p. 210.

trying. It was then that the summer soldiers and sunshine patriots really fell by the wayside.

Paine missed the big story in his *Crisis Papers,* Number I. He attacked the citizens of the middle colonies (New Jersey, Pennsylvania, New York) for being ambivalent about the Revolution, completely ignoring the divisions in the army. There were two groups: the *haves* and the *have-nots.* The *haves,* of whom General Washington was the spiritual leader, were antagonistic throughout the war to the *have-nots,* who didn't even have a leader.

A gifted writer like Paine could have explained to Washington that the poorer the soldier of any rank, the more dependent he will be upon the compensation he receives for his services—at least in a right wing revolution one of whose premises was respect for property rights. The rank and file (the *have-nots*) were no doubt more in need of money than their officers (the *haves*). When the money did not come, even in form of paper, they mutinied. The officers in the *have-not* group (not all of them had independent incomes) at least could resign.

In terms of the patriot's honor, this was an important distinction. When three hundred fifty members of the New Hampshire Regiment threatened to walk out on the Revolution in 1776, charging that Washington's inability to pay them from his depleted war chest was in reality nothing "less than a contrivance to cheat them of their wages," Brigadier-General Sullivan called them "worthless scoundrells."* They walked out anyway. The officers went home without disgrace, pleading pressing business affairs.

"So many resignations of officers," a surgeon was to write the next year, "that his Excellency expressed fears of being left alone with the soldiers."†

Without meaning to denigrate Tom Paine's ability as a reporter, more than likely he didn't know about Washington's expense account. As far as is known, Paine was even paying his own expenses on this trip. But he will win the respect of modern expense account writers later on in these pages with his under-the-table dealings with Robert Morris, the Secretary of the Treasury (see items Aug. 28, 1781, No. 94 to No. 95). He finally gained some common sense.

1777 — March 8

No 6

To Captn. Gibbs . . . Hd. Exps. $130*

---

* *This & every other sum which is charged in these accounts to Major Gibbs, will be found credited in his Book of Household Expenditures, which is given in as a voucher.* —[G. W.'s note]

* *Sullivan Papers,* I, p. 167.

† Dr. A. Waldo's Diary; in *Historical Magazine* (June 1861), p. 169.

I'm sure the General thought highly of Gibbs's voucher, which is reprinted here as submitted.

D^r .... Major Caleb Gibbs _ _ _ _ _ _

1776.		To Cash for Household Exp'ry	Dollars	Lawful
June	26	91. Dollars ... a 6/		27 6
July	8	To .. 120 .. Ditto		36
	15	To .. 200 .. D°		60
	23	To .. 200 .. D°		60
Aug	9	To .. 500 .. D°		150
Oct	10	To .. 500 .. D°		150
1777		1611. amounting to	£	483 6
Mar	8.	To Cash for the above purposes. 130 & 260 D° 390.		
Ap	11	To .. Ditto ... 1000		
May	22	To .. Ditto ... 1000		
Aug	8	To .. Ditto ... 1000		
	28	To .. Ditto ... 1000		
Oct	11.	To .. Ditto ... 1000	5390	
1778 Jan	29	To .. Ditto ... 2000		
Apl	10	To .. Ditto ... 1000		
June	16	To .. Ditto ... 2000		
Sept	2	To .. Ditto ... 1000		
Nov	20	To .. Ditto ... 2000		

Why would either of us want to publish bad writing? Not as encouragement to bad writers. Modern expense account writers have enough trouble understanding good writing, and as far as bad writing is concerned, they turn out enough of that without help.

Ebenezer Austin established the basic principle in accompanying vouchers that: *None should ever be the same.* When you take cabs to the airport, for example, you never write "$5.60, $5.60, $5.60." You write: "$5.60, $5.75, $5.45." It adds up to the same thing, but this style has the additional advantage of avoiding the suggestion of any irregularity in your expense account. There never is, but why waste the examining official's time by arousing his suspicions.

Gibbs carried Austin's work forward by breaking this rule as early as his third voucher. Notice the five straight items from April to October 1777. Gibbs didn't rest on his laurels. By August 1780, he had the account moving along nicely at $5,000. This is the most dramatic example of the principle of military escalation: *As the hopes for a short war diminish, the costs rise geometrically.* We will go into the details of what Gibbs spent as these great figures are rementioned in the account. Suffice it to say now, Gibbs played a role in the development of the *lulu,* a flat sum given to state legislators and others in lieu of expenses.

1777 — March 8
No 7

   Ditto . . . . *Ditto* *$260*

No 8

  To Mrs. Thompson, the Ho. Keeper for
like purposes *$10*

April 11
No 9

  To Captn. Gibbs . . . *Hd. Exps.* *$1,000*

No 10

  To Servants—at sev[eral] times *$46*

No 11

  To Benja. Hemmings's Acct. *$117.43*

[No 12 is missing]

April 19
_____

No 13

> *To specie to Majr. Genl. Greene for Secret*
> *Services* *$78*

May 22
_____
No 14

> *To Captn. Gibbs* . . . *Hd. Exps.* *$1,000*

At Morristown, Washington commanded approximately 3,000 men. Here he proved himself to have a fine talent for deception. "It was the one department of strategy in which he was an adept," the historian Woodward explained. He scattered his men in farmhouses for miles around Morristown, and kept changing them about like an accountant juggling figures. Even the shrewd country people who should have known better thought he had a large army. He instructed the adjutant general to prepare false returns, showing a force of 12,000 men, and with his blessings and a few guineas these papers fell into the hands of a British spy.

Item No. 13 may have covered this smart move, although nobody can be certain. Of all the innovations Washington had put in motion up to now, the secret service was working least smoothly.

It was a haphazard affair, Fitzpatrick says of the Morristown period, largely conducted by the commanders of the dragoon outposts and picket officers. While in New Jersey, he adds cryptically, "the secret intelligence was obtained through patriotic country folk, as there were then few regular secret service agents. Later in the war the service was developed into a machine that rendered invaluable assistance to the Commander-in-Chief."

The emergence of the professional, we will soon see, was partly responsible for the Continental Army defeats at Brandywine and Germantown. One of the feats of the secret service at this time involved a Mr. Smith (obviously a cover name), captured by the patriots and shipped into Philadelphia on the charge of being a British spy. Washington was enraged. Mr. Smith in reality was an American spy. The General ordered his freedom, with instructions that the release or escape must be managed so that no suspicion would be aroused as to the man's true character.

Morristown, the cloak and dagger center of America, although hardly worth mentioning in the same hushed tones as Paris, Vienna and London, at this time must have seemed to mysterious visitors like just another sleepy village at the foot of Thimble Mountain in New Jersey's Central Mountain range. Thimble was to be Washington's Sierra Maestra, where he could restore his troops and watch the movements of the enemy without fear of surprises. General Washington set up his headquarters in Arnold's Tavern; here he recovered from a brief illness that may have been gout. Unfortunately historians have not done a study on the incidence of gout amongst the rebels who lived on the expense account during the war. We do know that starvation, frostbite and smallpox were the major health threat at Morristown. But life goes on in war.

As early as January, Lt. James McMichael wrote that "the young ladies here are very fond of the soldiers, but much more so of the officers." The local girls were reinforced by the arrival of Martha Washington. In a more gossipy tone than item No. 9 has, Martha Dangerfield Bland, the wife of Col. Theodorick Bland of Virginia, described how the first lady of the army gave a shot in the arm to the social life at headquarters:

Now let me speak of our noble and agreeable commander (for he commands both sexes, one by his excellent skill in military matters, the other by his ability, politeness, and attention). We visit them twice or three times a week by particular invitation. Every day frequently from inclination. He is generally busy in the forenoon, but from dinner till night he is free for all company. His worthy Lady seems to be in perfect felicity, while she is by the side of her "Old Man," as she often calls him. We often make parties on horseback, the General, his Lady, Miss Livingston, and his aides-de-camp, who are Colonel [John] Fitzgerald, an agreeable, broad-shouldered Irishman; Colonel [George] Johnston . . . who is exceedingly witty at everybody's expense, but can't allow other people to be so at his own, though they often take the liberty; Colonel [Alexander] Hamilton, a sensible, genteel, polite, young fellow, a West Indian; Colonel [Richard Kidder] Meade; Colonel [Tench] Tilghman, a modest, worthy man who from his attachment to the General voluntarily lives in his family and acts in any capacity that is uppermost without fee or reward; Colonel [Robert Hanson] Harrison, brother of Billy Harrison that kept store in Petersburg and as much like him as possible, a worthy man; Captain [Caleb] Gibbs of the General's Guard, a good-natured Yankee who makes a thousand blunders in the Yankee style and keeps the dinner table in constant laugh. These are the General's family, all polite, sociable gentlemen, who make the day pass with a great deal of satisfaction to the visitors. But I have forgot my subject almost, this is our riding party, generally at which time General Washington throws off the hero and takes on the chatty, agreeable companion. He can be downright impudent sometimes, such impudence, Fanny, as you and I like, and really, I have wished for you often.*

Naturally, the troops not on the expense account faced economic deprivations during this period. On January 1, 1777, the following order was tacked up on the headquarter's bulletin board at Trenton:

* Martha Bland to Frances Randolph, May 12, 1777, New Jersey Historical Society *Proceedings,* LI (July, 1933), pp. 151–52.

His Excellency General Washington strictly forbids all the officers and soldiers of the Continental Army, of the militia and all recruiting parties, plundering any person whatsoever, whether Tories or others. The effects of such persons will be applied to public uses in a regular manner, and it is expected that humanity and tenderness to women and children will distinguish brave Americans, contending for liberty, from infamous mercenary ravagers, whether British or Hessians.

G. Washington.*

The "Ditto . . . Ditto" in item No. 7 is short for :
"To 5 geese . . . To 9 turkeys . . . To 30 eggs . . . To 1 gallon Rum . . . To Cash paid Servant Jenny . . . To 2 quarters veal . . . To 1 bushell Apples . . . To 1 Quarter mutton . . . To Cash paid Corporal Houston for a shirt your Servant Lanny had . . . To 6 Trouts . . . To 4 Lbs. Butter . . . To 10 Gallons rum to put to Cherries . . ."† These items are taken from the purchases of January 4, 7, 8, not from the entire stay at Morristown. You can see why brevity is the soul of great expense account writing.

1777 — June 1
_____
No 15

    To Secret Services to this date $4,356

No 16

    To Mr. Parke Custis Esq. for a Riding Horse . . $333⅓

August 4 [?]
_____
No 17

    To Colo. Moylan for Ditto, having lost
    two of mine with the distemper that raged $200

August 8
_____
No 18

    To Captn. Gibbs . . . *Hd. Exps.* $1,000

August 28
_____
No 19

    Ditto . . . . . *Ditto* $1,000

* *Writings of Washington*, ed. Fitzpatrick, VI, p. 466.
† Gibbs, daily expense memo, Library of Congress.

No 20

*To Secret Services while the two Armies
were Maneuvering in the Jerseys—& till
British sailed for the Head of Elk* $1,935

The language in item No. 16 does not make it clear whether the
General used his expense account to buy a horse *for* his stepson,
John (Jacky) Parke Custis, or *from* him. It would seem the latter
were true. Either way, this establishes the basic principle of doing
business with relatives, an old American custom which still flourishes in some of the nation's finest corporations.

Assuming that Jacky was wearing the three-cornered hat of a
supplier, we still don't know whether his horse was 30 percent better
than the one Col. Stephen Moylan sold the General, which might
also give Washington's seal of approval to favoritism. Fitzpatrick
says only that Quartermaster General Moylan *sold* his Excellency, a
horse *captured* from the British light cavalry.

Quartermaster General Moylan is a hero in expense account
writing because he is the first to employ the basic principle of *buying
low and selling high.* Still, this kind of business ethics in the law-and-
order contingent at headquarters must have confused those who
desired to follow strictly the letter of the General's orders on ex-
propriation (for his approach, see item No. 14, May 22, 1777).

Nepotism was in the saddle in the patriot army. "I have been
credibly informed," Captain Alexander Graydon wrote in *Memoirs
of His Own Time* (pp. 147–48), "that it is no unusual thing in the
army before Boston for a colonel to make drummer and fifers of his
sons, thereby not only being enabled to form a very snug, economi-
cal mess, but to aid also considerably the revenue of the family
chest. In short it appeared that the sordid spirit of gain was the vital
principle of this greater part of the army." General Washington
brought his stepson into what was the equivalent of a family business as an aide at headquarters. A principle still valid in business
today is: *There is always room at the top for a relative.*

Jacky served without official rank or appointment. Some historians say his place in the table of organization was sightseer.
Even then it wasn't until the final moments of glory—the Battle of
Yorktown in 1781, which took place down the road a piece from
Mount Vernon—that Jacky volunteered to the front. He was seen
by other participants at the siege, as it has been said, ordering
people around. This brief exposure to the rigors of war was too
much. He contracted camp fever at Yorktown, and died November
5, 1781, a final act of rebellion against his stern but generous stepfather.

Jacky was a good-natured, popular boy, no doubt spoiled as an
only son by wealth and lack of restraint by his mother. Old-fash-
ioned historians refer to him as "rather stupid," a reference to a
little difficulty he had with book-learning. When he was seventeen,
Washington described him to Rev. Jonathan A. Boucher, head-
master of a famous school at Annapolis: "He has little or no
knowledge of arithmetic and is totally ignorant of the mathematics"
—serious deficiencies by Washington's standards. Jacky knew a few
words of Latin, but "nothing of Greek," nor of French. Shipped
around from one school to another with his horses and *livery*
servant, he was finally taken by Washington himself to King's College (Columbia) in New York. But he dropped out soon after his
stepfather turned for home. It is a clear case of the student revolt
against permissive parents.

If Jacky had survived at the front a bit longer, he might have
played a major role in the first Washington administration. The
stout Federalist Henry Knox became the first Secretary of War.
Alexander Hamilton was Secretary of the Treasury. James Mc-
Henry, Tench Tilghman, and many of the other secretaries we read
about in the expense account followed the boss into politics. Bushrod Washington, the General's one-eyed nephew, even grew up to
become Supreme Court justice. Bushrod distinguished himself in
the law and order field by being the first to tear out pages of his
uncle's diaries, although this seems to have been done less with an
eye to cleaning up the records than giving away valuable souvenirs.
He can't be blamed on General Washington: John Adams appointed
him to the Supreme Court. Although President Washington was the
first to pack the court, he established the principle of ignoring
family and rewarding old political friends with judgeships. Perhaps
an L.B.J. or a Richard Nixon should not be too severely censured
for an Abe Fortas or a Clement Haynesworth.

1777 — August 28

No 21

> *To Expenditures per my Memm. Book on the*
> *March from Middle Brooke in the Jerseys*
> *to Smith's Cove—and from Smith Cove in*
> *the State of New York to the Cross Roads in*
> *Pennsy[lvani]a* $1,150.50

No 22

> *To expended in a trip to examine Mud Isl[an]d,*
> *Red Bank and Billingsford* $60⅔

No 23

> *To Ditto—going to Marcus Hook* *$86*

No 24

> *To Ditto on the March from the Cross Roads*
> *to Wilmington in the State of Delaware*
> *exclusive of other acc[oun]ts* *$234*

No 25

> *To the Expence of a Reconnoitre to the Head*
> *of Elk with a large party of Horse when*
> *the Enemy were ab[out] landing there.* *$588.90*

September 14

No 26

> *To Expenditures after the Battle of Brandy*
> *Wine until we arrived at German Town—per*
> *Memm. book* *$397.80*

No 27

> *To Cash advanced to Serv[an]ts at Sundry*
> *times* *$52*

October 11

No 28

> *To Captn. Gibbs for Hd. Exps.* *$1,000*

December 25

No 29

> *To Expenditures in the different & continual*
> *movements of the Army from the time of its*
> *March from Germantown Sept. 15th till we*
> *Hutted at Valley Forge the 25th of Dec. per*
> *Memm. Book* *$3,078*

This series of items is a thrilling, ironical chronicle of a guerrilla
band running away from the enemy one day to fight him on another.
Washington must have been like a Moses or a Mao Tse-tung,
holding his people together with the force of his charisma. The

months beginning with August 28 were for the army the forty years in the desert for the Israelites and the nine years in the hills of the Yuan for the Chinese Communists.

Patriotism for the expense account writer is the last refuge of scoundrels. For there is no explaining away the fact that here for the first time Washington shows signs of losing his quick touch. These passages are an old man's writing. They sag from the weight of the overwriting. In item No. 21, he tells us that Smith's Cove is "in the State of New York"; item No. 24 says that Wilmington is "in the State of Delaware." This is what is known as "padding an expense account," a practice which has been distorted by modern usage.

If it's facts Washington wanted to give his readers, he should have gone to his memorandum books. As Fitzpatrick says of these glorious feats:

July 29 a Mrs. Lowry was paid £1 2s. 6d. [$29.25], and that same day the troops began crossing the Delaware at Coryell's Ferry, sixteen miles above Trenton. August 1 Washington inspected the river defense of Philadelphia, Fort Mifflin on Mud Island, Fort Mercer at Red Bank . . . He was at Marcus Hook, now Linwood, eighteen miles southeast of Philadelphia, and dined and supped at Chester, Pa., that same day. . . . August 5 Daniel Smith was paid £263 4s. [this must be an error; otherwise it is highway robbery] for the use of his tavern during this period of uncertainty. August 6 Washington was at Germantown, and August 13 there is an item of 17s. 6d. [$22.75] paid to Colonel Henry Hill's servants in gratuities for their trouble in cleaning the house in Indian Queen Lane, one mile east of Schuylkill Falls, after Headquarters left it. At Neshaminy Camp, in Bucks County, Pa., Washington received word that the British fleet had been seen off Sinepuxent, Maryland. The army halted, and Washington established his headquarters at Mrs. Moland's house, a stone dwelling, about half a mile above Hartsville on the old York Road, known then as Cross Roads, Pa. Here he remained until August 23, when definite information was received that the British fleet was actually in the Chesapeake Bay. Mrs. Moland was paid £5 5s. [$136.50] for the use of her house and furniture . . . August 27 the accounts show an item of £63 12s. [$1,653.60] [this wasn't a bargain; it's an outrage] paid to George Forsythe, at Wilmington, for lodging . . . August 29 to September 2 Washington spent in examining the country, and the different roads, and the expense account from August 30 to September 2 shows bills at Elk, at Eagle Tavern, Chester, Derby, Ciscill's and Christiana Bridge . . . September 15, the orders are dated near Warren Tavern and expense account shows £3 10s. [$91] paid to Mr. George (?) Syngs for breakfast and £9 4s. [$239.20] to Mr. Waggoner at the Sorrel Horse Tavern, Radnor Township, Pa. The next day the Continental Army engaged the enemy near White Horse Tavern, when a heavy rain set in and rendered the ammunition useless. The Continentals then marched to Yellow Springs, five miles to the northward, and the expense account shows that Mr. Malin was paid on September 16 £7 10s. [$195] for the use of his house "and trouble—(rainy day)." On the 18th, £7 10s [$195] was paid to Mr. Olds at Reading Furnace and on the 19th Washington breakfasted at Mr. Kennedy's at Flatland Ford, the account being £3 10s. [$91] for sundries and trouble . . . September 29, £5 10s. [$143] was paid for the use of the house at "Paulin's Mill" and the extra trouble caused, and Washington reached Skippack September 30. October 2 at Worcester, Pa. . . . Joseph Smith's house was used by the Commander-in-Chief; the accounts show a payment of £2 5s. [$58.50] for this and the trouble caused and for sundries to the amount of £11 19s. 6d. [$311.35]. October 4 Headquarters were at Peter Wentz's and he was paid £2 10s. [$65] for butter, vegetables, etc. October 5, the Headquarters were at Perkiomen and on the 8th the Commander-in-Chief expended £5 [$130] for the use of a house and the trouble caused at that place. . . .

This was the Washington who makes the pulse of modern expense account writers beat fast! One might argue that he could have slept at a more expensive inn in Bucks County on such and such a day, but it would be quibbling. The four months "of making continual movements" are as close to perfection as could be expected under the conditions.

The expense account contains none of the mistakes one reads in the standard battlefield accounts of this period. The defeat at Brandywine, where his right flank was turned because he ignored a farmer's information that the British were coming as he waited for his paid volunteer spies to check in! The failure at Germantown because of an over-complex battle plan! General Howe faking out General Washington at Reading Furnace! The Quaker City was lost; but the General was alive and well in Bucks County.

These retreats may cause trouble for some idealists. We have already seen (item No. 27, Sept. 14, 1777, most recently) that it is all right to charge for servants in a battle. However, should public servants like soldiers continue to draw their pay when they are in the act of retreating? From a crassly commercial point of view, the primary mission of soldiers at a time like this is saving their own skin. A government does not hire soldiers to go backward, but forward. A retreat is prima facie evidence that the employee is not doing his job. Shouldn't he go off the payroll until he is ready, willing and able to perform the requirements of his job?

None of this applies to General Washington, but to the soldiers on the payroll who hutted at Valley Forge Christmas Day, 1777.

1778 — January [*?*]

No 30

To Secret Services—since the Enemy's Landing at the Head of Elk to the present date *$1,948*

January 29
_____
No 31

    To Captn. Gibbs—Hd. Exps. $2,000

April 10
_____
No 32

        Ditto . . . Ditto $1,000

June 5
_____
No 33

    To Captn. Barry—per Acct. $356

The group of items covering the first winter headquarters in eastern Pennsylvania are known in expense account writing lore as the Valley Forge Caper. It began on December 18, when General Washington issued a General Order, which read in part:

> The General ardently wishes it were now in his power to conduct the troops into the best winter quarters. But where are these to be found? Should we retire to the interior parts of the state, we should find them crowded with virtuous citizens, who sacrificing their all have left Philadelphia and fled thither for protection. To their distresses humanity forbids us to add. That is not all; we should leave a vast extant of fertile country to be despoiled and ravaged by the enemy from which they would draw vast supplies and where many of our firm friends would be exposed to all the miseries of the most insulting and wanton depredation. A train of evils might be enumerated but these will suffice.

The order went on to explain that at Valley Forge "with activity and diligence huts may be erected that will be warm and dry." He himself "will share in the hardship and partake of every inconvenience," it ended on a gloomy note.

The troops knew what Valley Forge would be like, and their anticipations were more than realized.

"I am sick, discontented, and out of humor," one veteran explained. "Cold weather. Fatigue, Nasty clothes. Nasty cookery. Vomit half my time. Smoked out of my senses. The Devils in it. I can't endure it. Why are we sent here to starve and freeze? What sweet felicities have I left at home, a charming wife, pretty children, good beds, good food, good cookery . . . Here all confusion, smoke and cold, hunger and filthiness. A pox on my bad luck.

"There comes a bowl of beef soup full of burnt leaves and dirt, sickish enough to make Hector spew. Away with it boys. I'll live like the chameleon upon air.*

In military language today this is what is known as bitching.

There were five reasons for picking Valley Forge, according to Dr. Waldo, who had his hands full with sick call during the winter of 1778:

1st. There is plenty of wood and water.

2dly. There are but few families for the soldierly to steal from—tho' far be it from a soldier to steal—

[3rd not given]

4ly. There are warm sides of hills to erect huts on.

5ly. They will be heavenly minded, like Jonah when in the belly of a great Fish.

6ly. They will not become home sick, as is sometimes the case when men live in the open world—since the reflection which must naturally arise from their present habitation will lead them to the more noble thoughts of employing their leisure hours in filling their knapsacks with such materials as may be necessary on the Journey to another Home.†

For some reason, probably because there wasn't a suitable tavern or house in the wooded area selected for winter headquarters, General Washington chose to live in a tent that first week. But this wasn't a betrayal of all the principles he set down earlier in the book. His was probably the custom-built tent with the marquees described in the 1776 junket to Philadelphia, purchased on the expense account for just such a contingency.

The expense account (item No. 29, Dec. 25, 1777) implied the army was hutted on December 25. This was another example of a harmless exaggeration. For in his diary of that day, Dr. Waldo writes, "We are still in tents when we ought to be in huts." More than likely, it referred to the fact that the first soldier in the land had been hutted.

Where General Washington got the information that food and provisions would be plentiful at the junction of Valley Creek and the Schuylkill, where stood symbolically the ruins of a forge, can be explained perhaps by item No. 30, January 1778. Washington's intelligence services seem to have set the standards by which the Central Intelligence Agency is judged today. All that chosen site offered was timberland to furnish wood for huts and a natural defensive area. Valley Forge was in the heart of a rich agricultural region, but the simple Quakers were taking their wheat and beef into Philadelphia, where the British paid gold. All Washington had at this time was Continental dollars.

* Waldo, Valley Forge 1777–8 Diary," *Pennsylvania Magazine of History*, XXI (1897), p. 306.

† Waldo's Diary; in *Historical Magazine* (May 1861) p. 131.

Still the expense account crowd survived. Caleb Gibbs's daily expense memo suggests that the General's table, while not as lavish as Morristown, was at least traditional. The day before Christmas Gibbs paid for geese, mutton, fowls, turkey, veal, butter, turnips, potatoes, carrots and cabbage. The vegetables helped prevent the rise of disease from a steady diet of meat, Bolton says of the army's health problems.

Gibbs's daily expense memos for the Valley Forge period can make your mouth water. Why they are buried away in the vaults of the Library of Congress is something of a mystery; they should be on display at the Freedom Foundation's memorial at Valley Forge. There are vouchers showing that Washington signed an agreement with Peggy Lee to do washing for the Commander in Chief for 40 shillings per month and to do the washing for the family at four shillings per dozen pieces. The daily expense account also shows that the band of Colonel Thomas Procter's 4th Continental Artillery apparently didn't take it upon itself to serenade the Commander in Chief on February 22, 1778: "Cash paid the 22 Inst. to Proct. band by the G.O. . . . 15s. [G.O. meaning, by the General's Order.]" This gig marks the government's first official celebration of Washington's Birthday.

By February of 1778 the army was at the point of dissolution. Four thousand men of Washington's force of 9,000 were unfit for duty on account of having no shoes or coats. He wrote that many men had to sit by the fire all night for lack of blankets. None of this was Washington's fault. He had written numerous appeals to Congress and the governors. He tried in every way possible to keep his army together, any historian will tell you that.

Washington's strongest asset was fortitude. "The fighter who stays in the ring as long as he can stand on his feet," Woodward said, "the man who keeps his business alive while his clothes are threadbare and his stomach empty, the captain who clings to his ship while there is a plank left afloat—that is Washington. This quality implies sincerity, courage and honesty of purpose, but it does not imply intellect or good judgment."

He may have been referring to a Congressional committee's blaming the Commissary General, Thomas Mifflin, for a breakdown in the army's distribution network. Warehouses in Boston and Newport filled with rotting clothing, blankets and shoes—400 miles away from the front; graft in dealing with suppliers; the usual revelations in any war-time investigation. For writing an "infamous letter" against a Colonel Brewer, a soldier was sentenced to stand in the pillory for an hour, where his comrades might be uplifted by witnessing his humiliation and suffering, according to Paul Lunt's diary. "In less than an hour, he fainted." (*The Private Under Washington,* p. 174.) The first of the expense account crowd, young

Mifflin was allowed to resign under fire. Paradoxically it is just this lack of judgment which led to Washington's greatness as an expense account writer.

In February, in the midst of all the distresses, there were some bright sides to the picture at Valley Forge. Mrs. Washington had the courage to follow her husband to Pennsylvania, on the theory that misery loves company. For an explanation of who picked up the travel expenses, see Washington's footnote to the Recapitulation (page 276).

Martha wrote to her sewing circle at Mount Vernon that on her second visit to the front the officers and men were "chiefly in Hutts, which they say is tolerably comfortable; the army are as healthy as can be well expected in general. The general's apartment is very small; he has had a log cabin built to dine in, which has made our quarters more tolerable than they were at first."

Mrs. Washington once again was a style leader. After her arrival, Valley Forge was an In-place. "Other ladies graced the scene," Duponceau, Baron von Steuben's secretary-valet, reported. "Among them was the lady of General Greene, a handsome, elegant and accomplished woman. Her dwelling was the resort of the foreign officers because she understood and spoke French . . . and was well versed in French literature. There were also Lady Stirling . . . her daughter Lady Kitty Alexander . . . and her companion, Miss Nancy Brown, then a distinguished belle. There was Mrs. Biddle, the wife of Colonel Clement Biddle, who was at the head of the forage department, and some other ladies, whose names I do not . . . recollect. They often met at each other's quarters and sometimes at General Washington's, where the evening was spent in conversation over a dish of tea or coffee." The only entertainment, according to Duponceau, was singing. "Every gentleman or lady who could sing was called upon in turn for a song."

After his exchange as a prisoner of war, even Maj. Gen. Charles Lee joined in the fun at Valley Forge. "He passed through the lines of officers and the army who all paid him the highest military honors to Headquarters, where Mrs. Washington was and there he was entertained with an elegant dinner and the music playing all the time," recalled Elias Boudinot, the super-spy. "A room was assigned to him back of Mrs. Washington's sitting room and all his baggage was stowed in it. The next morning he lay very late and breakfast was detained for him. When he came out, he looked dirty, as if he had been in the street all night. Soon after I discovered that he had brought a miserable dirty hussy with him from Philadelphia (a British sergeant's wife) and had actually taken her into his room by a back door, and she had slept with him that night." (Boudinot, *Journal,* p. 77.) This must have been Lee's idea of a joke on General and Mrs. Washington.

The daily routine at Valley Forge for the enlisted men also had its bright spots. Dressing for parade and the morning meal were dispensed with, as there was little to wear and less to eat. But the men were not allowed to grow soft with idleness either. There was Baron von Steuben's drill classes to attend. Bolton says the men also were ordered to have their beards close shaved, shoes cleaned and hands and faces washed. When an event of importance occurred the orders of the day mentioned the men *will* powder their hair. The troops' visits to the barbers were deducted from pay. (*Private Soldier Under Washington,* p. 237.)

Supper and dinner are not worth discussing. Sometimes there were no more than two kettles in which to prepare the meals for a company: The meat was broiled over the fire spitted on a bayonet and the bread was baked in hot ashes.

By May, the enlisted men no longer were quenching their thirst with snowballs, the amber waves of grain were sparkling again on the fruited plain, and His Excellency's purple mood vanished. The officers in the expense account crowd decided to give a play, which Washington and Lady Washington attended along with Lord and Lady Stirling, and Mrs. Greene.

For the first time in these pages, Congress expressed disapproval of an act of the Commander in Chief. A theater, in the eyes of the puritans in Congress, was a den of iniquity. The congressmen expressed their indignation and astonishment that patriotic officers, entrusted with the defense of their country and the freedom of all, should fall so deep in dissolute habits as to give a play on the stage. Hoping to head this shameful conduct off at the pass, Congress passed a firm resolution that said in part: "any person holding an office under the United States, who shall attend a theatrical performance shall be dismissed from the service."

This established the basic principle: *Never do anything on an expense account the boss wouldn't do; if you do, don't get caught.* The kill-joys in Congress never heard of another play at Valley Forge.

1778 — June 16

No *34*

To Maj. Gibbs—Hd. Exps. *$2,000*

Modern expense account writers should celebrate the promotion won by Caleb Gibbs, the first record of which is included in this item dated June 16. A day off from the office would be a suitable commemoration of the fact that a man can get ahead even if he is in the backrooms.

Subtract that smile from your face! Gibbs fought well on the battlefield, even if he was no liability in the less glamorous field of bookkeeping. Like West Point and Annapolis, the country needs a U.S. Accounting Academy to help prepare the military for battles in Congress over defense costs. When it is built, there should be a statue honoring Caleb Gibbs, done in gold leaf, which the accounting cadets could throw pennies at as they strolled with their dates down Deduction Walk.

1778 — June 18

No 35

> *To Secret Services—during the Enemy's hold[in]g. of Phila.* $6,170

August [?]

No 36

> *To Sundry Expenditures on the March of the Army from Valley Forge June 18th (by the way of Monmouth) till its arrival at the White plains the latter end of July* $1,520

September [?]

No 37

> *To Cash paid in Recong. the Country ab[ou]t the Plains, betw[ee]n the North and East Rivers* $133

This is another chapter modern expense account writers should read for amusement, not instruction. Item No. 36 covers the famous battle of Monmouth Court House, where Washington uncharacteristically slept on the battlefield, wrapped in his finely-made cloak, the equivalent of sleeping in the office. I don't think we can blame the General for this crime against expense accountry. His intelligence (possibly included in item No. 35) warned him the enemy was planning to resume the battle the next morning. At dawn, however, he found only the British dead and wounded on the field; Sir Henry Clinton and his army were gone.

There is nothing immoral about sleeping at the office, provided you charge for it in other ways. General Washington more than compensated for the failure at Monmouth Court House on the trip to White plains.

The Monmouth battle was marred in another way. A private in a gun battery reportedly had his wife giving him a hand at the office.

Private Hayes's wife, "Molly," was an illiterate who smoked and chewed tobacco, swore like a trooper, and throughout the battle worked as a gunner's mate. "While in the act of reaching for a cartridge," Pvt. Joseph Martin wrote in his journal, "and having one of her feet as far before the other as she could step, a cannon shot from the enemy passed directly between her legs, without doing any other damage than carrying away all the lower part of her petticoat. Looking at it with apparent unconcern, she observed that luckily it did not pass a little higher, for in that case it might have carried away something else, and continued her occupation." When Mrs. Hayes wasn't passing the ammo she was bringing around water to the troops on the cuff. "Molly Pitcher" was one of those women who had no head for business. Fortunately for modern expense account writers, the precedent didn't catch on at headquarters.

The trip north, as the General wrote, was an "inconceivably distressing march," twenty miles to Brunswick through deep, hot, sandy red and yellow dust, almost without a drop of water. The typical Jersey summer, however, did not lessen the enthusiastic celebration of the second anniversary of the Declaration of Independence. "We Selebrated the Independence of Amarica," wrote Private Elijah Fisher of the Commander's Guard, in his memoirs, "the howl army parraded . . . the artilery Discharged thirteen Cannon. we gave three Chears &c. At Night his Excelency and the gentlemen and Ladys had a Bawl at Headquarters with grate Pompe."*

On the march north to the new headquarters in Paramus, Washington and the expense account crowd paused at least once for a light repast. "The travelling canteens were immediately emptied," James McHenry noted in his diary. "With the assistance of a little spirit, we composed some grog over which we chatted away a very cheerful hour." The menu for the picnic included cold ham, tongue and "excellent bisquit."

When the General and his circle staggered into Paramus, they accepted the gracious offer of Mrs. Theodosia Prevost to set up headquarters in her red stone Gothic mansion, "The Hermitage." Mrs. Prevost's husband had recently died in the British service in the West Indies. She obviously now wanted to make up for her husband's past sins. Lt. Col. Aaron Burr, the sharpshooter, was in the expense account crowd by now, and immediately launched a campaign to win Mrs. Prevost to our side.

Paramus today is known as a discount shopping center, but in 1779 the small Dutch settlement must have been a winter resort. "At our new quarters we found some fair refugees from New York on a visit," McHenry wrote. "Here we talked and walked and laughed and frolicked and gallanted away four days and four nights and

---

* Fisher, "Diary" in Godfrey, *Commander-in-Chief's Guard*, p. 280.

would have gallanted and frolicked and laughed and walked and talked I believe forever, had not the General given orders for our departure" (*James McHenry Papers,* II, p. 10).

1778 — September [*?*]
No 38

To Expenditures in Visiting the Post at West Point $268.62

September 2
No 39

To Maj. Gibbs—Hd. Exps. $1,000

September 6
No 40

To 25 guineas sent Brigad [*ie*]*r Gen*[*era*]*l Scott—commanding the light Troops on the Lines—to enable him to engage some of the Inhabitants betw*[*ee*]*n him and the Enemy to watch their movem*[*ent*]*s, & apprize him of them—to prev*[*en*]*t Surprizes* $910

September 25
No 41

To 25 guineas sent him for the like purposes . . . $910

There were still some bugs in the General's intelligence network. Earlier in the year, for example, he was "Surprized" by the Conway Cabal. Political enemies in Congress and military enemies in the army had formed a bloc to unseat General Washington as Commander in Chief. As Jonathan D. Sergeant, Attorney General of Pennsylvania, explained in his critique of the way the war was being run: "Thousands of lives and millions of property are yearly sacrificed to the insufficiency of our Commander-in-Chief. Two battles he has lost for us by two such blunders as might have disgraced a soldier of three months standing, and yet we are so attached to this man that I fear we shall rather sink with him than throw him off our shoulders."* They really flung mud in those days.

The demand for a recall of Washington agitated Congress in

* Jonathan Sergeant to James Lovell, Nov. 20, 1777, MS letter, *Samuel Adams Papers,* New York Public Library.

Philadelphia, while the General suffered in Valley Forge. But the campaign for the election of "a Gates, a Lee or a Conway" never got off the ground. The General preferred to think of the major threat to his administration of the army as a "staff dispute." Nevertheless the cabal showed glaring defects in his intelligence apparatus. The lesson to be learned in this for modern expense account writers is: *Never trust anybody in your crowd.* You never know which fellow will turn out to be a Machiavelli of the water cooler.

This visit to West Point will be significant in terms of one of the biggest "Surprizes" in the war next year. No one had "apprized" General Washington yet that General Arnold was soft on the Revolution.

1778 — October 4

No 42

> To Exps. of Myself & Party of Horse from
> Fredericksb[ur]gh to Fishkiln, where I was
> detained two days on bus[iness] $449.60

No 43

> To Ditto to Danbury $240

October 22

No 44

> To 25 Guin[ea]s sent Brigr. Genl. Scott for
> the purposes above mentioned—Sett[le]d $910

November [?]

No 45

> To a second trip to Fishkiln $320

November 20

No 46

> To Maj. Gibbs—Hd. Exps. $2,000

No 47

> To the Expences which were paid by Myself
> on the March (sometimes with, & sometimes
> apart from the army) from Fredericksburgh
> to Middlebrook to our Winter Cantonm[en]t,
> & on My Return back to the No[rth] Riv[er]
> upon the movement of General Clinton [illegible] . $1,343

No 48

> *To Maj. Gibbs* . . . *Hd. Exps.* *$2,000*

Sir Henry Clinton's army was holed up in New York City the fall of 1779. But Washington gave no quarter. It was business as usual with him, as he rode across Dutchess County looking for suitable locations for his troop's winter quarters.

Comparing items No. 42 and No. 44, we see a good illustration of the basic principle, explained earlier, that two trips to the same place should never cost the same.

1779 — February 6

No 49

> *To My Exps. in Phild. to w[hi]ch place I was*
> *called by Congress, & remained from the*
> *22nd of Dec. to this date* *$1,913*

This must have been urgent business. The General rode from his winter headquarters in Middlebrook, New Jersey, to the nation's quondam capital at Philadelphia in a single day. Congress, which had rushed back to the City of Brotherly Love immediately after the British left without a fight earlier in the year, wanted to discuss the General's secret plans for a 1779 campaign. Martha Washington was a familiar face in the greeting committee. The couple took up residence at Henry Laurens's house. In the debates on the Conway Cabal the year before, Laurens had been Washington's cheerleader. The President of Congress at the time, Laurens denounced the conspirators as "prompters and actors, accomodators, Candle snuffers, Shifters of scenes and mutes."* Those were fighting words in 1778. The South Carolinian must have charged the Washingtons a stiff rent.

Philadelphia was founded by William Penn in 1682 as "His Holy Experiment." A master of the soft-sell, Penn promoted his new town in brochures he circulated in many languages across Europe with modest claims rather than over-statement. Its major attraction: it would be a plain place. The checkerboard city plan was the model of simplicity. To the Lancaster farmers who halted their Conestoga wagons to gawk at Christ Church downtown, however, Philadelphia in the mid-eighteenth century must have seemed the quintessence of beauty and costliness. By the 1760s it was the fastest growing city in America. Visitors still thought of the Bible when they came to

---

* Edmund Cody Burnett, *The Continental Congress*, p. 280.

Philadelphia. It was Gomorrah, with class. The pleasure capital of
the colonies was indolent in its leisure. The wealthy played cards
with great decorum. In the drawing rooms, crystal bowls of rum and
punch stood all day long awaiting any casual caller. The great ladies
flirted by means of fans and handkerchiefs. On walks through the
streets, they were followed by black slave boys of all ages carrying
toilet cases, bon-bon boxes and an extra wrap. Inside Philadelphia
houses, the rooms were lined with damask and pictures of the Fall
of Troy, the candlelight being reflected from the multitude of
mirrors and falling on white powdered heads bent in kissing obei-
sance over ladies' delicate hands.

The city had lost some of its plainness during the British occupation, but not much. There were petty alarms and minor shortages,
but the British troops were masters at muddling through. The
townspeople had made their peace with the conquerors.

"You can have no idea of the life of continued amusement I live
in," wrote Rebecca Franks, a Loyalist, to Mrs. William Paca, the
wife of a congressman exiled to the country. "I can scarce have a
moment to myself . . . and most elegently am I dressed for a ball
this evening at Smith's where we have one every Thursday . . . No
loss for partners, even I am engaged to seven different gentlemen,
for you must know 'tis a fixed rule never to dance but two dances at
a time with the same gentleman. Oh, how I wish Mr. P. would let
you come in for a week or two . . . I know you are as fond of a
gay life as myself. You'd have an opportunity of raking as much as
you choose, either at plays, balls, concerts or assemblies. I've been
but three evenings alone since we moved to town."*

These daughters of the American Revolution may have won the
war in Philadelphia. The rebel's fifth column danced the British
army to death. It is as good an explanation as any for why General
Howe's army never marched the twenty miles to Valley Forge to put
the rebel army out of its misery. There is little doubt that Howe's
troops were weakened by the insatiable taste for high living developed in Philadelphia. General Howe himself was often reported
to be "snoring with Mrs. Loring," his mistress. The role that capital
cities play in wartime has not been appreciated by military experts.
One wonders how long the war in Vietnam would continue if not for
the existence of Saigon, a city to which officers and government
officials on an expense account are not allowed to bring their
dependents.

General Washington was sickened by the way the Philadelphians
were conducting themselves even during this second visit. "If I was
to be called upon to draw a picture of the times and of the men,
from what I have seen, heard and in part know, I should in one
word say that idleness, dissipation and extravagance seem to have

* Rebecca Franks to Mrs. William Paca, Feb. 26, 1778, *Pennsylvania Magazine of History,* XVI (1892), pp. 216–17.

laid fast hold of most of them. That speculation, peculation and an insatiable thirst for riches seems to have gotten the better of every other consideration." He decided to stay for two months anyway.

Shortly after the British left town, and shortly before Washington marched in, Congress had resumed sitting in the capital. By day the General mended his fences in Congress. By night he helped brace the populace's sagging morale by dancing. One of his favorite dancing partners, Mrs. Bache, wrote to her father, *the* Dr. Franklin: "We danced at Mrs. Powell's [Powel] your birthday, or night I should say, in company together, and he told me it was the anniversary of his marriage . . . It was just 20 years that night." It must have been a scene right out of "Stage Door Canteen" with the wearied soldier pouring out his heart to a USO girl.

The General also saw a lot of his old friend, Benjamin Harrison. John Adams called the man who was the father of one President and the great-grandfather of another, "another Sir John Falstaff . . . his conversation disgusting to any man of delicacy or decorum." (Adams, *Works,* III, p. 35.) But Harrison's defenders make him sound like a pleasant traveling companion. A lover of good food, he was 6'4" tall and weighed 249 pounds. In later years, one biographer said, he tried dieting by "giving up good old Madeira for light French wines." It didn't work. Washington depended on Harrison for an occasional laugh. Not even the floor of Congress was safe from Harrison, a notorious joker of the earthy stag party variety. He disturbed decorum in 1775 when John Hancock was elected President of Congress by picking up the Massachusetts man's staid body in his arms and depositing him in the presiding officer's chair.

The vouchers accompanying this second junket to Philadelphia do not specify who recommended the washerwoman Washington hired. In the eighteenth century there was an acceptance of the general idea that any gentleman, as a matter of course, entertained himself, when occasion offered, with washerwomen or their daughters. Such a notion is English enough if one reads the memoirs of the times. But Washington, I think, idealized women. Psychiatrists will tell you that one of the well-known traits of highly masculine men is to put women on a pedestal. Washington was intensely masculine.

A ladies' man like Benjamin Franklin would stoop to kissing washerwomen or their daughters. "He was a firm believer in chastity and moderation," Woodward says, "but he was not a fanatic. Like Samuel Butler, he believed that vice has a purpose, and that its true function is to keep virtue within reasonable bounds. During the year his illegitimate son was born Franklin was deeply absorbed in a plan which he had conceived of writing a literary work to be called *The Art of Virtue.*" (*Washington,* p. 149.) In a series of one-liners for which he was to become famous in *Poor Richard's Almanac,* Franklin planned to indicate how virtue might be acquired—the way to be frugal, chaste, temperate. "But the plan was never carried out, though he fumbled with it for years," according to Woodward. The "sly old rogue" never was accepted by the better people of Philadelphia because of the lewd company he kept. Washington was Main Line.

1779 — February 15

No 50

To 50 Guineas sent Genl. McDougall at West
Point by Mr. Lawrence Esqr. for Secret
Services $1,820

March 3

No 51

To 150 Ditto—Sent Do. at Do. by Col.
Malcolm $5,460

March 15

No 52

To Maj. Gibbs. Money rec[eive]d by him of
Mr. Mitchell Esqr. D[eputy] Q[uartermaster]
Gen [era]l in Phila. to purchase Neccesaries
for the use of the Family $500

March 27

No 53

To Ditto . . . Hd. Exps. $2,000

April 29

No 54

Ditto . . . Ditto $2,000

The shopping bills for the junket to Philadelphia are covered in item No. 52, written by the General at his new field headquarters in Middlebrook, New Jersey. This establishes the basic principle: *Buy now; pay later.* That Washington's Birthday sales have become such an important part of department store merchandising strategies today is understandable.

When the General returned to the banks of the Raritan he found a gay social life that must have reminded him of Philadelphia. Although he had criticized dissipation in public, he hesitated about suppressing it in his midst. Some historians say he even encouraged it, a reversal which could be explained by the old double standard: *If you can't beat them, join them.* The social lion at Middlebrook was the artillery man Henry Knox, who presided with his equally rotund wife (the former Lucy Flucker) at the Jacobus de Veer House near Pluckemin, New Jersey. Here Knox and his gunner's mate were hosts at a grand celebration of the French Alliance. General Washington opened the ball with Lucy Knox. "Everybody allowed it to be the first of the kind ever exhibited in this state at least," the proud husband wrote. "We had about seventy ladies, all of the first *ton* in the state, and between three and four hundred gentlemen. We danced all night—an elegant room. The illuminating fireworks, etc. were more than pretty. . . ."*

In March, General Greene wrote to Jeremiah Wadsworth, "We had a little dance at my quarters a few evenings past. His Excellency and Mrs. Greene danced upwards of three hours without sitting down. Upon the whole, we had a pretty little frisk."†

After one of these "frisks," General Greene was rushed off to the front so quickly he didn't have time to say goodbye to Mrs. Greene. But the vivacious, dark-eyed Catherine Greene continued to draw admirers in swarms. The Greenes' temporary residence in the old Derrick van Veghten farmhouse was always bright with laughter.

The winter was the mildest of the war, but still the troops on the payroll complained. "We have been without bread or rice more than five days out of seven for these three weeks past," wrote Maj. Ebenezer Huntington," and the prospect remains as fair as it hath been."

1779 — June [?]

No 55

> *To Expences in going from the Cantonm[en]t*
> *at Middlebrook in the Jerseys to New*
> *Windsor & to West Point—preceeding the*
> *Army upon Gen. Clinton's Movem[en]t up*
> *the No[rth] River to Verplanks Point* $1,400

June 3

No 56

> *To Major Gibbs* . . . *Hd. Exps.* $2,000

---

* Drake, *Life and Correspondence of Henry Knox,* pp. 60–61.

† Nathanael Greene to Jeremiah Wadsworth, March 19, 1779, *Magazine of American History,* XX (Sept. 1888), p. 247.

July [?]
_____
No 57

To Expences in Recong. the Enemy's Post
at Stony Point previous to the assault of it,
& on a visit to it after it was taken $273

September 12
_____
No 58

To Major Gibbs . . . Hd. Exps. $2,000

October 14
_____
No 59

To 120 Guineas for Majr. Talmadge at
different times to date for the purpose of
Establishing a line of Com[mand] by the
way of Long Island & for defraying the
Expe. thereof with my Spies in New York . . . $4,368

This is not a paragraph by paragraph defense of General Washington's war record. Still I would like to try to explain away the facts that link General Washington's name with the alleged traitor, Benedict Arnold.

While the General was in the saddle riding around the countryside like a guide Michelin, moving his troops about and strengthening his secret service, General Arnold in May 1779 was opening negotiations which were to solve his financial problems. Major Andre, the British purchasing agent, left New York City on his assignment to buy General Arnold on September 20, 1780. It was to be one of the best kept secrets of the war.

Before Arnold sold his country short in the bear market of 1780, General Washington thought highly enough of him to serve as a character witness. As he told Congress in 1777, "[Arnold] has always distinguished himself, as a judicious, brave officer, of great activity, enterprize and perseverance." (Washington, *Writings,* VIII, pp. 47–48.) Arnold had been a militant radical in New Haven before the war and had been elected Captain of the local militia. Within twenty-four hours after hearing the shot fired at Lexington and Concord, he had his company on the road to Cambridge.

A trusted lieutenant of Washington, Arnold had an admirable war record until he became impatient with red tape, military-congressional politics, and his money problems. Mrs. Arnold, the former Peggy Shippen (of the Shippens of Philadelphia), complained bitterly of the hardships and deprivations in having to fight a revolution on a general's salary. The fun-loving, vivacious Peggy yearned for the dances and parties that had enlivened the British occupation before she married Arnold. In some ways General Washington's expense account is the forerunner of the welfare state for the rich. Had the blonde, gray-eyed, 18-year-old Tory socialite known of its existence, she might have urged her husband to notify Congress that he, too, wanted to go on relief.

Arnold went deeply into debt trying to live like General Washington on his salary. He had ridden into Philadelphia in June 1778, a military hero and a social nobody. "A swarthy horse jockey," they called him. As the commander of the occupation forces in Philadelphia, he moved into the mansion vacated by Howe and started practicing social-climbing. He was a miserable second to General Washington in this field of achievement. Eventually he enlisted a housekeeper, coachman, groom, and seven minor servants; he had a fine chariot with a handsome team of four with a livery attendant. His wine cellar was the height of presumption. Still, it convinced the right social people that Arnold was a real comer.

Hard-pressed financially, he dabbled in the usual dubious real-estate schemes, issuing passes to ships in which he later invested, and using government wagons to save his own property from capture. Arnold's moonlighting was not one of the many success stories which highlight this period in American history.

The Council of Pennsylvania preferred charges, and Arnold, on advice of Washington, demanded a court-martial. He was found guilty of two charges, issuing the ship passes and using government wagons. In April 1780, the Commander in Chief accordingly pronounced Arnold's conduct with respect to the passes "peculiarly reprehensible" and with respect to the wagons, "imprudent and improper."*

No matter what misgivings the Pennsylvania Council, Congress's internal security committee, and Washington's closest military advisers had about Arnold's honesty, the General never lost confidence in his associate's basic integrity. It's enough to gave pause to any zealous conservative who is quick to criticize our contemporary leaders for the rotten apple in their barrels.

It is to Washington's everlasting credit that in some way he did not wind up paying for Major Andre's travel expenses.

1779 — November 6

[No 60]

To Major Gibbs . . . Hd. Exps. $3,000

---

* Willard M. Wallace, *Traitorous Hero: The Life and Fortunes of Benedict Arnold,* pp. 169–92.

December 23
<hr/>

[*No 61*]

      Ditto . . . . . . *Ditto* *$3,000*

1780 — January 29
<hr/>

[*No 62*]

      To Major Gibbs . . . *Hd. Exps.* *$3,000*

March 14
<hr/>

[*No 63*]

      Ditto . . . . . . *Ditto* *$3,000*

March 28
<hr/>

[*No 64*]

      Ditto . . . . . *Ditto* *$3,000*

[*No 65 is missing.*]

April 14
<hr/>

No 66

    To Expences of a visit to Elizabeth Town & ye
    Posts on Lines *$298.25*

May 2
<hr/>

No 67

    To Major Gibbs . . . *Hd. Exp.* *$4,000*

May 13
<hr/>

No 68

      Ditto . . . . . . *Do* *$4,800*

June 1
<hr/>

No 69

      Ditto . . . . . . *Do* *$4,300*

June 15
<hr/>

No 70

    To Expenditures while the Army was moving
    ab[*ou*]*t Springfield—& the Enemy about*
    Elizabeth Town *$955.50*

August 20
No 71

> *To Major Gibbs* . . . *Hd. Exps.* $5,000

This collection of items could be called "The Best of Caleb Gibbs."

A small charge of £7 10s. for the expenses of Major Gibbs in going to meet Mrs. Washington and bringing her to Philadelphia, February 14, 1780. An entry of £487 10s. paid to some handymen for cleaning and stoning Mrs. Ford's well. (Mrs. Theodosia Ford was the widow of Jacob Ford, Jr., at whose house the Morristown headquarters was strategically located.) A £75 item for some plastering work done on this house. A dinner for the Commander in Chief and his suite at Springfield costing £21 7s. 6d. on April 7. Nothing worth apologizing for.

"I am in rags," wrote Lt. Col. Ebenezer Huntington, one of the men on the payroll without whom none of this high living would have been possible, "have lain in the rain on the ground for 40 hours past, and only a junk of fresh beef, and that without salt, to dine on this day. Received no pay since last December, and this for my cowardly countrymen who flinch at the very time when their exertions are wanted, and hold their purse strings as though they would damn the world, rather than part with a dollar to their army."

Who promoted Colonel Huntington?

The life of the average government employee at Morristown or Valley Forge could hardly have been considered luxurious or extravagant. Working conditions, nevertheless, took a further turn for the worse before the army broke this camp.

"We were absolutely litterally starved," wrote Private Joseph Martin in his recollections about the days when soldiers were soldiers. "I do solemnly declare that I did not put a single morsel of victuals into my mouth for four days and as many nights, except for a little black birch bark, which I knawed off a stick of wood, if that can be called victuals. I saw several . . . men roast their old shoes and eat them" (Martin, *Narrative,* p. 124). So much for the shortage of shoes.

1780 — August 29
No 72

> *To Col. Graham of the York State Troops—*
> *per Acct.* $313.41

September 2

No 73

> *To Colo. Meade's disbursem[ent]s per account*
> *rendered (including 1505 dollars returned to,*
> *& credited by—Maj. Gibbs in his Acc[ount])* . $10,000

September 11

No 74

> *To Richd. Humphreys's Acct. per Col.*
> *Biddle's [illegible]* $1,112.80

No 75

> *To the Expence of a Reconnoitre as far as*
> *the Town of Bergen—& into the Neck* $331.50

September 27

No 76

> *To Major Gibbs* . . . *Hd. Exps.* $5,000

By this time in the war, Washington's critics were saying that too much attention was being paid to paperwork at headquarters. The rattle of his sword, not the scratch of the pen, was what the Revolution needed. This item for $10,000 shows that he was not insensitive to criticism. It would have taken long hours to list the details; he slashed through to the bone by saying nothing.

More is known about item No. 74. Richard Humphreys, a Philadelphia merchant, sold the family tablespoons and cups. Col. Clement Biddle was the Commissary General of Forage until June 1780, and a friend of Washington to the bitter end.

1780 — September 27

No 77

> *To Col. Meade's Acc. of Expenditures to*
> *Hartford when I went to meet their Excellency*
> *Ch. de Rochambeau & Adm. de Terney—*
> *including 416 D [ollars] ret. to Maj. Gibbs &*
> *credited in his Acc[oun]t* $8,000

[*There is no No. 78.*]

_____

No 79

> *To Specie paid on my journey to Hartford &*
> *back, and during 4 days stay at the place* . . . *$892.66*

These items illustrate the basic principle: *An expense account trip shouldn't be canceled just because there is trouble back at the office.*

On the morning of the 25th of September 1780, General Washington sprang into his saddle and rode off to see for himself how General Arnold was preparing the defenses at West Point against a suspected British sneak attack. General Greene a few months earlier had asked to be relieved of the Quartermaster General's job. Washington had tried to give the plum to Arnold. The shrewd operator, pleading his three wounds, asked for the command of West Point instead.

"My God, this can't be true. This message must mean the Philippines," Secretary of the Navy Frank Knox cried on December 7, 1941. At the most serious failure of Intelligence prior to Pearl Harbor, General Washington reacted with more becoming dignity.

Arnold was out on business the morning the General and his suite arrived for the inspection. By afternoon Washington was disturbed by the absence which was soon explained when Alexander Hamilton handed him the packet of papers found in Andre's boot. The General shuffled the papers, according to people who were there, was "appalled, but not for a moment did he lose his accustomed composure." The rat had left the sinking ship. Quietly Washington ordered Hamilton and McHenry to spur after Arnold, and then sat down to dinner without a word to anyone about his disappearance.

As he rode to Newport and Hartford for business conferences with the French high command, and for months to come, Washington must have gone over and over again in his mind Arnold's betrayal. Where had he gone wrong in judging this rascal? Should he have known how vulnerable Arnold was, a man who would do anything for money? Such "enterprize"! Such a "surprizingly" poor value structure! His mind must have been on tobacco prices not to have seen through him.

Meanwhile, back at the fort, the army could talk of nothing else. The General Orders for the morning of September 26, written by General Greene, broke the news of the foul plot to the starving rebels:

> *Treason* of the blackest dye was yesterday discovered! General Arnold, who commanded at West Point, lost to every sentiment of honor, of public and private obligation, was about to deliver up that important post into the hands of the enemy. Such an event must have given the American cause a deadly wound, if not a fatal stab . . .

Great honor is due to the American army that this is the first instance of treason of the kind when many were to be expected from the nature of the dispute. And nothing is so bright an ornament in the character of the American soldier as their having been proof against all the arts and seduction of an insidious enemy . . .

His Excellency, the Commander in Chief, has arrived at West Point . . . and is no doubt taking the proper measures to unravel fully so hellish a plot.*

Greene certainly sounded black with rage. But he could have predicted that sooner or later a Benedict Arnold would develop in the patriots' ranks. "The common people," he explained of New Englanders, "are exceedingly avaricious; the genius of the people is commercial, from their long intercourse with trade."†

General Arnold, the swine, didn't blame his defection on a desire for easy money or on his weak character. He said he did it for the highest principles. He loved his country too much to see it fall under the French influence. At least that's what he told General Washington afterwards in a letter of apology. Arnold's attacks on the Quai d'Orsay may have later inspired General Washington's warning against foreign entanglements in his farewell address of 1796.

Virtue is supposed to be its own reward. The deal worked out for delivering West Point, however, showed Arnold had a fine business mind. His price had been 10,000 British pounds. Though he failed to deliver his part of the bargain, the British granted him the £6,000 that Major Andre had been empowered to offer before he was captured, plus £315 as expense money.

Like Washington, Arnold had been a businessman before the war. He was in apothecary shops in New Haven. According to the Arnold historian, Willard Wallace, he immediately invested £5,000 of the capital sum with the Court bankers for £7,000 worth of consolidated annuities at 4 percent. "The British likewise rewarded his family," Wallace writes. "In 1782, the King authorized an annual pension of £500 for Peggy. Each of Arnold's children by Peggy—and there were five who survived—received a pension of £100 . . . The crown subsequently awarded the traitor and his family a total of 13,400 acres from among its lands in Canada for American tories." All was not lost for Arnold, save honor.

Benedict Arnold must have secretly admired the British, as so many status-minded businessmen today do. If it was money alone he was after, the American army offered many golden opportunities for advancement. The man who replaced Arnold at West Point, General Greene, was to make a name for himself as a speculator in war materiels. Jeremiah Wadsworth, one in a long line of Com-

* *Writings of Washington,* ed. Fitzpatrick, XX, pp. 95–96.

† Greene to Ward, December 18, 1775; in Greene's *Nathanael Greene,* I, p. 126.

missary Generals short on supplies and ethics, was to be his secret partner. Thievery in the Continental Army was unbelievable, Bolton says. "Eighteen generals quit, many out of pique, some to escape arrest for taking double pay." Officers robbing their troops of pay was commonplace. Washington himself reported that "many of the surgeons are great rascals . . . often receiving bribes to certify indispositions and drawing medicines and stores in the most profuse and extravagant manner for private purposes."

Even Congress showed its support of the free enterprise system. Congressman Samuel Chase of Maryland took advantage of inside information to make a secret purchase of grain for the French fleet. Robert Morris, the Secretary of the Treasury himself, made numerous killings in the black and gray market. The founding fathers were not so much against conflict of interest as they were interested in conflicts.

Still, Washington retained his high moral standards in these expense account pages, regardless of his associates.

Of item No. 78, Fitzpatrick says, "There seem to be no receipts preserved of the expenses of this journey to Hartford."

1780 — October 16

No 80

> *To Cash paid Mr. Jn. Mercereau of*
> *Woodbridge in New Jersey (including 5*
> *guineas to Baker Hendricks) per receipts*
> *for exps. and rewards of himself & others*
> *(whom he was obliged to employ) to open &*
> *carry on a Correspondence with persons within*
> *the Enemy Lines by the way of Staten Island* . . . $7,943

No 81

> *To Ditto paid Majr. Talmadge towards the*
> *Expences of the Communication with New*
> *York by the way of Long Island* $1,456

In line with Washington's previously expressed desires, I have refrained from naming names in these items about informers. I can assure you, however, that I have papers in my possession indicating the prevailing market prices for the sale of souls during this period. A.R. went for four guineas a month. P.R. for six guineas a month. J.C. for seven guineas. Why go on? Suffice it to say that the list of names would compare favorably, if not identically, with the roster of the New Jersey and New York state chapters of the Daughters of the American Revolution. For some of the finest American families, fortunes were based on acts that the British public considered as treasonous as we found Benedict Arnold's. More interesting is the rise of technology in the spying profession underwritten by Washington in these shady items.

When Washington began dabbling in espionage, during the siege of Boston, the rebel Central Intelligence Agency had trouble getting daily intelligence reports. Colonel Loammi Baldwin (possibly another cover name), Freeman says, "had no glass worth focusing on the enemy. When one or other of the express horses at Chelsea was lame for lack of shoes, or was used to carry a man to get medicine from Cambridge, the dispatch of intelligence reports was rendered uncertain or was suspended altogether for the day."* Back Bay could have been our first Bay of Pigs.

By 1780, the rebels were into aliases. John Bolton was really Major James Tallmadge of the 2nd Continental Dragoons, and had been the director of secret services since 1779. One of the men on his mailing list was Sir James Jay, a brother of John Jay and an eminent scientist, who gave Washington a new secret formula for a super invisible ink. A message could be brought out only by painting the communication with a "counterpart" or reacting mixture. Many of the reports paid for in these accounts were written between the lines of ordinary letters in ordinary ink. A variation on this scheme was the sending of blank sheets, or sheets preceded by an inconsequential communication.

The research and development program under Washington still wasn't advanced enough to detect secret messages between members of the expense account crowd. This is one classic example of great writing between the lines, reported in Commager and Morris's *Spirit of Seventy-Six:*

Morristown, 11th of April 1780
. . . How stands our 298.37 with B.D.? Let me know as particularly as you can. Send the information in one letter and what you say upon it in another.

Yours
You Know Who

In breaking the code, we find that "298.37" stands for a company affair in the business partnership of Col. Jeremiah Wadsworth with "B.D." (Barnabas Dean) and "You Know Who" (Gen. Nathanael Greene).

As the General explained to the Colonel in requesting secrecy, "While we continue in the offices which we hold, I think it is prudent to appear as little in trade as possible. For however just and upright our conduct may be, the world will have suspicions to our

* *George Washington,* IV, p. 516.

disadvantage. By keeping the affair a secret I am confident we shall have it more in our power to serve the commercial connection than by publishing it. I have wrote to my brother Jacob Greene to pay you £5000 without informing him for what purpose or on what account."*

Now, of course, it is publish or perish.

1780 — October 10

No 82

To Col. Lewis—the Caughnawaga Indian—a
Pres[ent]. $62.40

Congress's policy of giving the Indians a few trinkets did not win the west for the patriots (see item No. 125). There are many examples of braves who fought gallantly for the stars and stripes, and their descendants are entitled to membership in organizations like the Daughters of the American Revolution. Mostly the hard-drinking, thieving, greedy Indians went to the highest bidder.

The Indians who took up the hatchet for the Bank of England often fought harder than the Hessians, although they didn't follow orders as well. The massacres at Wyoming Valley, Pennsylvania, and Cherry Valley, New York, occurred when the braves of the Six Nations ignored their British commander's instructions to take prisoners. They embarrassed the Foreign Office in London and enraged public opinion much the way our policy of bombing villages in Vietnam does today.

At about this time in the expense account General Washington issued orders to Gen. John Sullivan, then in Providence, to deal with the Indian problem. He wanted "the Six Nations not to be merely overrun, but destroyed." Sullivan's campaign on the Chemung River (near the present city of Elmira, New York) accomplished much. His soldiers burned more than 40 villages, 20,000 acres of corn and fruit trees, and killed thousands.

After a skirmish at the Indian village of Newtown, a Lt. William Barton of the First New Jersey Regiment led a small party to find some dead Indians. "Towards noon they found them," wrote the lieutenant in his *Journal,* "and skinned two of them from their hips down for boot legs, one pair for the major [Piatt], the other for myself."

Lt. Thomas Boyd of Morgan's Riflemen served on the search and destroy mission. While his men were disputing the possession of the

* Greene, "Letters," *Pennsylvania Magazine of History and Biography,* XXII, pp. 211–16.

scalp of an Indian they had slain, they were ambushed and 22 of them were killed by His Majesty's Indians. A rescue party discovered examples of the local arts and crafts program:

On entering the town we found the body of Lt. Boyd and another rifleman [wrote Lt. Erkuries Beatty in his journal]. They was both stripped naked and their heads cut off, and the flesh of Lt. Boyd's head was entirely taken off and his eyes punched out. The other man's head was not there. They was stabbed, I suppose, in forty different places in the body with a spear and great gashes cut in their flesh with knives, and Lt. Boyd's privates was nearly cut off and hanging down. His finger and toe nails was bruised off, and the dogs had eat part of their shoulders away. Likewise a knife was sticking in Lt. Boyd's body. They was immediately buried with the honor of war.*

There were hard feelings on both sides.

The money General Washington spent on Colonel Lewis, the chief of a New York tribe, had to be a wise investment. However, it could be argued that since the Caughnawaga was a close friend of Maj. Gen. Philip Schuyler, he was a "white" Indian, and that it would have been better to wine and dine one of the hostiles who were not already in our pay.

1780 — November [?]

No 83

> *To the Expenditures on a journey (after the Army left the field for Winter Quarters) to Morristown—Fleming Town—Hackets Town—New Germ[a]n Town—[illegible] House &c. to the Cantonment at New Windsors—Per Memomd.* $2,670.20

November 15

No 84

> *To Major Gibbs* . . . *Hd. Exp.* . . . . $1,000 *Received from Col. Pickering*

No 85

> *To Tayler's Acct. for my Servants* $745

If the patriot army's Criminal Investigation Division had taken a poll of the troops during this sixth winter of the war on who their

---

* Beatty, "Journal," New York Secretary of State, *Journals of the Military Expedition of Major General John Sullivan,* p. 32.

military heroes were, my guess is that the British general Howe would have finished first, with General Clinton a close second. The basic trouble with the common rebel soldier was that he had an insatiable taste for high living. Fortunately, they had received their basic training at Valley Forge in '77 and a refresher course at Morristown in '79 to toughen them up for the winter of '80.

The General worked through channels to better the situation. There are hundreds of letters to Congress attesting to his concern. While he and his writing aides flooded the mails in the warmth of some widow or other's house, he was also cognizant that his men were beginning to act like animals. Nothing could restrain them from foraging; they were eating anything that wasn't nailed down. A modern expense account writer who works near a buffet in a cocktail lounge knows how difficult it is to resist getting something for nothing. Especially when under tension, there is a tendency to run for food when the going is at its roughest. Washington knew hunger himself: in the French and Indian War he had starved with the best of them. But the General couldn't relax discipline now.

A militiaman named Jesse Pierce tried to take a no-expenses-paid trip home and was sentenced to run the gauntlet. Usually the brigade was drawn up in two lines to form a narrow line, sometimes a half mile long, through which the culprit ran naked to receive lashings from switches held by his comrades. If he was unpopular, he really got it from the fellows; if he was liked and was fast on his feet, he suffered little. A number of improvements on this crime preventive were introduced by reformers in the patriot camp. A soldier was ordered to point his bayonet at the guilty man's breast, then back slowly through the lines so that progress could not be too rapid for adequate punishment.

Historians do not say which gauntlet Jesse Pierce had to run. But the second half of the sentence must have really hurt: "to be confined in the dungeon for one month on bread and water." Fattened up, the deserter would have trouble adapting to his environment a month later.

Some may think the General thought up these punishments out of frustration. Congress had limited him (in November 1775) to degrading, cashiering, drumming out of the army, whipping not to exceed thirty-nine lashes, fines not to exceed two months' pay of the offender, and imprisonment not exceeding one month. In September 1776 the Articles of War were amended to allow 100 lashes. None of these remedies was able to eliminate crime in the streets of the army camp.

"However strange it may appear," wrote Dr. Thatcher, an army surgeon who was often on emergency duty at the whipping post, "a soldier will often receive the severest stripes without uttering a groan or once shrieking from the lash, even while the blood flows freely from his lacerated wounds. This must be ascribed to stubbornness or pride. They have, however, adopted a method which they say mitigates the anguish in some measure. It is by putting between the teeth a leaden bullet, on which they chew while under the lash, till it is made quite flat and jagged. In some instances of incorrigible villains, it is adjudged by the court that the culprit receive his punishment at several different times, a certain number of stripes repeated at intervals of two or three days, in which case the wounds are in a state of inflammation and the skin rendered more sensibly tender, and the terror of the punishment is greatly aggravated."*

For the crime of robbery, it was the gallows or the firing squad. Washington couldn't use the death sentence as much as it was needed. He would have had to fight the war alone.

Ebenezer Wild, in his Revolutionary War journal, refers to a variation which kept the army in a state of suspense. The doomed men were marched to the place of execution to the strains of the "Dead March," each one with his coffin borne before him. The brigade was then paraded, with the guilty men in front where they could be seen by all. The death sentence was read in a loud voice. Their graves were dug. The coffin lay beside them, and each man was commanded to kneel beside his future resting place in mother earth while the executors received their orders to load, take aim and—

Bolton says, in *Private Under Washington* (p. 173), that at this critical moment a messenger appeared with a reprieve which was read aloud. "This last all important act in the series was omitted often enough to strain the nerves of everyone present by leaving the result in doubt until the last instant."

A good hanging or shooting has always been high in the entertainment values of America; the demise of capital punishment in public has forced thrill-seekers to turn to sex, drugs, and business. Ebenezer Wild and his fellow patriots refer frequently in their diaries to punishments, and, as Bolton says, it is obvious that they interested him by their variety and terrible reality. It was either that at Morristown or listening to the sounds of dancing in the expense account crowd's quarters. Girls who were rugged enough to get through the mountainous snowdrifts, a historian wrote, were energetic enough to wring from Capt. Samuel Shaw a groan: "three nights going till after two o'clock have they made us keep it up." Shaw, who later became the first secretary-general of the veterans organization, the Society of the Cincinnati, was one of the 34 officers in the military elite, or dancing assembly, which met at Colonel Biddle's house.

One of the rumors that made the rounds at the enlisted men's smoking camp fires was that Washington, who as we have already

* James Thatcher, *A Military Journal during the American Revolutionary War,* 2nd ed. (Boston, 1827) p. 183.

seen loved to dance, fought a brisk skirmish with a Mrs. George Olney. "If he did not let go her hand," the story went, "she would tear out his eyes, or the hair from his head; and that though he was a general, he was but a man." In expense account lore, this ranks with the Samson and Delilah story of the Bible.

These items constitute Caleb Gibbs's farewell address to the expense account field. If we need further evidence of his achievements in the face of adversity, there is a note in the *Journals of the Continental Congress* about financial conditions during the winters of 1778 to 1780. "The Army was in such extremity for want of provisions that the Commander-in-Chief was reduced to the sad alternative either to suffer it, to disband, or to collect supplies by military force."*

General Washington must have been the only man in the army paying his way during these grim months.

1781 — February [?]

No 86

To Lieut. Colfax—Bal[anc]e of 9260 Dollr.
Rec[eive]d on a Warrant & retained in his
*hands** $3,260*

---

* This, and all the Sums which will be found charged to Lieut. Colfax in these accounts are credited on his accounts, which are herewith rendered as vouchers.—[G. W.'s note]

William Colfax enlisted as a private in the 13th Continental Infantry in May 1775. He was honorably discharged several times during the war, always re-enlisting at a higher rank. From 1781 on, he served as general superintendant at Headquarters and Washington's cashier. Lieutenant Colfax was wounded at White Plains and Yorktown and was said to have fought valiantly on the battlefield. Despite the General's standard disclaimer (see asterisk, item No. 86), Colfax did not distinguish himself in the field of expense account writing in any way.

1781 — March [?]

No 87

To the Expenditures on a journey to Rhode
Island on a Visit to the French Army—per
Colo. Tilghman $19,848½

* *Journals of the Continental Congress,* XIII, pp. 275–79; XIX, p. 410.

No 88

*To Specie Expenditures in this journey—per
my Memm. B[oo]k—where Paper [remainder
illegible]* *$1,768*

Possibly on the theory that misery doesn't love company, General
Washington left for the shore on March 2. Historians say this was
probably the most important trip the General made, since it was at
Newport that he, the Comte de Rochambeau, and Chevalier Des-
touches began discussing the strategy for finally ending the war. In
expense account writing, above items No. 87 and No. 88 are important because they set an all-time army record for spending. They
also end doubts that these traveling expenses may have been for the
whole army.

As we have already seen, the army was resting as comfortably as
could be expected in its winter cantonment. The General's party on
this trip included the French boy, Major General Marquis de
Lafayette, who had been on the expense account from time to time
since Washington first met him at a dinner on July 31, 1777 in
Philadelphia. Washington was so drawn to the smiling 19-year-old
nobleman, he immediately invited him to join his inner circle.
Lafayette was the equivalent of the fair-haired boy who becomes the
boss's right-hand man in business today. The Marquis was one of
the few foreign military adventurers who was a credit to his profession. He was invaluable on the trip to Newport, with his command
of the French language. From all reports, the General sat silently at
these conferences, looking from face to face.

At the conference a year earlier (see items No. 77, No. 79)
nothing had been decided. The General, however, did get to see, if
not talk to, Count Fersen, an aide to de Rochambeau, later famous
as the reputed lover of Marie Antoinette, the cake lady. General
Washington made such a good impression on the French military
that on his birthday, in 1781, they declared a holiday for the French
troops. It might have been just French politeness. Whatever the
reason, this was probably the first public celebration of Washington's Birthday. (The American troops worked on February 22.)

Much to Washington's vexation, this was the only military action
the French took the first year. Lying idle in Newport, the French
armed forces hadn't helped the Revolution appreciably, but they did
help Newport. The Rhode Island city had been a center of the
African slave trade before the war, and now it was also a cultural
center. It was here that General Washington learned about the
cocktail (from the ancient French word *coquetel*), ice cream, and
brass bands, the three major contributions the French made to
American civilization. French bread, a staple of the modern expense
account writers' diet, caught on only in fancy restaurants. ˴

When the French troops first landed, they were feared by the pious Newporters who worked the slave trade in the name of God. The French were wicked people with popish tongues who would fling their Protestant enemies into dungeons or burn them alive. But the locals saw that the French were also interested in curling their hair and painting their faces. In a few weeks Newport fell in love with the French, or at least their gold. People wore French colors; young laides practiced their French on the officers; everybody who had a spare room rented it; everybody who had a horse could sell it at a high price. "The only thing that Newport did not like about the French Army," a historian said, "was its size; if it had been twice as large it would have given the town more joy."

In light of the high prices, another man would have cut the talks short. Washington, however, stayed more than two weeks. Once again he demonstrated his determination to live the expense account life to the hilt.

We don't know which *coquetel* lounges he favored or how much ice cream was consumed (was he a chocolate man?). "The detailed expense account of this journey cannot be given," Fitzpatrick says, "as it was entered in Washington's Memorandum Book of Expenses, which is missing from the Washington Papers."

On March 20, he was back at New Windsor, Connecticut, ready to deal with a new army problem: mutiny. There had been a minor protest demonstration at Morristown in May 1780 by two avaricious Connecticut regiments on the pay issue. Nothing was trifling when it came to money, but the situation Washington faced now was far more serious. By 1781, virtually all of the idealistic hippie kids and young family men had left the army, their enlistments ended, or deserted (often with the excuse they had wives and little ones at home without firewood). The patriot army now was largely a professional army, like the Hessians in the sense that they worked for the state paying the highest bounty and expected their pay.

The Pennsylvania line was the first to revolt against management in January 1781. Joseph Reed, the President of Pennsylvania then, ended the mutiny by giving in to most of militants' demands. General Washington had been out of town. When the New Jersey line tried mutiny a few weeks later, Washington was as firm as a slaveowner.

"The fatal tendency of that spirit which has shown itself in the Pennsylvania and Jersey lines, and which derived so much encouragement from impunity in the case of the former determined me at all events to pursue a different conduct with respect to the latter," General Washington reported to the Commission for Redressing the Grievances of the New Jersey Line on January 27, 1781. "For this purpose I detached a body of troops under Major Genl. Howe with orders to compel the mutineers to unconditional submission and execute on the spot a few of the principal incendiaries. This has been effected this morning; and we have reason to believe the mutinous disposition of the troops is now completely subdued and succeeded by a genuine penitence."

The General wasn't what we would call an easygoing boss, but he was always open to employees' suggestions. "Whenever a complaint has been made to me," he closed his report to the commissioners, "I have invariably directed an inquiry, for I have considered it as not less impolitic than unjust in our service to use fraud in engaging or retraining men; but as I mentioned above the complaint has much oftener been found to originate in the levity of the soldier than in truth."*

1781 — May [?]

No 89

To the Expence of a journey to Weathersfield for the purpose of an Interview with the French gen[era]l and adm[ira]l—see Colonel Tilghman's account as above $8,376½

No 90

To Specie expended on this trip $933.40

This was the interview at which the final plans were drawn up to end the war.

Some of the General's critics may feel that the length of the campaign is a reflection on Washington's abilities as an executive. It had taken him six years to finish a job he estimated would take a few months. My theory is that General Washington was a fast worker; it would have taken the British generals twice as long to end the war.

In any reappraisal of why we won the war, credit must be given to the weakness of General Washington's opponents. The British War Office's blunders were much more impressive than ours. At the time, Britain also was fighting another more important war—in India. They were preoccupied, too, with keeping Ireland down. The Revolutionary War to the English was just a police action. Traditionally, the British people loved wars, but this one was very unpopular. A great debate raged in Parliament and in the universities about its wisdom.

On one side was a group we can call *Lambs*. They wanted to bring the boys home from America by Christmas, 1776, as the war minister, Lord George Germaine, had promised. The Lambs considered a land war in America madness. William Pitt, one of the

* *Writings of Washington*, ed. Fitzpatrick, XXI, pp. 147–48.

more outspoken Lambs in Parliament, said, "Get Out of Boston." Oxford and Cambridge students said they didn't want to fight in the jungles of Massachusetts. The poet Roger wore black till his death, mourning the Americans killed at Lexington and Concord. Recruiting for the American regiments went badly. Troops refused to go to Boston in the early days of the war. Vice Admiral Keppel of the Fleet refused to go. Lord Effingham resigned his commission when he discovered that his regiment was on orders for America. King George himself called on Sir Jeffrey Amherst to volunteer and offered him a peerage. Amherst refused to serve against the Americans.

That's why King George had to hire mercenaries. His first thought had been Catherine the Great's troops. By balking, the czarina indirectly must be a true daughter of the American Revolution; one shudders to think what those Cossacks would have done at Valley Forge.

The Lambs argued eloquently in Parliament. There was Mr. Pitt, Colonel Barre, Lord Camden. Edmund Burke made a five-hour anti-war speech. Adam Smith, the economist, was against the war because of the high cost. A new bridge was needed in London. The country needed a new set of national priorities.

Every year the British budget was strained by the war. Aside from the living costs of the troops the British War Office also had to pay the costs of dying. For every Hessian killed in America, the Landgrave of Hesse-Cassel received $55; for the wounded, $12. Presumably these bounties were to indemnify the Hessian leader for loss of service. As we are seeing with General Washington's expense account, these minor costs add up. The Landgrave closed his accounts at the end of the war with 8,000 dead, or roughly $440,000 in the Bank of England (without counting the spare change he picked up from the maimed on every casualty list, and the accrued interest for eight years).

The Lambs were opposed in Parliament by another group we can call the *Lions*. They believed the war could be won more quickly by escalation. It was the Lions in the House of Commons who suggested arresting the entire Massachusetts legislature and bringing them to England for a treason trial.

The Lions argued that England's honor was at stake in winning the war. The British Way of Life was threatened. Dominos were played in coffee houses in London, and the undersecretaries in the government were afraid that if England let the thirteen revolting colonies get away with it, a domino effect would take place in the British Empire. As Massachusetts (including Maine) went, so went Nova Scotia, Newfoundland, Canada, Bermuda, the Bahamas, Ireland, and eventually India.

Besides, the real enemy was another foreign power: France. America didn't mean anything to King George, compared to France.

He feared that France would infiltrate the colonies from Canada, then seize control of all North America. Even before the Alliance, the French were, at first, covertly and later openly, supplying the Americans with guns and ammunition on what could be called the Louis XIV Trail.

The Lions felt that the way to win the war in America was to send in more and more troops. First the War Office assured the Lambs in Parliament that 3,000 new troops were enough to pacify the countryside. Then 10,000. Then 20,000. And so forth. The Lions demanded the defoliation of the forests of Massachusetts and the destruction of Boston by cannon, in the mistaken belief that the Bay State Colony was the root of all un-English sentiment in America.

Ruling the waves, the British could land troops anywhere along the coast. But the Continental Army would disappear into the jungles. Sometimes the guerrillas were led by Insurgent General Washington. Sometimes he followed them, as in the retreats at Long Island, Harlem Heights, and Brandywine. Few Americans were ever taken prisoner. They moved too quickly. The British were always complaining about how hard it was to fight the guerrillas. They never knew when they were beaten. After fleeing they reformed in the woods and fought again, again, and again.

The most angry and militant Lion of them all was King George the Mad. He had two mental breakdowns—one during the Stamp Act crisis and the other when he learned that General Howe had called a Christmas Truce while the rebels were iced in and prussianized at Valley Forge in 1777. General Howe, who must have been a Lamb sympathizer, as we have already seen was too busy fraternizing with the natives in Philadelphia to run the sword through the miserable insurgents that winter.

There is some dispute amongst historians whether George was really mentally disturbed or just upset by politics. Recently one medical historian—without benefit of urine or blood samples—suggested that his strange actions were caused by a rare kidney disease. Others feel that the fact that King George had to be restrained from violating the women in his court, and wound up in a straight jacket after his ministers broached the idea of peace talks with the rebels, was a sign of some kind of abnormal mental condition. George the Mad was in favor of holding peace talks, but first he wanted to beat the guerrillas, or "bandits" as he called them, on the battlefield.

The strategy for Yorktown, which was to be England's Dienbienphu, was one of three alternatives hammered out at Weathersfield, Connecticut, by General Washington and our French allies during this appropriately costly interview. When he returned to New Windsor on May 25, he was under the impression that the joint attack was to take place against New York City.

1781 — August [?]

No 91

    To Secret Services **$3,796**

No 92

    To Cash advan[ce]d Cap. Dobbs & other
    Pilots, to carry them to Monmouth Cty.
    to await the arrival of the French Fleet,
    hourly expected **$485.33**

August 25

No 93

    To Cash paid Mrs. Thompson the
    Housekeeper, in part of her wages, viz—
    25 Guineas **$910**

Washington's intelligence during the war was meager, as item No. 92 suggests. Captain William Dobbs of Fishkill, New York, a sea captain and pilot; Daniel Shaw, Patrick Denis, and Abraham H. Martlings of Peekskill; and William Redfield of Connecticut were rounded up and sent to wait at "Baskingridge," New Jersey, for the expected French fleet under Comte de Grasse. Basking Ridge is about forty miles inland on my map, so the wait for the fleet would certainly have been a long one. It wasn't until the latter part of August that Washington guessed Chesapeake Bay, not New York Bay, was the intended French target. In business today, we call this a breakdown in communications. Money, Washington was to learn about the espionage business, can't buy everything.

"Where thousands of Loyalists were prepared to tell what they knew, why hire spies?" asks my old history professor Richard B. Morris in *The Spirit of Seventy-Six.* "Where tens of thousands of Americans were prepared to inform on the invaders, why build up an espionage system? Almost the only place where espionage was important was Europe; and London and Paris swarmed with spies and informers in the best cloak-and-dagger tradition."

I bow to the professor's superior wisdom on this point. My only suggestion is that, like most executives, Washington felt insecure and this spying apparatus was something of a security blanket.

1781 — August 28

No 94

    To Expenditures on my March from ye
    White Plains, or Dobbs's Ferry by ye way of
    Kings ferry to Brunswick inclusive **$1,007.50**

No 95

*To Washing & other sm[al]l Accounts at
Philadelphia* *$169*

The Continental Liberation Front was around Philadelphia now, waiting to spring the trap at Yorktown, which would need a miracle to pull off. The patriots and the French fleet were to arrive roughly the same week. The French do not have a reputation for making their ships run on time. Despite his anxieties and concern General Washington found time to stop off for some washing (see item No. 95, above).

By the summer of 1781, Philadelphia had felt the impact of the French Alliance. "War which keeps the spirits in motion has diffused a taste for gayety and dissipation," an English diplomat marooned there in 1780 reported. "The French Resident at Philadelphia gives a rout twice a week to the ladies of that city, amongst whom French hair dressers, milliners and dances are all the *ton*. The Virginia jig has given place to the cotillion, and minuet-de-la-cour."

As this is the last direct mention of washing in these accounts, I would like to submit my last piece of evidence that they do not conceal hank-panky. I have not read of a single birth announcement after General Washington had his clothes washed in any of the many places he slept at these eight years. Many children were named "George Washington" after the war, but these were mostly black children and couldn't have been connected with Washington in any way. Of course some historians claim he was sterile, from an attack of the mumps during his childhood, so this isn't much of a defense. It also weakens the childless Washington's right to be called the father of the country. If anybody deserved this honor it is Conrad Castor of Brock's Gap, Virginia, a soldier in the Revolutionary Army who was the father of 27. Of the political figures, Patrick Henry had twenty children. No one can argue, however, that General Washington wasn't a founding father figure in the eyes of the nation's women during his stay in Philadelphia.

He arrived on August 30, and went south for the battle on September 5.

One of the transactions between the lines of these items involved two of the General's associates. Tom Paine at this time was the guardian of Washington's reputation, an unpaid post. Robert Morris was the most powerful financier of the day, known as "The Man." A few days after Washington rode off to catch up with the troops, The Man summoned the pamphleteer Paine and proposed that "for the service of the country he should write and publish such Pieces respecting the propriety, necessity, and Utility of Taxation as might be likely to promote the Public Service of America as the war does and ultimately must rest on the Taxes to be raised in the U.S." Morris's diary does not mention whether Paine accepted money in advance of publication of this idea, which makes common sense today but was controversial in 1781. (Taxation was one of the issues the war was being fought over; the people were against it.) He didn't write it, that's for sure.

"In consequence of the information received from Mr. Thomas Paine of the intention of some Officers to promote a General Application by way of a Memorial to His Excellency General Washington respecting their Pay," Morris wrote in his diary for January 26, 1782, "I sent for Him and had a long Conversation on the various matters of a Public Nature; he observed that his service to the Public had Rather been neglected. I told him that I could wish his pen to be wielded in aid of such measures as I might be able to convince him were clearly calculated for the Service of the U.S., that I had no views but what were meant for the Public Good and that I should ask no man's assistance on any other ground; that it was true I had nothing in my power to offer in compensation for his Services but that Something might turn up and that I should have him in mind."

After the trap was sprung at Yorktown, the badly beaten and starved Americans had turned their attention to collecting their pay. Morris was trying to call the idealist Paine's attention to the fact that there was something in it for him if he would turn down the soldiers' request for his writing services. The power of his pen was widely known and appreciated and, like an honest businessman, Paine had told Morris of a previous offer.

Paine had violently and persistently attacked Morris on his most vulnerable points, fidelity to the trust. Acting on secret information given him by Arthur Lee, Paine had written that Morris was sometimes not able to put the public interest above his own personal interest. Yet Morris had the gall to try to buy Paine off at a time when he had nothing to pay. Paine wrote the Memorial for the soldiers, not for their Commander in Chief. But he later went to work for The Man. During the struggle over ratification of the Constitution in 1787 to 1788, Morris hired him to write a number of pro-Constitution pamphlets, even though he was on record as being against the Constitution because it deprived the people of too many of the things they fought the war for. Perhaps Paine's strange behavior might have been influenced by reading this expense account.

1781 — September 6

[*Not numbered*]

> *To Household Expences from the close of*
> *Major Gibbs's acc[oun]t Nov. 21, 1780 till*
> *the commencement of them by Lt. Colfax the*
> *6 of Sept. 1781—amounts from the best*
> *accounts & Estimates that can be had & from*
> *recollection (exclusive of what was obtained*
> *by bartering a little salt w[hi]ch was put into*
> *the hands of the Housekeeper for that purpose)*
> *to at least** $20,800

---

* This business during the above Interval was in such a variety of hands for want of a proper Steward (w[hi]ch in vain by myself & others endeavoured to obtain)—and the accounts were not only irregularly kept, but many of them were lost or mislaid, & some of them so defaced as not to be legible, that it is impossible for me to make out a statement of them; But as it comprehended that space of time in which the French & American armies formed one camp at Philipsburgh & our Expences were at the highest; and as this sum corrisponds [sic] as nearly as can be expected with the average Expenditures per Month as will appear by Lieut. Colfaxs acc[oun]ts since—The above sum is charged under these Circumstances, upon the principle which seems most equitable to do justice to the public, and no injustice to mysef—[G. W.'s note]

Nothing can be added to this gem, one of the greatest qualifying statements in expense account writing.

1781 — September 8

No 1

> *To Danl. Grant (Balt[imor]e) his acct.* $274.36

No 2

> *To my own Expences together with one A[ide-]*
> *D[e-]Camp & three Serv[ant]s on the Road*
> *from Baltim[or]e to my Ho[me]** $166.83

---

* "Home," i.e., Mount Vernon.

No 3

> *To my Secretary & two Aids their Exps.*
> *from Do. to Do.* $218.94

Washington's defense policy, with its quick marches and counter-marches, was hard on the foot soldiers. A passage in the journal of Elijah Fisher describes what it must have been like to keep up with the General's fast-changing mind:

About Dark it did begin to Storm, the wind being at the N.E., and the Artillery went before and Cut up the roads; and the Snow come about our shows [shoes] and then set into rain, and with all of which made it very teges [tedious] . . . At twelve at night we come into a wood and had order to bild ourselves shelters to brake of [off?] the storm and make ourselves as Comforteble as we could, but jest as we got a shelter bilt, and got a good fire and Dried some of our cloths, and began to have things a little Comfurteble, though but poor at the best, thare Come orders to march and leave all we had taken so much pains for . . .*

In the summer, on the road to Virginia, the men couldn't complain about the snow. Heat is somewhat easier to bear than the cold. The foot soldiers who still had uniforms were forced to cut them in half to get relief; from the extra cloth, they made shoes of a sort.† At the Yorktown theater of action, French troops made jokes about the nudity of the Continental Army. This undress uniform may have inspired the radicals in the American theater today. One of the performers in the last act of the war predicted: "If the war is continued through the winter, the British troops will be scared at the sight of our men, for as they never fought with naked men, the novelty of it will terrify them."‡

The marches were irksome to the General and the expense account crowd, too. Every night the taverns had to be reconnoitered, and weighed as to the superiority of the table and bed. Daniel Grant was the owner of the Fountain Inn, which won the competition in Baltimore (item No. 1, Sept. 8, 1781). His bill included eight dinners for the Washington suite and seven dinners for servants. Sixteen horses were cared for by the innkeeper on September 9.

The second item strongly suggests that the expense account crowd also detoured for a visit to Mount Vernon, while the armies were taking their siege positions before Yorktown. Of the nature of the military business transacted here during the General's first visit to the home office in six years, I can only guess. Undoubtedly he checked the mail and observed how his underlings had been minding the store while he was out of town. In General Lee's opinion, however, the General and his staff used the Washington slaves

* "Military Diary, May 1775–February 1785," p. 7; in Godfrey, *The Commander-in-Chief's Guard.*

† E. Wild's Journal, May 2, 1781; in Massachusetts Historical Society *Proceedings,* October, 1890, p. 137.

‡ M. Morris, Private's Journal, p. 16; in Bolton, *The Private Under Washington,* p. 104.

badly. He cited a so-called "letter of invitation" that the General had purportedly sent to his comrade-in-arms, General Lafayette. As an inducement for a visit to Mount Vernon, he is supposed to have listed the allurements of an octoroon slave girl. Fitzpatrick says this was a product of Lee's warped mind, the sort of thing that could be expected from a man who preferred the company of dogs. The same letter is said to have been written to Jefferson, yet again to Alexander Hamilton. By a curious inversion, Fitzpatrick points out that the exact letter is also said to have been written by Jefferson to Washington, by Hamilton to Washington and so forth. All of this may sound like the goings-on in the average medium-sized corporation today. That these stories persisted and kept reappearing in books, like Joseph's coat, is proof that nobody likes a winner. If you think that men who have been at war for six years and were heading to their possible death at Yorktown would fool around with slave girls at this climactic moment in American history, that's *your* sex problem.

1781 — September 17

No 4

> *To Exps. on the Road per Col. Smith* [*list of different currencies*] *together—is* $2,431.71

No 5

> *To Sundries exclusive of the above, paid by myself on the Road to W* [*illia*]*msburgh in w* [*hi*]*ch C* [*omt*]*e de Rochambeaus Exps., who travelled in Compa* [*ny*] *with me were generally included* $1,547.60

To mount—and be off to the front, via a short detour to Williamsburg, the Paris of Virginia, for another conference.

While the General attended to high-level matters, labor agitators were doing their dirty work en route to Yorktown. Twelve goons stepped out before the regiments and persuaded the men to refuse to march any further because the financial promises made to them had not been honored. General ("Mad") Anthony Wayne addressed the workers earnestly, urging them to end the sit-down. He asked a platoon of soldiers to fire either on him or the agitators. Wayne had been humiliated by the mutiny of his troops in the Pennsylvania line the year before; he seemed to fear less facing his men now than facing General Washington later. At the word of command, the platoon presented and fired—killing six of twelve of the leading agitators. General Wayne must have sighed in relief.

"One of the remaining six was badly maimed and Wayne ordered a soldier to use his bayonet,'" Bolton says. "This the man refused to do, claiming that the mutineer was his comrade. The General instantly drew his pistol and would have shot the soldier had he refused longer to carry out the order. General Wayne then maneuvered the regiments about the lifeless bodies and ordered the five remaining mutineers to be hanged" (*The Private Under Washington,* p. 141).

1781 — September 17

No 6

To the Expences of a Trip to the French Fleet
of Cape Henry—to fix upon a Plan of operation
with Count de Grass[e] $650

No 7

To Washing & other small Exps. at
Will[ia]msburgh $132.60

After an inspection tour in 1781, Quartermaster General Timothy Pickering wrote to the President of Congress that everything in the state of Virginia was being impressed, "even breakfast for officers and soldiers." It was useless for the people to object, Pickering observed, "because the soldiery had the force."*

I don't believe anyone can force a woman to wash clothes, if she doesn't want to.

1781 — October [?]

No 8

To Secret Services $1,996

October 31

No 9

To Taylor's Account for Serv[ant]s $63.70

No 10

To an Express $109.20

* *Pickering Papers,* XXXIII, Massachusetts Historical Society, p. 331.

No 11

> *To Expended on a Second Visit to the French*
> *Fleet after the Seige of York*[town] *$565.60*

With his usual modesty, Washington does not mention the surrender of the British at Yorktown on October 18, which ended the war.

"To Taylor's Account for Servants" is the way the British would have preferred to remember this dismal chapter in the empire's war record. As George Washington might have explained Yorktown to the correspondent for the London *Financial Times,* "William Riley did the tailoring work, a pair of riding breeches for my servant William."

1781 — November 1

No 12

> *To John Likley's Acct. for 20 lbs. of Tea—*
> *it being for Public Use* *$468*

This is an example of the problems a modern expense account writer can run into when he doesn't resist the temptation to expand his remarks.

John Likely was a Philadelphia merchant. The tea was purchased when the victorious army passed through the city. By citing, for the first time, the quantity of a commodity purchased, Washington is vulnerable to the charge of being had by a shopkeeper. Even Nova Scotia salmon doesn't cost that much today, his critics might argue. My theory is that at $23 a pound, Washington bought very good tea.

This is also the first example of what today is known as a federal handout. Super-patriots who are against things like free lunches for the poor today are, thus, showing disrespect to the memory of Washington.

1781 — December 1

No 13

> *To Col. Trumbull's acc*[oun]*t of Travelling*
> *Expences from York Town in Virginia to*
> *Mount Vernon—& from Mount Vernon to*
> *Phila.* [lists currencies] *and together* *$2,283.23*

No 14

> *To Colo. Smith for his Expenditures on the*
> *said Jour[ne]y* *$398.78*

No 15

> *To Cash paid by Myself on Ditto* *$474.50*

The war ended abruptly at Yorktown.

What would have happened to the rebel cause if the French fleet had arrived late or if one of the hundreds of other pieces in the Franco-American strategy had not fallen exactly into place? The answer to this puzzle can be found in the first New Jersey campaign (1776 to 1777). Washington at the time was running to save the remnant of his army, and Cornwallis was pursuing in a stumbling manner. One British officer observed, "As we go forward into the country the rebels fly before us and when we come back, they always follow us; 'tis almost impossible to catch them. They will neither fight, nor totally run away. But they keep at such a distance that we are always above a day's march from them. We seem to be playing at Bo-Peep."*

The General was following tactics later to be adopted by Mao Tse-tung and Fidel Castro. A story made the rounds in the Continental Liberation Front's camp one night that he asked Colonel Reed, "Should we retreat to the back parts of Pennsylvania, will the Pennsylvanians support us?" Reed answered, "If the lower [eastern] counties are subdued and give up, the back counties will do the same."

Washington reportedly passed his hand over his throat and said, "My neck does not feel as though it was made for a halter. We must retire to Augusta County, in Virginia . . . and if overpowered, we must pass the Allegheny Mountains."

I don't doubt that he would have gone to the Poconos or Catskill mountains, and stayed there as long as this expense account held out. That a man can work wonders with an unlimited expense account behind him is a well-known fact in the world of business.

1781 — December 1

No 16

> *To Ditto paid Mrs. Thompson—Housekeeper* . . *$910*

---

* Bamford, "Diary," *Maryland Historical Magazine,* XXVIII (March 1933), p. 18.

December 16

No 17

> *To Ditto advanced Lieut. Colfax for Household*
> *Expenses from Septemr., Inclusive to the date* . . $4,747.60

No 18

> *To Ditto advanced Ditto upon a Warrant* . . . $7,800

For those who may think they have seen everything in the art of expense account writing, I call your attention to item No. 18, an example of what could be called expense account overkill.

1782 — January 7

[*Not numbered*]

> *To Saddlers Account* $67.60

February [*?*]

No 19

> *To Lieut. Colfax—Warr*[*an*]*t on the*
> *Treasury* $7,800

March 20

No 20

> *To Genl. Lincoln—Col. John Laurens draft for*
> *35 Guineas—amount of Tin Plates—a*
> *Telescope &ca. brought from France for*
> *my use* $1,274

No 21

> *To Lieut Colfax—received from the Treasury*
> *for Household Expences* $7,800

Poorer expense account writers by this point of the war would have been tempted to insert a note, "Going Out of Business," and abruptly ended this chronicle. An army of patriotic citizens was now coming out of the woodwork in every town Washington passed through, greeting and treating the old soldier like a new King George. But Washington stuck to his guns, as these items suggest.

This would have been an appropriate moment, too, for Washington to hold a going-out-of-business sale, clearing his shelves of all the equipment he had purchased during the war. "A GREAT SACRIFICE" sale might have raised money for the nation's public coffers, now bare.

George Washington wasn't the first soldier to walk off with the government's property, like the telescope in item No. 20. This is what we call khaki-collar crime today, and was a problem for congressional watchdogs during the Revolutionary War. They passed a law in 1780 that made the misappropriation of public stores an act "punishable by death, or such other punishment as a court martial should deem equal to the punishment of the defendent." Under the code of military justice prevailing, that law was probably meant to apply only to enlisted men anyway.

The wrinkle Washington added in this area of accomplishment is that he was probably the first to charge the government express fees for shipping the materiel home.

On the gloomy side is the fact that the General neglected to charge for the sentimental value attached to equipment he may have lost on the retreats. I don't know how to account for this negligence, except that the government originally paid for the missing items. *Two wrongs,* a basic law of expense account writing runs, *can make a right.*

1782 — March 20

No 22

To Sundry small acc[oun]ts and Expenditures during my Residence in Philadel[phi]a from the Month of Novr. to the date *$1,211.60*

Quartermaster General Timothy Pickering wrote in 1782 that the cash expended by federal officers in the Middle States was "but as the dust of the ballance." In New York he claimed one hardly met a man who was not a public creditor for services or supplies rendered the army. "The business of my department in all the posts in this state and in the Jerseys when the army has been there has been effected almost wholly by persuasion and impress."*

On behalf of my coauthor, who is no longer around to explain this charge in Philadelphia and other expenditures, like the purchase of a pair of bearskins in the next item, I would like to take the Fifth Amendment.

The last basic principle of expense account writing is: *Know your Constitutional Rights.*

* Pickering to Maj. Richard Claiborne, Jan. 16, 1782, Pickering, *Letterbooks,* Revolutionary War Mss., No. 83, National Archives.

1782 — March [?]
_____
No 23

    To Wm. Eagle's Rec[*eip*]*t* $36.40

May [?]
_____
No 24

    To Servants—viz Phila. Wamsley &
    others Their Wages $416

June [?]
_____
No 25

    To My Expenditures in a Tour to Albany—
    Saratoga & Schenectady on a visit to our
    Northern Posts $842.40

July [?]
_____
No 26

    To my Expences in going to the Interview
    with Count de Rochambeau at Phila
    [*break down of who paid the money*] $2,903.44

August 17
_____
No 27

    To Capt. Pray—per Rec[*eipt*]*s* $364

September [?]
_____
No 28

    To Majr. Talmadge—Do. $234

No 29

    To the Expences of a Reconnoitre as far as
    Philipsburg & then across from Dobbs ferry
    to ye Sound with a large Party of Hosse $842.40

October 10
_____
No 30

    To the Expenses of a Visit to the Post
    at Dobbs's ferry—&c. $195

November 1

No 31

> *To Secret Services to the date—per Memm. Book* . $4,450

(No 87 & 89)

> *To Col. Tilghman for old Contin.[ental?]*
> *Money Returned & now handed in* $27,775

See the U.S. Constitution, Amendment No. 5

1782 — November [?]

No 32

> *To the Expences of a tour to Poughkeepsy*
> *—thence to Esopus & along the Western Frontier*
> *of the State of New York* $1,031.03

To Ditto . . . Ditto. . . .

1783 — January 1

No 33

> *To Sundry Sums advanced Lieut. Colfax*
> *for Household Expen[ce]s betw[ee]n the Mo[nth]*
> *of June & the pres[en]t date [lists of*
> *currencies]* $11,900.85

March 10

No 34

> *To ——— Sheldon's Acct. per Colo. Trumbulls*
> *Recs.* $165.75

Do . . . Do. . . .

1783 — April [?]

No 35

> *To the Expences of a Trip to meet the Secretary*
> *at War at Ringwood for the purpose of making*
> *arrangements of liberating the Prisoners—&c.* . $222.46

No 36

> *To Expenditures upon an Interview with Sir*
> *Guy Carleton at Orange Town, exclusive of what*
> *was paid by the Contractors [list of exceptions]* . $635.70

> Do . . . Do. . . .

1783 — May
_____

July 1

No 37

> *To Cash advanced Lieut. Colfax for Household*
> *Expences between period of Jan. 7 and this*
> *date per his accounts* $11,535.05

[Not numbered]

> *To Ballance—unaccounted for* $18

1783 — July 1
_____

[sub]
[TOTALS]

Dollars & Lawful

Amount of the Expenditures for
the Years 1777,8, &9 and 1780,
1 & 2—and to the pres[en]t date. $160,074 £7070/15/4[*]

_____

> * *£7070/15/4 @ $26 = $183,839.93. $343,913.93. The General*
> *adds these six years to 1775 and 1776 in the Recapitulation to*
> *follow.*

_____

Excepted
G. Washington [Signature]
July 1st, 1783

Note,

  Before these Accounts are finally closed, Justice and propriety call upon me to signify that there are Persons within the British Lines—if they are not dead or removed, who have a claim upon the Public under the strongest assurances of Compensation from me, for their Services in conveying me private Intelligence, and which when exhibited, I shall think myself in honor bound to pay.—
  Why these claims have not made their appearance 'ere this unless

from either of the causes above mentioned—is from a disinclination in them to come forth till the B. [British] force is entirely removed from the United States, I know not—but I have thought it an encumbent duty on me to bring the matter to view that it may be held in remembrance in case such claims shall hereafter appear.

—G. Wn.

I know not the reason either.

But I would guess it had something to do with how high passions ran after the war. These political differences were to be found in every town and hamlet, and split even my own block in Leonia, New Jersey (established 1668).

The Jerseys had more than their share of militants, one of whom lived in a Revolutionary War house several houses down from mine, the Cole House. Old man Cole was a Tory, a man who wanted to maintain the status quo. Most of the others in the surrounding area were Bolsheviks, who favored the violent overthrow of the government. The British foraging parties who came through the area raided the radicals' cattle. Old Man Cole, according to a League of Women Voters pamphlet (*Know Your Leonia*), offered to take the neighbors' cattle into his barn where they would have a safe haven. The neighbors went along with the plan. A few days later Old Man Cole sold the cattle to the British, named names of loyalty risks, and fled town. Eight years after the war, when passions everywhere had cooled, Old Man Cole returned to Leonia and began life anew. The next morning he was found hanging from an oak tree in front of the house. The tree is still there, a constant reminder of how seriously Leonians take their politics.

That was a long time ago. Now that the descendants and the executors of the great American informers have read Washington's expense account and the note about the monies being held in escrow, they might consider stepping forward and putting in for the money still owed them. It could add up to a large sum now, with the interest and, as Washington himself would put it, "&C."

Haym Solomon, as everybody knows, advanced $350,000 to the government without interest during the period covered by Washington's expense account. What scheme the Philadelphia financier was up to was never fully discovered. He died in 1785 without cashing in his promissory note on the country. In the early 19th century, his heirs made an attempt to have the debt, which already must have been in the millions, liquidated. Solomon's vouchers from the government were lost by some government official to whom they were entrusted for the purpose of verification. His descendants, then wealthy New York internationalist bankers, abandoned their claims.

The vouchers for Washington's informers are still in the Library of Congress. Should anyone now want to step forward, I stand ready to help him present his claim. I would pay it myself, out of Washington's share of the profits from republishing this account book. If there were any. Neither of us is accepting any fee or royalties for this work—only expenses.

But not to claim the money would be false pride. George Washington would have wanted the matter cleared up. It would close these accounts finally, and the man would sleep soundly.

—M. Kn.

RECAPITULATION *or* GENERAL STATEMENT
of the Accounts for the Years 1775, 6, 7, 8, & 9—
and for 1780, 1, 2 & 3

	Dollars		Lawful
To Household Expences (Exclusive of the Provisions had from the Commissaries & Contractors —and Liquors &c. from them & others) viz			
Mr. Austins Acct. . . . No. 1			
Mrs. Smiths—Do. . . . 2			
Major Gibbs's 3			
Captn. Colfax 4			
Total Hd. Expenditures—69,250	&	88,080.64
Expended for Secret Intelligence .	7,617	&	55,145.00
Ditto in Reconnoitring—& in travelling —sometimes with, & sometimes without the Army—but generally with a Party of Horse	42,755⅔	&	38,735.27
Miscellaneous charges amounts per Accts. to	40,457½	&	76,765.12
Total . . .	160,074		258,725.03

To 160,074 Dollars extended in Lawful money according to the Scale of depreciation—

per Contra . . . . [ALREADY INCLUDED IN LAWFUL COLUMN]

Expenditures of 8 Years $414,108.21[†]

---

* *200 Guineas advanced Genl. McDougall for the like purpose is not included in this sum as I have had no controul of it & know nothing of the Application.—*[G. W.'s note.]

† *See next page for additional expenditures.*

1783 — July 1

To Interest of £ 599 19s. 11d. being the
Bal[lanc]e due me Dec. 31, 1776—the amount
having been applied to Public uses in the
preceeding years—from whence to wit[?]
July 1, 1775 I charge Int. at 6 p[er] c[ent]
per Ann[um] $7,488

To Mrs. Washington's travell[ing] Exps. in
coming to & returning from my Winter
Quarters per accts. rendered.—The Money to
defray which being taken from my private
Purse & brought with her from Virginia* . . $27,665.30

* Altho' I kept Mem[orandu]ms of these Expenditures I did
not introduce them into my Public Accounts as they occurred
—the reason was, it appeared at first view, in the commencement of them, to have the complexion of a private charge—I
had my doubts therefore of the propriety of mak[in]g it
—But the peculiar circumstances attending my Command,
and the embarrassed situation of our Public Affairs which
obliged me (to the no small detriment of my private Interest) to postpone the visit every year contemplated to
make my Family between the close of one Campaign and
opening of Another—and this expence was incidental thereto,
& consequent of my self denial, I have, as of right I think I
ought, upon due consideration adjudged the charge as just
with respect to the Public as it is convenient with respect to
Myself; and I make it with less reluctance as I find upon
the final adjustment of these Accts. (which have, as will
appear, been long unsettled) that I am a considerable
looser [sic]—My disbursements falling a good deal short of
my Receipts, & the money I had upon hand of my own—
For besides the Sum I carried with me to Cambridge (and
which exceeded the aforementioned Ballance of £ 599 19s
11d.) I received Monies afterwards on private Accts in 1777
and since which, except small Sums that I had occasion now
& then to apply to private uses, were also expended in the
Public Service—and thro' hurry, I suppose, & the perplexity
of business (for I know not how else to acct. for the deficiency) I have omitted to charge—whilst every debit
against me is here credited.
                                        —G. Washington
July 1, 1783

The only conflict in the book is found in the last sentence of George Washington's footnote. He wrestled with his conscience, and won. This is what we know in literature as "a happy ending."

I asked my accountant what an Internal Revenue Bureau agent would say about Washington's decision to throw in an extra $27,665.30 item for the expenses of having the founding mother visit him at the Valley Forge Holiday Inn or other battlefield motels. "They would want to hear more details about the soul searching," the CPA explained. "If he was my client, I would have advised him to attach a transcript of the debate he had with himself."

V

CONCLUSION

*"If he does really think that there
is no distinction between virtue and
vice, why, Sir, when he leaves our
houses let us count our spoons."*
—SAMUEL JOHNSON

THERE is a moral in all of this for young people who don't know anything about expense accounts and happen to be advancing their education by reading this instead of more important history books. It is not to refuse to stay home from school next Washington's Birthday. It is that George Washington wasn't less a hero because of his highly creative expense account. It just proves he was human.

George Washington didn't have to go into the army. Some of the finest men of his day were slackers. The Cabots and Lodges of Boston, Thomas Jefferson, the majority of Declaration of Independence and the Constitution signers found excuses—some quite real—not to bear arms. As C. F. Browne (Artemus Ward) said in *Artemus Ward: His Book* in 1862: "I have alreddy given 2 cousins to the war, & I stand Reddy to sacrifiss my wife's brother ruther'n not see the rebelyin krusht."

John Hancock had expected John Adams to nominate him as Commander in Chief when the Braintree orator began his "man who" nominating speech. The military qualities he was describing must have struck Hancock as his own résumé, and he was reportedly dismayed when Adams ended it with the George Washington name. Hancock immediately wrote to Washington asking for a berth in the army. "I am determined to act under you, if it be to take the firelock and join the ranks as a volunteer." Washington dodged the matter gracefully, and Hancock did not take the firelock, although he did show up at one battle in Rhode Island in 1781 in a uniform which put General Washington's tailor to shame. The nation's military stock remained at rock bottom, but historians say Hancock's laughing stock rose.

The few extra dollars Washington may have picked up on his expense account was penny ante stuff compared to what an accomplished smuggler and insurance man like Hancock made out of the war. Washington may have been buying up deeds for the land Congress was giving the troops on the payroll in lieu of cash at Valley Forge at a nickel an acre, as some historians have suggested. He may have first seen the land he bought in western New York in partnership with Governor Clinton while on an expense account trip (see item No. 32, Nov. 1782) in 1782. It later became part of the route for the Erie Canal. And his old army buddies may have served on the interlocking directorates of the military-industrial-government complex which founded the country. But these are the vicissitudes of war.

George Washington, as it has been pointed out for centuries, was willing to make every sacrifice for liberty. Except one: reducing his standard of living. Even here, he may have sincerely been unaware of the incongruity of his actions. "No person wishes more to save money to the public, than I do," he wrote to the President of Congress on April 23, 1776, "and no person has aimed more at it . . . I give in to no kind of amusements myself; and consequently those about me can have none." Washington's attitude is puzzling, until we realize that he was just another congressman at heart. They always want economy for the nation, but they like a little prosperity for their own states and districts even more. Few of our representatives are willing to go so far in their love for economy as to sacrifice the trivial boondoggle for their home district out of the military pork barrel.

Besides it wasn't until President Kennedy that men were supposed to ask not what your country can do for you, but what you can do for your country. Poor people shouldn't go into the army in the first place.

None of these explanations, rationalizations, apologies and excuses for what General Washington wrote during the war, I fear, will satisfy the stuffed shirts in the ivory towers, the non-expense account crowd. They are apt to render a judgment, based on the man's previous record and high reputation, of "not guilty—but don't do it again."

For those of us in the expense account crowd who must grapple every day with the same moral problems George Washington coped with so well, there remains one professional criticism. What Washington was doing with this expense account could be called market research on the tolerance of lows and highs. He was testing the point at which the proper—or improper—authorities would ask questions. The most amazing thing about this expense account may be that Washington kept his spending so low.

The President of the Continental Congress in 1783, when the expense account was turned in, was Elias Boudinot, the superspy. The presidency came his way not because he was a statesman of the first magnitude but because under the seniority system it was Boudinot's turn. Later Boudinot became Director of the Mint. The congressional committee that scrutinized the General's ledger, admirers of great expense account writing will be pleased to learn, approved the document without haggling.

There is evidence the accounts were gone over with a fine tooth comb. The skilled accountants of the Treasury Department found there was a discrepancy of 89/90 of one dollar more due Washington than his accounts showed. Nevertheless, James Milligan, then Comptroller of the Treasury, complimented the General in an unusual way. Carried away with the enthusiasm of the trained accountant for the amateur, he sent all the supporting evidence back to Mount Vernon.

"As all accounts when liquidated are regularly entered in the Treasury Books, and the original papers carefully filed," Milligan wrote in a letter of January 13, 1784, "it is not deemed necessary, for Accountants to receive any official papers, unless a Warrant for the balance if any due; But your Excellency having in your Accounts, clearly displayed that degree of Candor & truth, and that attention you have constantly paid to every denomination of Civil Establishments, which invariably distinguish all your actions, I could not resist the inclination I felt of transmitting you these papers, in hopes it may prove a Matter of some satisfaction to you."

Awed by the remarkable accuracy and precision in keeping straight a complicated mass of accounts throughout a period of eight stormy and trying years, it appears the Treasury Department only checked the General's arithmetic and gave him an A+. George Washington knew his market. What a golden opportunity was missed to soar to even greater highs, or lows, depending on your point of view.

Actually this lack of attention to detail on the part of the examining bodies may have started a tradition of concern the government has shown for its leader's financial problems. After Thomas Jefferson's second administration, the government ran a lottery for him so he wouldn't have to return to the soil. James Monroe's private papers were purchased by government bodies over and over again.

The promptness with which General Washington's accounts were settled was unusual, too. By 1790, some war veterans who didn't have expense accounts were still writing pamphlets like Pekelach Webster's *Plea from a Poor Soldier; or an Essay to Demonstrate that the Soldiers and other Public Creditors Who Really and Actually Supported the Burden of the Late War Have Not Been Paid! Ought to Be Paid! Can Be and Must Be Paid!*

I don't mean to imply that the Congress and the Treasury were unaware of the general nature of Washington's philosophy of expense account writing. When he offered the same deal to the country after his election as the first President—no salary, but only expenses—Congress turned George Washington down flat. They humbly begged him to accept instead a salary of $25,000 (at a time when the salary of the Secretary of State, Thomas Jefferson, was fixed at $3,500).

It was the country's first economy wave.